To Tom,
To receive me with the
hospitality and spirit
that you have given me
a joy that, only friendship
can give!
The Lord bless you
and Barbara for making
me feel at home on
Awasco Lake .....
— Ken

# THE
# Pessimist's Journal

## OF

# Very, Very Bad Days

### OF THE

# 1980s

Compiled by
**Jess M. Brallier and
Richard P. McDonough**

Illustrated by
**Seth Feinberg**

Designed by
**Janis Owens**

**Little, Brown and Company**
Boston ~ Toronto ~ London

for JK and Hugh
—JMB

à les plein d'espoir
—RPM

First Edition

10 9 8 7 6 5 4 3 2 1

BP

Published simultaneously in Canada by
Little, Brown & Company (Canada) Limited

Printed in the United States of America

# "It was the worst of times,

and it was the worst of times." That was the spirit and conviction we had always hoped to bring to our work, but for The Pessimist, confronting the 1980s was more than a little daunting. The very premise on which the gentleman had built his view—that the world was going to hell in a handbasket—seemed to be under siege. The personnel who year after year had never failed to disappoint were no longer there for us. Nixon was not in office, John Connally was looking for work, Engelbert Humperdinck was no longer novel, Henry Kissinger was sniffing around the cuffs of those in power but getting little attention, and Annette Funicello was "history." Walter Mondale's weak smile seemed promising, but hell, being pitiful is not enough.

And then, in the nick of time, along came the Trumps, Lawyers, Anita Bryant, Jane Byrne and Mary Calderone, Leona Helmsley, Post-Modernism, the Wave at football games, an oft-married, emaciated English woman called Collins, Coleco, and Ronald Reagan. The reprises of Robert Vesco and Edward Teller were welcome clouds on a bright horizon. Fertile times were upon us. Auto Alarms, Joan Rivers, Laurie Anderson, Lyndon Larouche goons in the airports, "Awwwlll rrriiiight!," "world class" creeping into the language, and everyone "going for it." Those deeply personal catalog letters from Sharper Image's Richard. The creepily compelling tear-jerking television advertisements for using the telephone. Consider them. We did and before long our faith was restored.

We now offer you on The Pessimist's behalf the best bad days of the '80s as your own personal little black lifesaver bobbing on the sea of life. And in such a "user friendly" (another '80s gift) format! We've booked the '80s, if you don't mind our verbing a noun.

Still, one haunting question of those dear dead days remains: did Ronald Reagan ever finish that California freeway story he started in the early eighties???

Have a nice day.

*Jess and Dick**

*(Oh, yeah. They started calling you by your first name, remember?)

# CODE KEY

**❷** Can't confirm exact date. The local librarian refuses to help because she didn't like my first book, *The Pessimist's Journal of Very, Very Bad Days*.

**🐿** Can't remember the exact date. Can hardly think. There's loud rock 'n' roll playing outside. Twenty-four hours a day. It's been almost a week. It's driving me nuts. I may have to make a run for it.

**☢** Unwilling to confirm the exact date on this. What's the use? Remember the funny noise down at the power plant? Well, it's back—and louder than ever.

—The Pessimist

January 1990

# January

• • •

I would like to suggest that Ronald Reagan is politically dead.

—NBC political correspondent
Tom Pettit in 1980

# JANUARY

**1** The Massachusetts Department of Public Works now officially refers to road signs as "ground-mounted confirmatory route markers." (1988) ✎

**2** Two hundred thousand baseball card packages are recalled when the children of America discover an obscenity painted on Orioles' Bill Ripkin's bat handle. (1989)

**3** Claiming she could no longer "stand him wearing that tutu around the house all day," a Palm Beach society matron seeks to divorce the man she had married to be assured of an escort for "fancy parties and things like that." (1985)

**4** "A lot of its readers are of an age where they forget to cancel." — Jerry Della Femina, on the wide circulation of *Reader's Digest* (1987)

**5** Sandra Jarvinen's former husband asks if he could bury his second wife in Ms. Jarvinen's backyard, but she turns him down, explaining that it isn't "a good idea to bury anybody on my property because I have a high water table." (1989)

**6** We discover that, after having piloted his firm to a 43% drop in earnings in 1982, Mobil Chairman Rawlins gets a 36% increase in salary. ☢

**7** The Trapp Family Reunion is being held up there in Stowe, Vermont. Neighbors report lots of singing. (1984)

**8** After stuffing $25,000 in cash into his pocket (while being secretly videotaped by the FBI), Congressman Richard Kelly says, "Does it show?" (1980)

**9** Clara Peller says, "Where's the beef?" (1984)

**10** The Morgan Guaranty Trust Company instructs its employees to "avoid saying 'hello.' This elsewhere pleasant and familiar greeting is out of place in the world of business." (1983) ☢

**11** Marianne Faithfull reports that (1) she's beaten her drug problem, and (2) she's been getting by on royalties from the Stones' "Sister Morphine," for which she wrote the lyrics. (1980)

**12** ABC introduces *Dynasty*, featuring lots of glamour and greed, and it becomes a big hit throughout the Reagan years. (1981)

## 13

In his customarily modest way, Jerry Lewis is sure "people hate me because I am a multifaceted, talented, wealthy, internationally famous genius." (1980)

## 14

Rex Hunt, British Governor of Falkland Islands, argues his case with an Argentine general: "I think it very uncivilized to invade British territory." (1983) ❷

## 15

Senator Orrin Hatch explains that "capital punishment is our society's recognition of the sanctity of human life." (1988)

## 16

Publication date, 1983, of a Spanish phrase book for California farm owners wishing to speak in the same language as their hired help. The book includes translations of helpful phrases like "Don't throw the beer bottles in the field" and "Clean up this camp, you live like a pig." ❷

## 17

After his ex–business partner is shot but not killed, Staff Sergeant Barry "Ballad-of-the-Green-Berets" Sadler is arrested for attempted murder. Sadler pleads innocent, his justification being "I'm a Green Beret. If I'd shot him, he'd be dead." (1981) ☛

## 18

According to *People* magazine, because he has begun sketching a 22-mile-long work to be assembled in Rumania, "Salvador Dali has put a stop to all the gossip that he had become senile." (1981)

**19** Reverend Louis Sheldon announces that he is against textbooks that treat evolution as scientific fact, because "when you teach kids that they come from monkeys, that's a dead, dinosaural kind of thing. It's not a warm, fuzzy kind of thing." (1989)

**20** The Reagan-Bush team's now in office and Panamanian leader Manuel Noriega's back on the CIA payroll. (1981)

**21** After conducting a phone poll, DC Comics goes along with the callers and kills off Robin, Boy Wonder. HOLY DICK GRAYSON!!! (1986)❷

**22** They're wearing the new red-framed power glasses. (1987)

**23** Rupert Murdoch is now a U.S. citizen. (1986)

**24** Marvel releases its Mother Teresa comics format biography. (1985) ➤

# JANUARY

**25** When it is pointed out that a Republican National Committee's advertisement misrepresented the facts, a stunned Republican official asks, "Since when is a commercial supposed to be accurate?" (1982)

**26** "It now becomes my responsibility to pick up the torch!" —would-be presidential candidate Jerry Brown on hearing of a Ted Kennedy primary loss (1980)

**27** "My T-shirts sold out by nine o'clock!" —would-be presidential candidate Jerry Brown (1980)

**28** Muhammad "The Greatest" Ali is on TV hawking a cockroach killer. (1981)

**29** Four hundred pets on Long Island are invited to a "bark mitzvah" for Greggie "Lump Lump" Taylor, a 13-year-old female mutt. (1982) ❧

**30** It's Olympics time again. Not only will Leroy Neiman be back but you will still not know what Dick Button's talking about when he says, "That was a beautiful double axel." (1984)

**31**

Phyllis George is now coanchor of the *CBS Morning News*. (1985)

# February

### ...

The future can only be secured by a
President who dares to be bold, not
cautious.

—Gary Hart in 1984

**1** "People don't want to be apologetic for their pets' looks. It's amazing what you can do with animal skin that you can't do with a person's." —Dr. Bill Sanders, who performs plastic surgery on pets (1989)

**2** Suction-cupped Garfield the Cat dolls. (1982)

**3** Alfred Bloomingdale and Vicki Morgan. (1982)

**4** "I believe the world is going to end— by an act of God, I hope — but every day I think that time is running out." — Secretary of Defense Caspar Weinberger (1982)

**5** "I must say acting was good training for the political life which lay ahead for us." —Nancy Reagan (1980)

**6** "We cannot reduce women to equality." —Phyllis Schlafly (1980)

**7** After being wrongly charged, convicted, and jailed for over ten years, and then released from prison on the strength of evidence in the documentary *The Thin Blue Line*, Randall Adams sues the film's maker, Errol Morris, for using his story. (1989) ❷

**8** "My supporters were at their daughters' coming-out parties." — George Bush on what went wrong in an Iowa straw poll (1988)

**9** After being arrested for driving 125 mph, José Canseco points out that the problem is that his Jaguar runs so well he thought he was only going 50. (1989) ✏

**10** Look out, here come the white Zinfandels! (1987)

**11** "One way I save energy is by asking my servants not to turn on the self-cleaning oven until after seven in the morning." —Betsy Bloomingdale, Nancy Reagan friend and confidante (1982)

**12** Oprah Winfrey goes national. (1983)

**13** Pachelbel's Canon is being used to sell everything from snapshot film to personal hygiene products. And it is just beginning. (1982)

**14** "If you are intent on submitting a final report that makes sense, his testimony becomes essential but not absolutely necessary." —Senator Daniel Inouye, chairman of the Iran-Contra committee, on Oliver North (1987)

**15** *Saturday Night Live* is still on television. (1987)

**16** Larry Speakes reminds Marlin Fitzwater, the new White House spokesman, "...you don't have to explain what you don't say." (1987)

**17** "Sex education is the principal cause of teenage pregnancy." —Phyllis Schlafly (1982) ❷

**18** *The A Team* now reigns as America's most watched TV show. (1984)

**19** Spiro Agnew asks California if it's all right to deduct the fines resulting from his bribery conviction in Maryland. (1989)

**20** Caspar Weinberger is spotted in Grenada taking photos with the lens cap on. (1986)

**21** When Ed Koch breaks his 1981 promise not to run for governor, his political guru, David Garth, notes, "I don't believe that the people really believe that he didn't believe that when he said it." (1982)

**22** Socialite C. Z. Guest shares her child-raising secrets: "I think children are better brought up with a governess.... That doesn't mean I never saw them. Of course I saw them. I went fox hunting with them." (1983)

**23** Roxanne and Peter Pulitzer. (1982)

**24** The new Ali MacGraw movie, *Just Tell Me What You Want*, is out. (1980)

## 25

Donna Summer allows that "God had to create disco music so that I could be born and be successful." (1980)

## 26

Over at the Defense Department, they're now calling a tent a "frame-supported tension structure." (1986)

## 27

In 1987, Interior Secretary Donald Hodel argues against controls to save the earth's ozone layer, proposing instead a program of "personal protection" against radiation, making use of wider hats, more sunglasses, and better sunscreen lotions.

## 28

Although what's on tape is obviously President Reagan calling reporters "sons of bitches," White House press secretary Larry Speakes insists Reagan is saying, "It's sunny and you're rich." (1986) ✒

## 29

"You don't have many suspects who are innocent of a crime. That's contradictory. If a person is innocent of a crime, then he is not a suspect. Miranda only helps guilty defendants," says the prime law enforcer of the country, Attorney General Ed Meese. (1985)

# March

...

I think it's upsetting to people that Donald and I have it all.

—Ivana Trump in the '80s

# MARCH

**1** Manhattan's Charles Hamilton Gallery is preparing to auction a Frank Sinatra painting (24" x 20", oil on canvas) from his "Ava Gardner period," according to the catalog, "when, obviously, Sinatra was in a state of depression, and thus the somber hues." A $7000 minimum has been set. (1984)

**2** Pompadoured Bob Graham ships Nobel Prize winners' sperm to promising female Mensa members. (1980)

**3** "There are various groups that think you can ban certain kinds of guns. And I am not in that mode. I am in the mode of being deeply concerned." —President George Bush on assault rifles (1989)

**4** Diane Keaton's photographs of empty hotel interiors—rooms, lobbies, lounges— can now be seen at Castelli Graphics in Manhattan. (1980)

**5** Financial analyst Bruce Collins reports on a study that links heavy program trading with whatever Vanna White wears. If she shows up in a white strapless dress, a "buy" program follows; whereas with a neck-high outfit, a "sell" program develops. (1987)

**6** "Approximately 80% of our air pollution stems from hydro-carbons released by vegetation. So let's not go overboard in setting and enforcing tough emissions standards for man-made sources." —Ronald Reagan (1981)

**7** "My life is a vehicle to explore the media and ethics...it's a woman's story. It's about trying to maintain a balance in life between marriage and a career. Any stupid publisher who doesn't want it has his head up his butt!" —Donna Rice (1989)

**8** Actors dressed in Rambo costumes begin delivering "Rambo-grams." (1985)

**9** President Reagan's Department of Agriculture declares that ketchup is a vegetable and can now "be counted as one of the two vegetables required as part of the school lunch program." (1981)

**10** Mayor Ed Koch notes that "graffiti on the walls of trains or bad subway stations create bad karma." (1989)

**11** Pee Wee Herman starts showing up. (1984)

**12** It's 1983 and an anonymous U.S. Office of Civil Defense official announces the bright side of things: "Nuclear war could alleviate some of the factors leading to today's ecological disturbances that are due to current high-population concentrations and heavy industrial production."

**13** Two pieces of bad news for lovers of good writing. Russell Baker publishes his last Sunday column in the *New York Times*. William Safire does not follow suit. (1988)

**14** The U.S. Air Force and Army field communications systems, the kind of thing you would use to talk to each other during combat, for instance, are discovered to be incompatible, but it'll only cost $30 million to modify them. (1985) ❷

**15** Los Angeles police chief Daryl Gates suggests why so many blacks seem to die from police use of the carotid choke hold: "We may be finding that in some blacks when it [the hold] is applied, the veins or arteries do not open up like...in normal people." (1982)

**16** Because of powerful U.S. Navy radio waves, for the fifth day in a row, San Francisco suburbanites are forced to manually open their automatic garage doors. (1989)

**17** The International Bluejean Institute in New York is finalizing its plan to open a museum featuring jeans worn by movers and shakers like Elton John, Joe Namath, Jimmy Carter, and Woody Allen; each display will include a brief summary of the wearer's "philosophy of bluejeanism." (1980)

**18** The Sea Grant Institute announces the availability—to fishermen with fax machines—of current weather satellite photos of Lake Michigan so that the sportsmen can determine the confluence of cold and warm water where the steelheads hang out. (1989)

**19** Oscar de la Renta redesigns the Boy Scout uniform and Jerry Hall models the summer shorts outfit. (1980)

**20** After spending eleven million dollars ($11,000,000.00), John Connally quits the race for the Republican nomination for President and releases all his delegates: Ada Mills, of Clarksville, Arkansas. (1980) ♣

**21** Ronald Goldstock of the New York State Organized Crime Task Force reflects upon the good old days: "The people who join the mob now...don't have the values their predecessors had." (1987)

**22** "I want to show women how to decorate the home by using contact paper, spray paint and getting the good deals in the bargain rooms at stores where Jim and I buy most of our furniture." —Tammy Bakker (1981)

**23** Annie Robinson recently got Virginia Edmondson's neck operation, while Virginia got Annie's parathyroidectomy. (1980)

**24** "I think we have a little problem here." — Captain Joseph Hazelwood of the *Exxon Valdez* (1989)

**25** After several Ecuadoran soldiers were killed by faulty ammunition sold by the U.S., a U.S. Army inspection team goes to that country and discovers 400 additional dangerous rounds. They bill the Ecuadorans $180,000 for the inspection plus the cost of 400 replacement rounds. (1987)

**26** Mr. T. (1982)

**27** Fancy jelly beans are now a big item, along with power breakfasts. (1981)

**28** In Chicago, Verona Berkley and her boyfriend, Willie Bradly, can't agree on what to watch—*The Thorn Birds* or a basketball game—so she kills him. (1983)

**29** City commissioner John Williams shares his view of Hollywood, Florida's, indigents: "When I grew up in the Depression, we didn't call these people homeless; we called them bums. I don't see any reason why not to still call them that." (1989)

**30** Suddenly, without warning, oatmeal, condoms, and Jackie Mason are back. (1988)

**31** With no cash but with $5.4 billion in junk bonds, Ted Turner goes after CBS. (1985)

# April

...

He's an intellectual from Yale, but
he's very intelligent.

—Pete Rose on
Bart Giamatti in 1989

# APRIL

**1** Donald Regan warns that imposing sanctions on South Africa would hurt the United States because the "women of America are not prepared to give up their jewelry." (1986)

**2** Ralph Engelstead, Imperial Palace Hotel and Casino operator, holds a theme party to boost employee morale. The theme: Adolf Hitler's birthday. (1986, and again in 1988)

**3** "I brake for animals" bumper stickers start showing up. (1983)

**4** With her husband still very much alive, Imelda Marcos announces that she will have him embalmed and displayed in Hawaii...after he is dead. She adds, "It will be a spectacle, an international spectacle." (1989)

**5** Gaston, South Carolina, installs its first stoplight and a couple of hours later a motorist tries to run it and causes a four-car accident. (1985) ☛

**6** "I think my wife is getting off lightly, which I am happy about, as I am very pro-women's equal rights." —Peter Holm, estranged husband of Joan Collins, on why he doesn't consider $80,000 a month too much alimony for him to receive (1987)

# APRIL

**7** ABC starts putting Ted Koppel on after the 11 o'clock news but does nothing about his hair. (1980)

**8** In Alabama, a medical student is about to begin dissection on a female cadaver when she recognizes the body. It's her great-aunt. (1982)

**9** "The environmentalists' real thrust is not clean air, or clean water, or parks, or wildlife but the form of government under which America will live...look what happened to Germany in the 1930s. The dignity of man was subordinated to the powers of Nazism. The dignity of man was subordinated in Russia...those are the forces that this thing can evolve into." —Secretary of the Interior James Watt (1983)

**10** New Age candidate Tiny Tim, age 66, withdraws his candidacy for mayor of New York. (1989)

**11** When asked about Ed Koch's comment that Jews "would be crazy" to vote for the Rev. Jesse Jackson, presidential candidate Albert Gore replies, "My contract with David Garth prohibits me from commenting." (1988)

**12** The Environmental Protection Agency instructs its employees to quit using the term "acid rain" and instead substitute "poorly buffered precipitation." (1982)

**13** *Washington Post* reporter Janet Cooke wins the Pulitzer Prize for making up a story about an eight-year-old heroin addict. (1981)

**14** In 1989, the *New York Times* announces that the Fresh Kills Landfill on Staten Island, when completed in sixteen years, will dwarf the Great Pyramid of Khufu, cover 339 acres, rise 505 feet, and contain nearly 80 million cubic yards of trash.

**15** It's income tax day! Let's see, in 1987, Michael R. Milken earned $1,046 every minute of every day or, that's uh, let's say, in a round figure, $550 million. (1988)

**16** "You can be happy on a lot less money." —Donald Trump, on Michael Milken's 1988 income

**17** After President Reagan's air strikes against Libya result in little more than the killing of Qaddafi's infant daughter, Frank Sinatra sends the White House a telegram reading, "Encore, encore, encore. Francis Albert." (1986)

**18** "Newport is not happy about it. Newport will never be happy about it." —Newport hotel owner on the Claus von Bulow trial (1985)

FRESH KILLS LANDFILL

**19** Rosie Ruiz wins the Boston Marathon...sort of. (1980)

**20** "I can do anything. In *GQ*, I appeared as a man." —Boy George (1986)

**21** The Pentagon begins calling peace "permanent pre-hostility." (1984)

**22** Elizabeth Ray, now 40, reports that she still can't type. (1984)

**23** The $519,750 bottle of Château Margaux believed to have been Thomas Jefferson's is inadvertently broken by consignee wine merchant William Sokolin, who watches it dribble out onto the rug at New York's Four Seasons. (1989)

**24** Coca-Cola Chairman Roberto Goizueta introduces a new "smoother, rounder, yet bolder" Coke. (1985)

**25** Although some mistake them for threats instead of marriage vows, Maureen Reagan and Dennis Revell insist on writing their own for today's wedding: "I love you because you're going to let me be me." (1981)

**26** *The Brady Bunch* still in syndication. (1988)

**27** Phillip D. Wyman of California introduces a bill in the state legislature that would require warnings on any albums that might ever be found actually to contain backward-recorded messages singing the specific praises of Satan. (1982)

**28** "I don't want to know what the law is, I want to know who the judge is." —Roy Cohn (1980)

**29** Sally Quinn is still alluded to as a journalist. (1980)

**30** "How'm I doin'?" —Ed Koch (all through the 1980s)

# May

●●●

We are not leaving Lebanon. The
Marines are merely being deployed
two or three miles to the west.

—Caspar Weinberger when
American troops are evacuated
from Lebanon to ships
offshore in 1984

# MAY

**1** "You all look like happy campers to me. Happy campers you are, happy campers you have been, and, as far as I am concerned, happy campers you will always be." —Dan Quayle in American Samoa addressing a group of Samoans. (1989)

**2** "Follow me around. I don't care. If anybody wants to put a tail on me, go ahead. They'd be very bored." — Gary Hart (1987)

**3** Andy Warhol's "Red Marilyn," 20 painted panels of Marilyn Monroe's face, sold for $4 million, inclusive of the buyer's 10% to Christie's, of course. (1989)

**4** In California, Buffums department store is now issuing credit cards—to children. (1984)

**5** An advertisement in the *New York Times* promises us that the "Sally Jessy Raphael Talking Advice Doll" will soon be available. (1989)

**6** With $900 worth of stolen merchandise and a long lead on the pursuing police, thieves back up to an unattended Coconut Creek, Florida, tollbooth to pay the 50-cent toll, allowing police just enough time to nab the thugs. (1989)

**7** Richard Secord tells those at the Iran-Contra hearings how Oliver North stands at attention while talking to the President on the phone. (1987)

**8** Police arrest John Griffith for driving his Cadillac with a live squirrel tied to the windshield wipers. (1989)

**9** Barney L. Cobb of Birmingham, Alabama, is found guilty of beating his wife over the head with her pet Chihuahua. (1983) ☣

**10** Massachusetts inmate Gordon Benjamin turns down parole rather than miss the chance to play Lancelot in a prison production of "Camelot." (1989)

**11** Mistaking a blind man's folded cane for an outlawed martial arts weapon, Hayward, California, police training officer Eric Ristrim and trainee Marie Yin beat the blind man into submission. (1989)

**12** Psychiatrist Graziella Margherini of Florence discovers a new emotional disorder that results in disorientation and hallucinations in non-Italians in the presence of great art. She calls it the Stendahl Syndrome. (1989)

**13** Ann Beattie's second novel published. (1980)

**14** Philip Abrams of the Housing Department explains that it's not because of poverty that Hispanics live in crowded homes but because "they don't mind and they prefer, some prefer, doubling up...it's a cultural preference, I'm told." (1984)

**15** Jerry Jeff Walker announces he's quit drinking and won't start up again until Iran releases the American hostages. (1980)☣

**16** So as to absolutely discredit "those reports claiming President Reagan is increasingly out of touch with reality," Senator Alan Simpson notes, "I even saw him do a cowboy doodle the other day, and I haven't seen him do that in years. He used to do that when he was in his prime." (1987)

**17** "Boy, they were big on crematoriums, weren't they?" — George Bush after touring the Auschwitz death camp. (1987)

**18** Media adviser Doug Watts is hard at work developing ethnic advertising for President Reagan's reelection campaign: "We'll have this nice couple in an ordinary house. Something good will happen to them, and the guy will say, 'Hey, honey, now that we've got so much money, let's go out for a steak.' But in the Hispanic version we'll have the guy say, 'Let's go out for a taco.'" (1984)

**19** Pac-Man. (1983)

**20** In Muskogee, Oklahoma, a man randomly selected by a "perfectly objective computerized system" for jury duty on a murder trial turns out to be the defendant. (1989)

**21** After demanding a list of homosexuals in state government, endorsing a book in which Afro-American children are called "pickaninnies," canceling the Martin Luther King, Jr., holiday, and appointing an education adviser who wants to tell kids the earth is flat, Arizona Governor Evan Mecham declares, "I'm doing things that haven't been done before." (1987)

**22** Eight times a week for over the past three years, a curly-headed little starlet's been singing that song "Tomorrow!" (1980)

**23** People now call radio talk shows and argue—from their car phones. While driving. (1984)

**24** "I liked the Remington Microscreen Shaver so much, I bought the company!" —Victor Kiam (1984 and seemingly ever thereafter)

**25** In Abilene, Texas, the Yellow Pages lists the Elliot-Hamil Funeral Home under "Wholesale Frozen Foods." (1980)

**26** Pia Zadora starts showing up. (1982)

**27** Liposuction. (1988)

**28** Four days ago Anita Bryant, homosexual deprogrammer and defender of the sacredness of the family, filed for divorce. (1980)

**29** The official portrait of former inmate John Mitchell is hung at the Justice Department. (1985)

**30** A Grosse Pointe Woods, Michigan, boy pulls a gun on an orthodontist and orders him to remove his braces. (1985)

## 31

"Everywhere we go Nancy makes the world a little better."
—President Ronald Reagan on his wife (1984)

# June

...

Jim is handsome and has good
manners, and I used to think that
every talented young woman that
walked through the door was
making a pass at my husband, and
that was a very real fear to me. I
finally had to come to the point
where I made up my mind that I was
going to trust Jim with these
beautiful, young, talented women.

—Tammy Bakker in the early '80s

**1** "Who does that dame think she is?" —Nancy Reagan on Raisa Gorbachev (1988)

**2** Oops. Philip Morris' Kraft division discovers there are over 100 winners of its "one and only" grand prize—a $17,000 Dodge Caravan. (1989)

**3** "I never said I had no idea about most of the things you said I said I had no idea about." —Elliott Abrams, during the Iran-Contra hearings (1987)

**4** Keep 2:30–4:00 open today. The seventh annual *Daytime Emmy Awards* show is on NBC. (1980)

**5** Alan Dershowitz. (1981)

**6** Several people have recently started talking about themselves in the third person, and there are signs that this may be catching on. (1987)

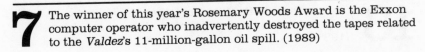

**7** The winner of this year's Rosemary Woods Award is the Exxon computer operator who inadvertently destroyed the tapes related to the *Valdez*'s 11-million-gallon oil spill. (1989)

**8** Tama Janowitz and Fran Lebowitz. (1987)

**9** Following his fabled instincts and a nose for the next good idea, Coca-Cola Chairman Roberto Goizueta leaves a screening of *Ghostbusters*, certain that his Columbia film subsidiary is going to "lose a bundle." (1984)

**10** A 97-year-old Wisconsin man seeks a divorce from his 91-year-old wife because "she just isn't fun anymore." (1982)

**11** Exiled Idi Amin takes the sun at poolside in Jidda. (1980)

**12** "...we'd go to my dad's house in the Berkshires...we were too poor to have our own summer houses."
—Jay McInerney (1989)

**13** Sixteen-year-old Hal Warden, father of two, explains why he just got divorced for the second time: "I got sick of it." (1987)

**14** Philip Johnson's AT&T headquarters building in NYC, the one that looks like Sears' plastic Chippendale door chimes, is completed and open. (1983)

**15** In 1987, Joe Biden gives a Neil Kinnock speech. 🖙

**16** On the 100th anniversary of James Joyce's birthday, officials of political and literary Dublin, accompanied by press representatives from all over the world, arrive to install a commemorative plaque at the house where Joyce lived. However, the lady of the house is not at home and the assembled folks have to wait until she's back from the grocer. (1982)

**17** Bernhard Goetz appeals his 6-month sentence for illegal gun possession and gets instead a 12-month sentence. (1987)

**18** The paperback bestseller list includes seven Garfield the Cat books. (1982)

# JUNE

**19** *Money* magazine declares the home computer a dumb idea. (1980) ❷

**20** Advice columnist Abigail van Buren sues Kinky Friedman over his song about Abbie Hoffman entitled "Dear Abbie." The matter confuses many. (1981)

**21** Bloomingdale's is advertising its Michael Jackson rhinestone-studded white glove for $9.95. (1984)

**22** There will soon be 7 million personal beepers in America. (1983)

**23** The newest Kennedy is Arnold Schwarzenegger. (1985)

**24** The Defense Department now officially refers to hammers as "manually powered fastener-driving impact devices." (1986)

# JUNE

**25** Disneyland Records' latest release, *Mickey Mouse Disco* —featuring disco versions of "It's a Small World" and "Zip-a-Dee-Doo-Dah," as well as new songs like "Macho Duck" and "Disco Mickey Mouse"—just moved onto *Record World*'s Top Fifteen list. (1980)

**26** "Have a nice day!" (1980)

**27** In an effort to turn the tide of violence, the Rev. Marshall Gourley of Denver offers $100 to anyone who turns over a firearm to him...so Robin Heid buys a handgun for $40, collects his $100, and uses it as down payment on an assault rifle. (1989)☣

**28** The following appears in the Warrenton, Virginia, newspaper (1981):

IMPORTANT NOTICE. If you are one of the hundreds of parachuting enthusiasts who bought our *Easy Sky Diving* book please make the following correction: on page 8, line 7, the words "state zip code" should have read "pull rip cord." ❷

**29** His audience actually bursts into uncontrollable laughter when Ed Meese says, "We don't care about the political or ideological allegiance of a prospective judge." (1987)

**30** Mary Cunningham and Bill Agee. (1981)

# July

...

It's better than gold.

—John De Lorean, on tape while
opening a suitcase full of
cocaine in 1982

**1** On a proposal to decapitate drug dealers, drug czar William Bennett says, "There's no moral problem there. I used to teach ethics." (1989)

**2** "You know, your nose looks just like Danny Thomas'." —President Ronald Reagan, in 1984, to the Lebanese foreign minister, in response to a careful and authoritative briefing on the situation in terrorist-ridden Beirut

**3** A Miami taxi company is beginning to get worried about Sheik Mohammed Al Fassi's unpaid tab of $15,700.00. (1982)

**4** Thousands of fundamentalists call the Donahue and Griffin television shows to expose Procter and Gamble as a devil-worshipping firm because of its quarter-moon-and-stars logo. (1982)

**5** "I can't see the point of those drips, and I think he couldn't do anything else particularly well." —Francis Bacon on Jackson Pollock (1989)

**6** Christopher Reeve's live-in companion, Gae Exton, shares her traditional values with us, saying, "One illegitimate child is fine, but two is [sic], well, tacky!" (1981)

**7** "Look, I'm trying to run for President! I can't sit here and debate free trade v. fair trade!" —Pat Robertson (1988)

**8** At the Carlyle Hotel in New York, there's now a fax machine in every guest room. (1989)

**9** Bruce Willis. Cybill Shepherd. *Moonlighting*. (1985)

**10** New York City covers over all those boarded-up windows next to the Cross-Bronx Expressway...with scenic decals. (1988)

**11** A court for the first time orders a wife (Neva Rockefeller) to pay alimony to a husband. (1981)

**12** A robber in Dundalk, Maryland, tells a bank employee, "Give me $418, but no ones." (1989)

**13** An executive vice president for Arms Corporation of America explains how they can't keep up with orders for semiautomatic M-14s since the Bush administration banned the sale of foreign models. (1989)

**14** Billy Carter registers as an agent of Libya. (1980)

**15** Business consultant John Hudson announces his intent to manufacture an Oliver North doll, pointing out that "it's impossible for it not to sell." (1987)

**16** Simon and Schuster announces that it will publish Richard M. Nixon's autobiography in the spring of 1990 in a regular trade edition and at least two deluxe editions. And on audio cassettes. (1989)

**17** Bess Myerson pleaded guilty to shoplifting two days ago. (1987) ☢

**18** Domino's Pizza spokesperson Ron Hingst, on being confronted with the fact that there were 18 speeding deaths of Domino's "we'll-get-it-to-you-within-thirty-minutes" delivery drivers, allowed as how that worked out to only about one death per 11.5 million pizzas in 1988.

## JULY

**19**

"If they get rid of tailgating, what else is there to do?"
—New York Giants fan, on being told beer would no longer
be sold at night games (1989)

**20**

Search for an honest congressman rewarded when Florida
representative Sam Gibbons publicly says of the 1981 (yes,
1981) savings and loan bailout, "This is one of the worst
pieces of legislation I ever introduced."

**21**

In San Francisco today, the Fourth Annual Anarchists'
Convention opens. (1989)

**22**

Imelda Marcos releases her first record album and says,
"It's nice to be recognized for something positive." (1989)

**23**

Look out United States Football League, Trump's got an eye
on you. (1983)

**24**

In response to Mrs. Boesky's comments on the beauty of
the moon on a Paris night, Ivan says, "What good is the
moon if you can't buy it or sell it?" (1984)

**25** Washington, D.C., police, committed to ridding their beat of prostitutes, drive 24 of the ladies over into Virginia and dump them; the ladies take cabs back to work in D.C. (1989)

**26** One of the things executives do these days is pay as much as $30 to be locked up in a dark tank full of saltwater. (1980)

**27** "Outside of the killings, we have one of the lowest crime rates in the country." —Washington, D.C., Mayor Marion Barry (1989)

**28** On being asked why he was invited to the White House dinner for Indian prime minister Indira Gandhi, Wayne Newton says, "I'm an American Indian." (1982)

**29** George Bush says he can negotiate confidently with the Russians if Congress spends at least $72 billion to build the Stealth bomber. (1989)

**30** Nobody has any idea, with $22.5 billion spent and another $72 billion requested, whether the Stealth bomber will fly, but they do know that if it does it will achieve a top speed of 500 mph and "may be" harder to detect on radar than other airplanes. (1989)

## 31

A Brooklyn bank robber is nearly two blocks away from his successful hold-up when a mugger jumps him and steals his $2,100.00 take. (1989)

# August

...

If I can make Willie Horton a household name we can win the election.

—Lee Atwater in 1989

# AUGUST

**1** A blind man robs a bank in California, but being unable to find his way back out... (1989)

**2** The few aging hippies who do show up for the Woodstock 20th anniversary concerts bring lawn furniture. (1989)

**3** After losing his wallet in the Rockhaven Campground outhouse, a Lawrence, Kansas, man tries to retrieve it with his toes, but falls in and, stuck there, spends the night. (1989)

**4** Few notice when, today, Marine Corps Major Oliver North is assigned to the National Security Council. (1981)

**5** The U.S. Court of Appeals for the Ninth Circuit finds it OK to make up quotations by public figures. (1989)

**6** A market analyst says that Disney's film *Tron* may be one of the highest-grossing films of the summer. *Tron*? (1982)

**7** A five-year-old future Alan Dershowitz from Indiana sues Borden for a Cracker Jack box with no prize. (1982)

**8** "I need something like Sister Mary Theresa and Madame Curie and, uh, Irma La Douce, a little bit of everything." —Sylvester Stallone, on what he needs in the right girl (1989)

**9** "What kind of a Mickey Mouse operation are we getting into here?" —angry Disney World executive to representatives of troubled Delta Airlines, with which Disney had recently entered into an agreement (1987)

**10** Bruce Rice, president of Rice Aircraft, Inc., pleads guilty to selling doctored aircraft parts—mostly rivets and other fasteners that hold airplanes together. (1989)

**11** "Just Say No." (1984)

**12** "I'd like to see us open up that Alaska refuge, and that is important, because it was said once, remember, when they built the pipeline, 'Don't build the pipeline, you get rid of the caribou.' The caribou love it. They rub up against it, and they have babies. There are more caribou in Alaska than you can shake a stick at." —George Bush (1988)

# AUGUST

**13** "Magic" Johnson throws a birthday party for himself and then asks his guests for five minutes of silence in his honor. (1986)

**14** An order from Joan Rohlfs of the Metropolitan Council of Governments for the District of Columbia—where there's one lawyer per 22 real people—bans the use of yellow legal pads. (1989)

**15** In 1982, U.S. Postal Service's Ralph Jussell warns Americans that Special Delivery, Registered, and Express mail will be suspended for a while in the event of a nuclear war. First-class deliveries, however, will continue.

**16** New Age devotees gather at sacred sites around the world and meditate at dawn to usher in an era of world peace. (1987)

**17** The National Archives sells the use of its name in advertising to the Philip Morris companies. (1989)

**18** Pachecho, California, police raid a card game at the local trailer court and the deaf retirees in the game have to ask the officers to please repeat—"FREEZE! YOU'RE UNDER ARREST!!" (1981)

**19**
Malcolm Forbes flies hundreds of guests to Tangiers to celebrate his birthday. Forbes wears a kilt and that smile. (1989)

**20**
"His sense of humor is horseshit, and I feel sorry for him."
—Bryant Gumbel on David Letterman (1982)

**21**
"When Dan gets back from vacation, we're going to rehearse it, look at it and, if we like it, we will then do it," says the *CBS Evening News* executive producer regarding discussions under way to have Dan Rather stand during his news broadcasts. (1989)

**22**
Now people are out there videorecording their damn vacations. (1984)

**23**
The first of those Maxwell House commercials airs, the ones featuring Linda Ellerbee, the one who built her career on integrity. (1987) ☢

**24**
They're done counting!—157.6 million viewers throughout the world watched Independent Television News coverage of the Hugh Hefner–Kimberly Conrad wedding. (1989)

**25** "I've never been qualified for anything I've done." —Sonny Bono, on his running for mayor of Palm Springs. (1987)

**26** It's now not unusual to see grown-ups yelling "Awwwlll rrriiiight!" and slapping each other's hands in midair. (1984)

**27** "If Mr. Ghorbanifar, an Iranian, made one of your President's most important policies up in a bathroom, I'm sorry for the United States," says Manucher Ghorbanifar, disputing Oliver North's testimony—and speaking of himself in the third person. (1987)

**28** People are hanging on to rocks and climbing the outside of buildings. (1987)

**29** "Meet Bess Myerson, the next senator from the great state of New York!!!" — a Bess Myerson advance man, megaphone in hand, alerting bathers at Far Rockaway Beach (1980)

**30** Leona Helmsley is found not guilty on 8 of 41 tax evasion charges. (1989)

**31** Rainbow Bright and Twink. (1987)

# September

## •••

I can't understand all the fuss about
student grants. Carol managed to
save out of hers. Of course, we paid
for her skiing holidays.

> —Margaret Thatcher in 1984

# SEPTEMBER

**1** So that President Bush can hold actual illegal drugs in his hands during his address to the nation, the administration decides to score some crack. First, the drug dealer doesn't show up; then, the undercover drug agent's body microphone doesn't work; finally, today, on the administration's third try, they get the drugs but the cameraman videotaping the deal misses the action when he's assaulted by a homeless person. (1989)

**2** In Pittsfield, Massachusetts, the General Electric Corporation begins construction on civilization's first all-plastic house. (1988)

**3** "There is absolutely no doubt in my mind that rap music spurs violence." — John Norton, Pittsburgh Public Safety Commissioner (1986) ☻

**4** Explaining why *five weeks ago* he voted against a bill making the Veterans Administration a cabinet-level agency, Dan Quayle calls it "a youthful indiscretion." (1988)

**5** In a full-page advertisement in the *New York Times*, Whittles Communications enters history as the word "impactfully" first sees the light of day. (1989)

**6** Reverend Lee claims that the report earlier in the week from Reverend Abernathy that Reverend King had sex with two women the night before Reverend King was killed has to be a lie because Reverend Abernathy had passed out drunk that night. God bless. (1989)

"The caribou love it. They rub up against it, and they have babies. There are more caribou in Alaska than you can shake a stick at."

— George Bush (1988)

**7** In 1981, John Hinckley writes to the *Washington Post*, insisting that they cease to call him a "drifter" because his travels were due to his need to follow Jodie Foster around.

**8** In New Orleans lifeguards throw a party to celebrate their first drowning-free swimming season. At the end of the party, a body is found at the bottom of the pool. (1985)

**9** Kitty Kelley's latest literary endeavor tells how Frank Sinatra considers Ronald Reagan "a real right-wing John Birch Society nut—dumb and dangerous" and his wife Nancy "a dope with fat ankles who could never make it as an actress." (1986)

**10** "I ran the wrong kind of business, but I did it with integrity." —Sydney Biddle Barrows, madam (1986)

**11** "Though I don't mean to blame others for my drug abuse, more and more those glamorous Palm Beach nights with such sparklers as Alfred Bloomingdale created a need for some diversion to get me through to the dessert course." —Roxanne Pulitzer (1987)

**12** At the Miss America Pageant, Miss Delaware declares her favorite author to be "Steven Spielberg." (1987)

**13** Sabrina Aset— a.k.a. Most High Goddess, a.k.a. Mary Ellen Tracy—who's just been arrested for prostitution, explains the confusion: "I've always been very willing to do what God required, whether to be monogamous or to have sex with a few thousand men." (1989) ☙

**14** Deborah Gore Dean, who took eight years to graduate 507th (in a class of 509) from Georgetown University, is now in charge of the Department of Housing and Urban Development whenever Sam Pierce is busy watching *All My Children*. (1985)

**15** Look out, People's Express, here comes Frank Lorenzo!! (1986)

**16** *Miami Vice* premieres. (1984)

**17** A Pittsburgh man who finds several pounds of boneless flesh and a human lung in a plastic garbage bag says, "This is quite an unusual find for this part of town." (1988) ☙

**18** On being billed with the Easter show at Radio City Music Hall, an angry Liberace says, "You can have either the Resurrection or you can have Liberace. But you can't have both." (1986)

**19**
After Donald "Tony the Greek" Frankos confirms that Jimmy Hoffa is buried under the artificial turf in Giants Stadium, right next to the end zone, New York Giants punter Sean Lendetta notes how that "puts a whole new meaning in the term 'coffin corner.'" (1989)

**20**
"I was shot down, and I was floating around in a little yellow raft setting a record for paddling. I thought of my family, my mom and dad, and the strength I got from them. I thought of my faith, the separation of church and state." —George Bush, in 1987, recalling his thoughts after being shot down over Japanese waters during World War II

**21**
Otherwise perfectly nice and well-coiffed women in clothes from Anne Klein, Chanel, and Missoni are seen going to the office in sneakers. (1982)

**22**
The Marina del Rey, California, fire department rushes a 56-year-old man to the hospital who injured his neck while masturbating. (1986)

**23**
Peking gets its own Maxim's of Paris but the Chinese can't eat there without a special permit. (1983)

**24**
Senator Dan Quayle introduces a special tax break for golf pros. (1987) ♣

**25** Tomorrow the producers of *Dallas* will reveal that Bobby wasn't really killed after all. His death last season was only Pam's bad dream. (1986)

**26** Milo Stephens, who got himself a $650,000 settlement in 1977 from the New York subways when he threw himself in front a train entering a station, does not have the same luck this year—he throws himself into the pit and is un-scathed. (1982) ☞

**27** "Clearly you don't get as much pleasure out of food that you microwave. But food today is more of a maintenance function than a pleasurable experience." —Richard Nelson, director of market research services, Campbell's Soup (1989)

**28** An Arby's in Denver installs computers so customers can punch in their own orders and save even more seconds that would otherwise be spent speaking their order to a clerk. (1989)

**29** *thirtysomething* debuts, proving that (1) whining's OK, and (2) many people this age once read e.e. cummings. (1987)

**30** For the first time, the federal debt limit is raised to the $1 trillion level. (1982) ☞

# October

•••

There are too many Pollyannas
around. There should be more
pessimism.

—Wall Street analyst
Harry Laubscher after the
Dow Jones average fell 190 points
on Friday the 13th, October 1989

## OCTOBER

**1** "...in muted hues of pink, blue and green, done not quite in Empire style and without either a court train or redingote, but flared about the bottom in an Alençon lace effect and sprinkled throughout with tiny pink dots not unlike stephanotis adorning the Plaza Hotel's Grand Ballroom." —introduction of world's first designer diaper (1984)

**2** Pat Buchanan's photograph appears twice in the Mt. Vernon, New York, *Daily Argus*. (1989)

**3** In Los Angeles, a check-forging suspect successfully posts bail with a bad check. (1989)

**4** "Hanging someone wasn't really something in our knowledge base." —an official of the Washington State corrections department on trying to find a hangman for its first execution in 26 years (1989)

**5** Having promised Tammy Bakker that He will serve on Jim's jury as its 13th member, He delivers, and Jim is convicted. (1989)

**6** In an advertisement for *The Lost Writings of George Orwell*, Arbor House identifies Orwell as the author of *Animal House*. (1985)

**7** Redskins fullback John Riggins tells Supreme Court justice Sandra Day O'Connor, "Come on, Sandy, baby, loosen up. You're too tight." Then he passes out on the floor. (1985) ❷

**8** "My experience with blacks is that they're basically anti-Semitic. Now, I want to be fair about it. I think whites are basically anti-black." —Ed Koch (1984)

**9** Soviet scientists confirm that a spaceship with tiny-headed, 13-foot aliens inside touched down in Voronezh and vaporized a Soviet boy. (1989) ✒

**10** After being charged with torturing and killing 77 cats, a Decatur, Georgia, man blames the entire matter on stress caused by his failure to pass the state bar examination. (1989)

**11** "Rural Americans are real Americans. There's no doubt about that. You can't always be sure with other Americans. Not all of them are real." —Dan Quayle (1988)

**12** "Get me a woman." — Jim Bakker to the Reverend John Wesley Fletcher (1980)

# OCTOBER

**13** "Presleynost" is launched when Kolya Vasin—the Ambassador of Russian Rock 'n' Roll—steps off an airplane in Memphis wearing blue suede shoes and clutching an exit visa issued solely for a visit to Graceland. (1989)

**14** Evangelist Billy Graham joins Hollywood Boulevard's "Sidewalk of Stars." He goes in next to Wayne Newton. (1989) ✒

**15** The following correction runs in the *Sacramento Bee* : "The recipe for Elaine Corn's Southwestern chicken salad recipe should call for 2, not 21, jalapeño peppers." (1989) ❷

**16** Full-page ads in the nation's major newspapers announce Larry Flynt's candidacy for the presidency. (1983)

**17** Brooks Brothers puts pleats in its trousers! (1989)

**18** When an earthquake jolts the San Francisco area, killing over 200 and injuring hundreds more, George Bush sends in Marilyn Quayle. (1989)

**19** The California earthquake causes the World Series at Candlestick Park to be postponed, and Giants' radio announcer Hank Greenwald notes, "Distressingly, this may have been the best chance we had of getting rid of this ballpark." (1989)

**20** Presidential candidate Ronald Reagan drops a note of reassurance to the Air Traffic Controllers Union, promising that "my administration will work very closely with you to bring about a spirit of cooperation." (1980)

**21** The IRS quarterly Statistics of Income reports that 595 people with incomes in 1987 of over $600,000 didn't have to pay any federal income tax. (1989)

**22** Silent Witness sunglasses—you know, the ones with the gold-plated religious symbol—have a new spokesperson: Anita Bryant. (1983)

**23** "I feel great. We passed a wonderful pro-life bill. Notre Dame beat Southern Cal. God is in Heaven and all is right with the world." —Pennsylvania State Representative Stephen Freind (1989) ☘

**24** ABC orders 13 episodes of a new sitcom starring Dr. Ruth Westheimer. (1989)

**25** If this is a third Tuesday, a Navy officer with top-secret photographs and charts is making his way to a clairvoyant so the Navy can have her predictions of Soviet submarine movements. Honest. (1980)

**26** Coleco introduces its Adam computer. Pessimist buys Coleco stock. (1983)

**27** After issuing the 15,000th violation of quality assurance, the Nuclear Regulatory Commission thinks there might be a safety issue at the Moscow, Ohio, nuclear plant. (1983)

**28** In 1989, the following appears in the *Latrobe* (Pennsylvania) *Bulletin*:

LOST DOG
One eye, one leg missing, no tail, neutered
Answers to Lucky
Call Ron at Latrobe Armory

**29** In Raleigh, North Carolina, a banner in the room where a task force meets in an effort to improve the state's Scholastic Aptitude Test scores proclaims, "Excellance In Secondary Education." (1989)

**30** Pat Robertson says, "We ought to close Halloween down. Do you want your children dressing up like witches? They are acting out Satanic rituals." (1986)

**31**

An Iowa licensing board refuses to reopen the case of an optometrist who was placed on probation for having women strip to the waist for their eye examinations. (1989)

Special Delivery, Registered, and Express mail will be suspended for a while in the event of a nuclear war. First-class deliveries, however, will continue.

# November

• • •

Warhol spent most of the fifties
drawing shoes. These shoe drawings
are often described contemptuously
or dismissively; the fact is that shoes
are famously difficult to draw....

—Adam Gopnick in
*The New Yorker*
(yes, *The New Yorker*)

# NOVEMBER

**1** In New York City, Floyd Flow shows up in court to answer a weapons charge but forgets about the 76 vials of crack he's got with him. Floyd is arrested. (1986)

**2** While signing the bill making Martin Luther King, Jr.'s, birthday a national holiday, Ronald Reagan defends Jesse Helms' "sincerity" in believing that King was a communist sympathizer. (1983)

**3** Yesterday, the Senate—led by Jesse Helms—passed a "private" law restoring convicted felon Oliver North's $23,000 military pension; which is $2,000 less than he earns every time he speaks. (1989)

**4** Tonight, on a split screen, Joe Franklin interviews himself. (1988)

**5** "Let me emphasize that all of this will be done with the respect and dignity it deserves." — Chip Rieger of American Licensing on the use of Ernest Hemingway's name and image on fragrances and clothing (1989)

**6** Rockefeller Center, including Radio City Music Hall, is now owned by the Japanese. (1989)

# NOVEMBER

**7** Using a pseudonym and a call-girl agency, a Tel Aviv dentist arranges for a prostitute; when he shows up at the designated motel room, the prostitute turns out to be his wife. (1989)

**8** The Elvis Presley MasterCard is now available. (1988)

**9** Ed Meese announces that he wants employers to spy on workers in "locker rooms, parking lots, shipping and mail room areas and even the nearby taverns" so as to catch them using drugs. (1986)

**10** In Chicago today—for reasons unknown—Dan Rather stuck his head out of a speeding cab, waved his arms repeatedly, and screamed that he was being kidnapped. (1980)

**11** It's Veterans Day, which causes Bob Hope to note that the day "brings back a lot of memories to me 'cause, you know, I saw nine years of...those kids laughing and cheering... but I never realized till I saw *Platoon* what really went on with the serious stuff." (1987)

**12** "Cheap! For sale! Hey, baby! Right here! The Berlin wall! Just arrived! A chunk or a chip! Seven dollars an ounce!" —New York City street peddler (1989)

# NOVEMBER

**13** The CIA now refers to its mercenary soldiers in Nicaragua as "unilaterally controlled Latino assets." (1984)

**14** "When I hear people talking about money, it's usually people who don't have any." —GOP finance chairman Richard DeVos, countering criticism of the Reagan administration's economic plans (1981)

**15** After $47 million and five months of publication, Time Inc. folds *TV-Cable Week*. (1983) ☏

**16** "It is the end of civilization as we know it." —columnist Robert Novak, on a new (1987) directive forbidding executive branch employees from accepting meals or drinks from journalists. ☢

**17** Twenty-year-old Manhattan multimillionaire Arthur Rinwalt Rupley IV dreams that "someday I'll be like Helmsley and the rest of the big ones." (1980)

**18** In 1985, Allen Neuharth, founder of *USA Today*, proudly points out that "we look like television in print."

**19** Bernie Cornfield is back and this time he's selling vitamins. (1984)

**20** "This has been the best year of my life," says Shirley MacLaine. (1984)

**21** "Some people are a little better at it than others." — convicted murderer Aladena "Jimmy the Weasel" Fratianno, when asked if he was a good killer (1980)

**22** "[You] don't have to go to college to achieve success. We need the people who do the hard physical work of our society." —George Bush, addressing Hispanic East L.A. high school students (1989)

**23** Oh, boy, Colgate introduces the toothpaste pump! (1984) ❷

**24** Kenner's Christmas toy line includes in its "Building Blaster" series a nice little shuttle model that blows up, just like the real one. (1989)

# NOVEMBER

**25** General Electric marks down its U.S. Navy screwdriver from $780 to only $45. (1983)

**26** Bob Vesco is currently tying up his yacht as a guest of the nation in Cuba. (1983)

**27** On learning that free passage would now be allowed his countrymen, an East German border guard shouts, "But what about my job?" (1989)

**28** In Chanhassen, Minnesota, a woman without the cash to pay for her gas leaves her 5-month-old girl for collateral. (1989)

**29** The film directed, produced, cowritten, and starred in by Barbra Streisand, *Yentl*, is at a theater near you! (1983)

**30** Pittsburgh, Pennsylvania, city councilman Otis Lyons explains why he refuses to support abortion in cases of incest: "Some of the great leaders in the Bible married their sisters." (1989)

# December

• • •

May our nation continue to be the beakon of hope to the world.

—Marilyn and Dan Quayle,
Christmas 1989

## DECEMBER

**1** "F_ _ _ it, blow them up." —Donald Trump's purported order to destroy the deco art at Manhattan's Bonwit Teller building (1980) ❷

**2** Because an EMT was wearing a pair of their shoes when he got caught up in the midst of the prison riot in which dozens were injured—some stabbed and brutally beaten—and half the prison was going up in flames, the Bostonian Shoe Company is proud to announce (in all seriousness) their new advertising slogan: "What Does the Well-Dressed Man Wear to a Prison Riot?" (1989)

**3** A story produced for NBC's *Today* show, claiming that General Electric Corporation uses shoddy nuts and bolts in the airplane engines it builds, is edited to delete all references to NBC's owner, the General Electric Corporation. (1989)

**4** *The Morton Downey Jr. Show* premiered 47 days ago. (1987)

**5** "One billion toothbrushes and two billion armpits." —New York marketing executive in 1980, on "the China potential"

**6** "If this country ever loses its interest in fishing, we got real trouble." —George Bush (1988)

# DECEMBER

**7**  After Rona Barrett complains to Soviet spokesman Vladimir Posner about those ugly "fur hats" that Russians wear, Posner points out that the hats are worn to keep warm. (1989)

**8**  Hunter Thompson is now a war correspondent for *Rolling Stone*. Just like Ernie Pyle. (1983)

**9**  Taking time out from his own preparations for the most sacred of Christian holidays, Edwin Meese says, "...people go to soup kitchens because the food is free and that's easier than paying for it." (1983)

**10**  The $1,775 datebook is available at Saks, but only in burgundy. (1983)

**11**  "I think of my secret of success as being that I never was a pretentious person." —Geraldo Rivera (1987)

**12**  When police interrupt their theft of a pickup truck, three thugs escape by scaling a fence into San Quentin prison. (1989) ❧

**13** Laurie Anderson's *United States Live, Parts I-IV* is now available on the Warner label. (1984)

**14** Business consultant John Hudson announces he's adding more stuffing and a birthmark to his unsold Oliver North dolls and selling them as Gorbachev dolls. (1987)

**15** Catherine Deneuve plays a 3,000-year-old bisexual vampire in her latest film. (1983)

**16** CBS Sports commentator Jimmy "The Greek" Snyder points out that "the black is a better athlete to begin with because he has been bred to be that way since the days of slavery." Furthermore, he notes, if more blacks become coaches, "there's not going to be anything left for white people." (1987)

**17** On being asked if she thought that class barriers had broken down in Britain, Barbara Cartland responds, "Of course they have, or I wouldn't be sitting here talking to someone like you." (1982)

**18** After waiting in line eight hours for a Wilkes-Barre department store to open, a woman suffers a broken leg in the stampede to buy a Cabbage Patch doll. (1983)

# DECEMBER

**19**

In Chicago, a lost school bus driver stops her bus in mid-route, drives back to the deserted school building, dumps the students into the freezing weather, and drives away. One six-year-old child reports that the driver told them, "You're supposed to be gifted children. You figure out how to get home." (1989)

**20**

The *New York Times* reports that dozens of rural Americans are killed each year after they drink too much, lie down in the middle of the highway, and get run over. (1986) ☙

**21**

It's Thursday and Nicolae Ceauçescu has called a rally for this evening. (1989)

**22**

Pessimist buys a Sony Betamax format videoplayer. (1984)

**23**

Congress passes 1,379 pages of tax simplification. (1985) ☙

**24**

Philip Glass Glass Glass Glass Glass Glass Glass Glass Glass Glass Glass Glass Glass Glass Glass. (1982)

**25** Having just gotten a $34,900 raise, the U.S. House of Representatives announces the result of its annual Christmas charity drive. From its 435 representatives and 11,000 employees, it raised a grand $1,700 for the needy, or 15 cents per contributor. (1989)

**26** Elliott Abrams announces that the United States would fund a powerful radio station to promote anti-Sandinista ideas, because "there isn't any way for the people of Nicaragua to find out what's going on in Nicaragua." (1986)

**27** The long-awaited AT&T breakup is on and you will spend the next year trying to figure out how to choose your long-distance carrier. (1983)

**28** "We thought Didi was stupid, but evidently she lies around and thinks a lot." — Californian Jean Roper, on communing with her dog via a psychic whose specialty is pets (1987)

**29** If you missed the last Molly Ringwald movie, don't worry, because there's probably a new one playing near you and you won't notice the difference. (1980–1989)

**30** The United States continues to play loud rock 'n' roll music outside the Vatican embassy in Panama. (1989)

**31** "Finally, and most importantly, I want to tell you how sorry I am that this accident took place." —Exxon Chairman L.G. Rawl on the Prince William Sound oil spill (1989)

On learning that free passage would now be allowed his countrymen, an East German border guard shouts, "But what about my job?" (1989)

# GOOD GRIEF,
# ANOTHER INCREDIBLE
# OFFER!!
# (So?)

As the shameless pessimists listed below will tell you, and despite The Pessimist's inclinations, they reluctantly received free copies of this book because we used their nominated Bad Days. The same could happen to you if you aren't careful.

Share your Bad Days. Put your nomination on a postcard with your name and address and send it to The Pessimist, Box 1950, Boston, MA 02130.

As in the past, if we use your Bad Day we'll send you the next Pessimist book, if we can find someone to publish it. Where there are duplicates, the first one in will be the one to get the book. Trust us, because, as Spiro Agnew said, what does a man have but his integrity?

—JMB and RPM

Our special thanks to the following pessimists for their contributions to this travesty: Gayle Shadduck, Lillian Dobkin, Gerald Howard, Carol and Gary, Wayne Ishikawa, David Hoffmann, Deborah Friedman, Steve Drake, Anne Laszlo, John Durkin, Bill Luehning, and the most pessimistic of them all, Colleen Mohyde.

# SLURRY TRENCH CONSTRUCTION
# FOR POLLUTION MIGRATION CONTROL

# SLURRY TRENCH CONSTRUCTION FOR POLLUTION MIGRATION CONTROL

by

**Philip Spooner, Roger Wetzel, Constance Spooner,
Claudia Furman, Edward Tokarski, Gary Hunt,
Virginia Hodge, Thomas Robinson**

JRB Associates
McLean, Virginia

**NOYES PUBLICATIONS**
Park Ridge, New Jersey, U.S.A.

Published in the United States of America by
Noyes Publications
Mill Road, Park Ridge, New Jersey 07656

10 9 8 7 6 5 4 3 2 1

Library of Congress Cataloging in Publication Data
Main entry under title:

Slurry trench construction for pollution migration
    control.

    (Pollution technology review, ISSN 0090-516X ;
no. 118)
    Includes bibliographical references and index.
    1. Waste disposal sites--Design and construction--
Handbooks, manuals, etc. 2. Slurry trench construction--
Handbooks, manuals, etc. 3. Water, Underground--
Pollution--Handbooks, manuals, etc. I. Spooner, P.A.
II. Series.
TD743.S68   1985     628.4'456     84-22747
ISBN 0-8155-1020-9

# Foreword

This book is an in-depth description of the current state of the art of slurry trench construction. Background material for the evaluation of pollution migration control by slurry walls, as well as construction techniques and cost data, are included.

In recent years, increased efforts have focused on the problems caused by improper land disposal of wastes. The need to clean up disposal sites, and the need to site new, more secure facilities, have resulted in the innovation and adaptation of a wide variety of engineered measures to waste site remediation. One such measure is slurry trenching. The low permeability cut-off, or slurry wall, has been used as part of the remedial efforts at both hazardous and solid waste disposal sites. This handbook was developed so that the use of slurry walls for pollution control might be better understood.

After the presentation of the fundamentals of slurry wall use, the procedures for planning a slurry wall installation are given. These include, site investigation procedures for characterizing the surface and subsurface conditions, as well as waste and leachate characterization. The factors considered in slurry wall design are then presented, followed by an outline of accepted construction practices. The necessary methods to monitor and maintain a completed slurry wall are also included, along with the factors that influence costs. The handbook concludes with a series of evaluation criteria that correspond to the stages of a slurry wall installation.

The information in the book is from *Slurry Trench Construction for Pollution Migration Control,* prepared by Philip Spooner, Roger Wetzel, Constance Spooner, Claudia Furman, Edward Tokarski, Gary Hunt, Virginia Hodge, and Thomas Robinson of JRB Associates for the U.S. Environmental Protection Agency, February 1984.

The table of contents is organized in such a way as to serve as a subject index and provides easy access to the information contained in the book.

## NOTICE

# Acknowledgments

This document was prepared by JRB Associates for EPA's Office of Research and Development. Dr. Walter Grube, of the Municipal Environmental Research Laboratory, Solid and Hazardous Waste Research Division, was the EPA Project Officer. Philip Spooner was Task Manager and principal author for JRB. Other major contributors include Roger Wetzel, Constance Spooner, Claudia Furman, Edward Tokarski, Gary Hunt, Virginia Hodge, and Thomas Robinson, of JRB. Preparation of this handbook was aided greatly by the constructive contributions of the following reviewers:

| | |
|---|---|
| Herbert Pahren | U.S. EPA MERL |
| Douglass Ammon | U.S. EPA MERL |
| Jon Herrmann | U.S. EPA MERL |
| Richard Stanford | U.S. EPA OERR |
| Ann Tate | U.S. EPA CERI |
| Dr. David Daniel | Civil Engineer |
| S. Paul Miller | U.S. Army COE, Waterways Experiment Station |
| Nicholas Cavalli | ICOS Corporation of America |
| S. Geoffrey Shallard | Engineered Construction International, Inc. |
| George Alther | IMC Corporation |
| T. Leo Collins | General Electric Company |

The technical contributions of the following individuals were greatly appreciated.

| | |
|---|---|
| John Ayres | GZA Corporation |
| Robert Coneybear | Engineered Construction International, Inc. |
| David D'Appolonia | Engineered Construction International, Inc. |
| Jeffrey Evans | Woodward-Clyde Consultants |
| Donald Hentz | Federal Bentonite |

| David Lager | Case International Company |
| Christopher Ryan | Geo-Con, Inc. |
| Glen Schwartz | Engineered Construction International, Inc. |
| Enzo Zoratto | Engineered Construction International, Inc. |

Appreciation is also extended to the numerous other individuals from Federal, State and industry organizations who were contacted on matters related to this handbook.

# Contents and Subject Index

# 1. Introduction

1.1  Purpose of This Handbook

In recent years, an increased effort has been focused on the problems
caused by the improper land disposal of wastes.  The need to clean up thousands of these disposal sites, and the need to site new, more secure facilities, has resulted in the innovation and adaptation of a wide variety of
engineered measures to waste sites and their remediation.  One such engineered
measure is the technique of slurry trenching.  By this method, a trench of the
desired configuration is excavated using a bentonite and water slurry to
support the sides.  The trench is then backfilled with materials having far
lower permeability than the surrounding ground.  The low permeability cut-off,
or slurry wall, has been used as part of the remedial efforts at both hazardous and solid waste disposal sites.  This handbook was developed so that the
use of slurry walls for pollution control might be better understood.

This handbook is intended for use by individuals responsible for reviewing the scientific and technical aspects of slurry walls used for the control
of pollutants.  These individuals, from federal, state or local governments,
or from private organizations, may use this handbook to become familiar with
what slurry walls can and cannot be expected to do to help control pollution
migration.

This handbook is not intended to replace the services of a qualified
design engineer, nor is it intended to make inexperienced construction firms
qualified to install slurry walls.  Both the design and installation of slurry
walls are as much an art as a science, and the state-of-the-art is evolving
rapidly.

1.1.1  Organization and Use

This handbook is organized primarily to meet the needs of individuals
reviewing the technical aspects of slurry walls included in proposed waste
site remedial action plans.  These reviewers will need to become thoroughly
familiar with the entire handbook and probably some of the most commonly cited
references as well.  These reviewers may wish to follow the suggested review
procedures given in Section 8 of this handbook, or use the handbook contents
to develop procedures better suited to their own needs.

Other users of this handbook may be interested in only certain aspects of slurry wall use, and can refer to sections on:

- Background
- Theory
- Applications
- Related Remedial Measures
- Site Characterization
- Design and Construction
- Monitoring and Maintenance
- Major Cost Elements.

These sections cover nearly all aspects of slurry wall use for pollution control, and show how complex certain of these aspects are. Where differences of opinion exist on scientific or technical points, they are reported with as much documentation as possible. Nonetheless, the state-of-the-art in slurry walls for pollution control is rapidly changing. At this writing,, a committee of the American Society For Testing and Materials (ASTM) is beginning to develop new standards for slurry walls which will replace or modify many of the standards and procedures in use today. Measuring units used in the slurry wall industry are commonly expressed in the International System of Units (S.I.), except for hydraulic conductivity which is expressed in cm/sec. Therefore, S.I. units are used here. A conversion table is included following Section 8.

1.2  Background

This section provides a brief overview of slurry trench construction; what it is capable of, what its limitations are, and its history.

1.2.1  Slurry Trench Construction Techniques

As stated earlier, slurry trenching is a means of placing a low permeability, sub-surface, cut-off or wall, near a polluting waste source in order to capture or contain resulting contamination. These walls are described by the material used to backfill the slurry trench. Soil-Bentonite (SB) cut-off walls are composed of soil materials (often the trench spoils) mixed with small amounts of the bentonite slurry from the trench. Cement-bentonite (CB) cut-off walls are excavated using a slurry of Portland Cement and bentonite which is left to set, or harden, to form the final wall. Diaphragm walls are composed of pre-cast or cast-in-place reinforced concrete panels (diaphragms) installed using slurry trenching. Each of these, as well as hybrids of the three, has different characteristics and applications.

In general, SB walls can be expected to have the lowest permeability, the widest range of waste compatibilities, and the least cost. They also offer the least structural strength (highest compressibility), usually require the largest work area, and are restricted to relatively flat topography.

Cement-Bentonite cut-off walls can be installed at sites where there is insufficient work area to mix and place soil-bentonite backfill, and, by allowing wall sections to harden and then continuing the wall at a higher or lower elevation, are adaptable to more extreme topography. Although CB walls are stronger than SB walls, they are at least an order of magnitude more permeable, resistant to fewer chemicals, and more costly.

Diaphragm walls are structurally the strongest of the three types as well as the most costly. Provided the joints between panels are installed correctly, diaphragm walls have about the same permeability as cement-bentonite and because of a similarity of materials, about the same chemical compatibilities. Because of the higher expense and higher permeability of diaphragm walls, they are seldom used for pollution control.

Combinations of these three major backfill types may be included within the same wall. For example, a soil-bentonite backfill may be used for the majority of a wall, with cement-bentonite being used for a portion, such as a road or rail crossing, that requires greater strength. Being able to combine the various types of walls makes this technique adaptable to a wider range of site characteristics.

Depending on the situation in which they are employed, slurry walls may be keyed into an underlying, low permeability zone, such as a clay layer or bedrock, or, in the case of floating contaminants, may be only deep enough to intercept the upper few feet of the water table. These "hanging" slurry walls have been used to capture and recover floating petroleum products at several locations.

A number of other construction techniques can be used with slurry walls to widen their range of applicability. Among these are grouts, used to help key the wall into fractured bedrock; and sheet piles, used to protect the wall from stream erosion. Another technique involves placing a synthetic membrane within a cement-bentonite wall to lower its permeability and increase its resistance to attack by certain chemicals. This is a newly developed technique and is not yet documented in the literature. Also, no cost information is yet available.

### 1.2.2  History of Slurry Trench Construction

Slurry trench construction originated over 30 years ago in Italy and the United States. This technique is now in use throughout the world to meet a variety of engineering needs.

### 1.2.2.1  Technique Development

Slurry trench construction developed out of the use of slurries and muds in oil well drilling operations.  The early 1900's marked the first use of clay mud suspensions in the drilling of oil wells (Nash 1976).  The next 20 to 30 years involved investigations of slurry properties, such as thixotropy, and experimentation with additives to control the viscosity of drilling muds (Xanthakos 1979).  In 1929, bentonite clays were first used in drilling operations to stabilize deep wells in unconsolidated materials and to bring cuttings to the surface (Nash 1976).

In the late 1930's, Veder, in Milan, Italy, developed the concept of a continuous diaphragm wall constructed in a slurry-supported trench (U.S. Army Corps of Engineers 1978).  This concept evolved from a combination of two systems already in use; the mud-filled borehole, and the continuous bored-pile wall (Xanthakos 1979).  By the late 1940's, Veder tested structural slurry trenches and used slurry trenches in construction of the Milan subway (U.S. Army Corps of Engineers 1978, Winter 1976).

The U.S. Corps of Engineers also used slurry trench construction in the late 1940's.  At Terminal Island in California, the Corps constructed a slurry trench backfilled with plastic material to control salt water intrusion into a freshwater zone (Nash 1974).  The Corps also installed slurry trench cut-offs under Mississippi River levees for control of underseepage and piping (U.S. Army Corps of Engineers 1978).

The 1950's marked a period of continuous development and improvement of the slurry trench technique.  These activities were accompanied by laboratory research into the supporting properties of bentonite in excavations (Veder 1963).  In the early 1950's, concrete diaphragm walls were installed at dams in Italy to control seepage flow and support vertical loads (U.S. Army Corps of Engineers 1978).  In the United States, a soil backfilled cutoff trench was constructed beneath the Wanapum Dam in 1959; this represented the first use of this technique in the United States for seepage control at a major dam (Meier 1978, Jones 1978, Wilson and Squier 1969).

By the mid-1960's, slurry trench cutoffs had become an established method for use in earth dam construction as an alternative to traditional foundation methods.  A major improvement in slurry trench cut-off construction occurred in 1969 with the development of a self-hardening slurry.  This slurry is termed "coulis" and consists of cement, bentonite and water.  It is used both as a stabilizing fluid for trench construction and as the cut-off wall.  The slurry hardens in place to form a continuous, jointless wall (Soletanche 1977).

### 1.2.2.2  Applications

Early applications of diaphragm walls were as impermeable barriers below earth dams in sand and gravel, and water barriers to make reservoirs watertight (Veder 1963). Slurry trench methods were first adopted in pile and caisson construction and eventually led to the development of cast-in-place continuous concrete diaphragm walls (Soletanche 1977).

The use of slurry trench techniques developed in different directions in Europe and the United States. Primary uses of slurry trench techniques in Europe were the construction of structural walls and load bearing foundations (U.S. Army Corps of Engineers 1978). Additionally, European slurry trench methods generally involved cement-bentonite cut-off walls (Miller and Salzman 1980, Sommerer and Kitchens 1980). In the United States, slurry trench applications have been oriented toward earth-filled cut-offs for seepage control and dewatering purposes (U.S. Army Corps of Engineers 1978).

In many cases, slurry walls were initially used as temporary structures with the permanent structure built inside (Regan 1980). Diaphragm walls were considered dangerous as permanent structures because of their relative rigidity, susceptibility to cracking, and ability to induce cracking of earth-fill due to differential settlement. However, the development of procedures and materials to construct jointless, continuous diaphragm walls that are impermeable and have physical characteristics compatible with earth materials has led to the use of slurry walls as permanent structures (Soletanche 1977).

There are many applications for use of slurry walls for seepage control and for groundwater diversion during site dewatering. Present applications of slurry trench construction include:

- Retaining structures
- Load-bearing elements
- Underground facilities, transit stations, tunnels, etc.
- Docks and waterfront installations
- Cut-offs under dams
- Repair of leaky dams
- Pollution migration control.

For pollution control, slurry trenches have been constructed to control sewage, acid mine wastes, chemical wastes and sanitary landfill leachate (Ryan 1980a). Slurry cut-off walls have also been constructed to control the lateral movement of oily wastes. As of 1980, approximately 10 slurry cut-off walls have been constructed as spill control barriers (Ryan 1980b).

1.3  Limitations

Slurry walls have been installed to retard the movement of groundwater and leachate at numerous waste sites. These walls have been constructed at sites having widely divergent geologic, hydrologic, climatic and demographic characteristics. Slurry cut-off walls are applicable to numerous situations

involving hazardous wastes. They are not, however, an answer to all waste
site problems.

Slurry cut-off walls are not impermeable, and some leakage through them
is inevitable. Permeability values range from less than $10^{-8}$ cm/sec for a
well designed SB wall, to over $10^{-5}$ cm/sec for a CB wall. For this reason, and
the fact that they are usually less costly, SB walls are the most commonly
applied to waste site remediation.

A second limitation to the use of slurry cut-off walls is that exposure
to the wastes at some sites may cause increases in wall permeability. Wall
failure may occur if the slurry wall is not designed or installed well enough
to withstand exposure to the chemical constituents of the permeating solutions
or the hydraulic gradients at the site. Certain chemicals have been shown to
have pronounced effects on both bentonite and Portland cement, and even brief
exposure of some walls to high strength leachates can seriously threaten their
integrity.

The use of slurry walls is also limited by the need for heavy construction equipment, sufficient maneuvering area and suitable access. At some
disposal sites, the degree of complexity in the design and installation of a
slurry wall caused by site conditions may reduce its viability as a remedial
alternative. For example, if a disposal site was located in a congested urban
area, the cost of the added design and construction effort needed to deal with
nearby cultural features or other obstruction, could make some other alternative, such as excavation and secure reburial, more attractive.

Slurry walls will seldom, if ever, be the only remedial measure applied
to a site. They are usually accompanied by other measures, such as surface
sealing, or drains and collectors, as part of an overall engineered solution
to the site's problems. Some of these measures can extend the effectiveness
of the slurry wall beyond what it would be without them. For example, if a
waste site were to be surrounded by a slurry wall, and the site dewatered by
capping and pumping, the net flow of groundwater would be toward the interior
of the wall. In this way, some waste/wall compatibility problems can be overcome because the wall is being permeated with groundwater and not leachate.
The amount of leachate in the enclosed area is greatly reduced, and the life
expectancy of the wall is increased. Also, an extraction well or drain network can act as a back-up containment measure if, for some reason, the wall is
breached.

Most of the slurry walls that have been installed for pollution control
have been in the private sector, and the majority have been in place for a
relatively short time. In most cases, the firms for which these walls have
been installed are not willing to provide the monitoring data that are needed
to evaluate the performance of pollution control slurry walls. Slurry cut-off
walls used in other applications, such as dam projects, have yielded enough
data to evaluate short and long term geotechnical performance. Long term
performance of the walls in the presence of chemical contaminants, however, is
not as well documented. The best indications of the ability of slurry walls
to withstand chemical degradation over time comes from laboratory studies.

These studies have begun to better define the range of chemical compatibilities but have not, and may never, replace the need for extensive, site specific testing and long term monitoring.


1.4  Summary


This handbook is intended to provide reviewers of remedial actions with the means of evaluating technical aspects of slurry walls. Although these groundwater cut-off barriers have been in use for decades, the last several years have seen a rapid increase in their use for pollution control. Although slurry walls are versatile and adaptable control measures, they are not suited to all waste sites or waste types.

# 2. Theory of Slurry and Backfill Function

During construction of slurry walls, a slurry containing bentonite is placed in the open trench to support the trench walls. After excavation is completed, a mixture of bentonite slurry and soil, or a mixture of cement, bentonite, and water is placed in the trench to form the completed wall. To become familiar with slurry trench construction techniques, it is helpful to understand several key theoretical considerations. These can best be presented in the five questions listed below.

- Why is bentonite used in slurries and cut-off walls, and how can bentonite's behavior in slurries be explained?

- What factors affect bentonite slurry properties?

- What factors affect soil-bentonite wall performance?

- What factors affect cement bentonite slurry properties?

- What factors affect cement-bentonite wall performance?

Each of these questions is addressed in this section. The theoretical aspects of slurry functioning and slurry wall performance are emphasized. The practical applications of these theoretical aspects are presented in the Design portion of Section 5.

## 2.1 Bentonite

Bentonite is a soft, soapy-feeling rock found in commercial quantities in several areas of the United States. The rock is composed primarily of the clay mineral montmorillonite or smectite, as it is frequently called, with about 10 percent impurities, such as iron oxides and native sediments (Boyes 1975). Finely ground bentonite is mixed with water to form the slurry that is kept in the trench during excavation. Although there have been attempts to use locally available native clays in place of commercial bentonites, the evidence presented below illustrates why these attempts have not met with great success.

2.1.1   Rationale for Bentonite Use

The bentonite performs two functions when used in slurry trench construction.  First, it coats the sides of the trench with a thin, slippery layer
called a filter cake.  This low-permeability layer minimizes slurry seepage
out of the trench and groundwater seepage into the trench.  It also forms a
plane against which the weight of the slurry can push against the trench
sides.  The lateral pressure of the slurry against the filter cake on the
trench walls holds the trench open.  Thus, the first function of the bentonite
in the slurry is to form the filter cake.

The second function of the bentonite is to maintain slurry density.  The
bentonite particles must not settle out of the water and the slurry must hold
in suspension small particles of soil that inadvertantly fall into the slurry
during excavation.  The density of the bentonite is only slightly higher than
that of the water.  The density of the trench spoils is, however, much higher.
When the slurry holds particles of trench spoil in suspension, the density of
the slurry is increased.  The reason the slurry must be denser than water is
that a higher density slurry pushes against the trench walls with greater
force and assists in maintaining trench stability, particularly where
groundwater levels are high (Xanthakos 1979).

2.1.2   Bentonite Properties

The major properties of bentonite that are of interest in slurry trench
construction are:

- Swelling and hydration

- Extensive dispersion

- Thixotropy.

These properties are expressed when bentonite comes in contact with water.

2.1.2.1   Swelling and Hydration

When finely ground bentonite is mixed with water, both the exterior and
interior of the particles become wetted.  Water becomes attached to the surfaces of the clay particles in the bentonite through electrochemical interactions that will be described in detail later in this section.  Water also
penetrates the interior of the clay particles and forces each clay particle to
expand in volume, or swell.  In addition, the cations that are associated with
the clay particles become hydrated.  Thus the water reacts with both the
exterior and interior clay surfaces as well as the associated cations.  As a
result, the bentonite increases in volume.  Dry bentonite can swell as much as
10 to 12 times its original volume when wetted (Case 1982).  This swelling

continues until the bentonite is fully hydrated, which can take as long as a full week (Boyes 1975).

### 2.1.2.2  Dispersion

The surfaces of the clay particles in bentonite are predominately negatively charged. When two of these clay surfaces are in close proximity to one another, they repel each other due to long-range coulombic forces (Mustafa 1979). The causes of this repulsion will be discussed in Section 2.1.3.1. The effect of this repulsion is that the clay particles remain for the most part dispersed throughout the slurry. This dispersion allows the intimate mixture of bentonite and water to be maintained.

### 2.1.2.3  Thixotropy

When a mixture containing 5 percent by weight bentonite and 95 percent water is allowed to stand undisturbed for a few minutes, it changes from a viscous solution to a gel-like substance. When agitated or vibrated, the gel reverts to a slurry. The gel will reform each time the agitation ceases. This behavior is the result of a property called thixotropy.

Thixotropy is important in slurry trench construction because the gel structure is what keeps the particles of trench spoils in suspension in the slurry.

Thixotropy is measured by determining how strong of a gel structure is formed over a set period of time. As the strength of the gel structure increases and the speed of gel formation increases, the degree of thixotropy is said to increase. The strength of the gel structure (called the gel strength) is measured using a Fann Viscometer. Measurements are taken at 10 seconds and 10 minutes. In a high quality bentonite, the 10-minute gel strength should be only slightly higher than the 10 second gel strength (Boyes 1975).

### 2.1.3  Factors Affecting Bentonite Performance

Because bentonite is a natural, rather than manmade substance, its quality, and therefore its performance, is likely to vary from deposit to deposit. Several factors influence the performance of bentonites in slurry trench construction. These factors include:

- Montmorillonite content and properties
- Relative sodium and calcium concentrations

- Fineness of grinding of the raw material
- Chemical additives.

### 2.1.3.1  Montmorillonite Content

As mentioned previously, bentonite contains about 90 percent montmorillonite and 10 percent impurities (Boyes 1975).  Montmorillonite, or smectite,
is the crystalline material that gives bentonite its unique properties.  To
understand the behavior of this mineral, it is necessary to know its general
structure and some of the interactions between montmorillonite crystals, water
molecules, and cations.  A description of montmorillonite structure is given
below, followed by a detailed discussion of clay-water and clay-cation
interactions as they affect the physical properties of montmorillonite.

### a.  Montmorillonite Crystal Structure

Crystals of this clay are composed of three distinct layers, as shown in
Figure 2-1.  The outer layers are a tetrahedral arrangement of silicon and
oxygen molecules.  Some of the silicon atoms in these layers have been
replaced by aluminum.  Sandwiched between the silica layers is a layer of
aluminum atoms surrounded by six hydroxyl or oxygen atoms in an octahedral
shape.  Some of the aluminum atoms in this layer have been replaced by
magnesium.  Because of the substitutions in the three layers, unsatisfied
bonds exist within the crystal, resulting in a high net negative charge.  To
satisfy this charge, cations and water molecules are adsorbed onto the
internal and external surfaces of the clay crystals.  These surfaces comprise
the exchange complex of the clay.  The types of cations adsorbed on the
exchange complex have a great influence on the properties of the clay (Brady
1974).

The characteristics of bentonite slurries are caused to a large extent by
the properties of the montmorillonite they contain.  As described previously,
three sets of properties are particularly relevant to slurry function.  These
are:

- Degree of hydration and swelling
- Flocculation and dispersion characteristics
- Gel strength and thixotropy.

The extent to which these montmorillonite properties are expressed varies
considerably, depending on the types of cations adsorbed to the surface of the
clay.  Although numerous cations and organic molecules can be adsorbed, two
cations are of primary interest in slurry trenching situations.  These are
sodium and calcium.

## Figure 2-1.
## Montmorillonite Crystal Lattice, Showing Adsorbed Cations and Oriented Water Molecules

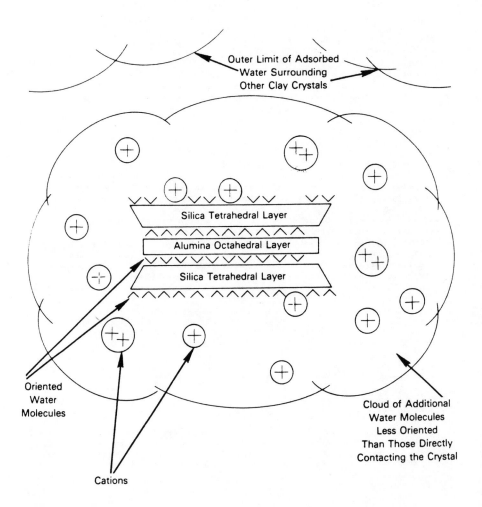

Note: Not to Scale
Source: Based on Grim, 1968

Sodium-saturated montmorillonites behave quite differently than the calcium-saturated varieties. These differences are summarized in Table 2-1. Theories governing the reasons for these differences are described in detail below.

### b.  Theory of Clay Hydration and Swelling

During hydration of montmorillonite, water molecules are adsorbed to the clay crystal surface by the attraction between the hydrogen atoms on the water molecules and the hydroxyls or oxygens on the outer clay surface and in between the silicate layers. This is illustrated in Figure 2-1. The adsorbed water is held so strongly by the clay that it may be thought of as a non-liquid, or a semi-crystalline substance. Even the water molecules that do not directly contact the clay surface are influenced by the montmorillonite crystals. This is because the water molecules that are bonded to the clay surface form partially covalent bonds with a second layer of molecules. In addition, the second layer of water molecules forms partially covalent bonds with a third layer, which bonds to a fourth layer, and so on. The water in these layers surrounding the crystal surface is oriented, forming what may be thought of as a semi-rigid structure (Grim 1968).

The number of layers of water molecules and the regularity of their configuration is dependent upon the types and concentrations of cations associated with the clay. The cations tend to disrupt water adsorption, and the degree of disruption depends on the size of the hydrated cation, its valence, and its tendency to disassociate with the clay surface during hydration (Grim 1968).

Sodium ions disrupt hydration much less than calcium ions. For example, sodium-saturated montmorillonites have been found to influence the orientation of water molecules more than 100 Angstroms from their crystal faces. This corresponds to about 40 molecular layers of water. In contrast, calcium-saturated montmorillonites have much smaller spheres of influence, on the order of 15 Angstroms, or about 6 molecular layers of water (Grim 1968).

The observable effects of these sub-microscopic interactions are that sodium montmorillonites adsorb much more water and swell far more than do calcium montmorillonites. As a result, as the amount of sodium on the exchange complex of montmorillonite increases, the amount of swelling increases (Rowell, Payne and Ahmad 1969). In addition, a 5 percent solution of highly hydrated sodium montmorillonite has a much higher viscosity than a 5 percent calcium montmorillonite solution. In fact, a 5 percent solution of sodium bentonite in water can exhibit a viscosity of 15 centipoise, but it takes 12 percent calcium montmorillonite in a solution to obtain the same viscosity (Grim and Guven 1978). This is illustrated in Figure 2-2.

TABLE 2-1

COMPARISON OF SODIUM AND CALCIUM-SATURATED MONTMORILLONITES

| Parameter | Sodium-Saturated Montmorillonite | Calcium-Saturated Montmorillonite |
|---|---|---|
| Swelling upon hydration, $cm^3$/g of clay | 11 (1) | 2.5 (1) |
| | (Wyoming sodium bentonite) | (4 base-exchanged bentonites tested)* |
| Hydration rate, 5% solution (2) | Hydrated to ~9cP in 10 min., stabilized at 9.2cP by 20 min. | hydrated to ~13cP in 10 min., stabilized at ~14 to 18 cP in 4 hours.* |
| | 3% solution of polymer treated sodium bentonite hydrated to 17.2cP in 10 min., then stabilized. | |
| Cation exchange Capacity, meq/100g. | 80-150 (3) | 60-100 (2) |
| Degree of thixotropy | high (2) | low (6) |
| Liquid limit | 300-700 (4, 5) | 155-177 (4) |
| Plastic Limit (4) | 75-97 | 65-90 |
| Yield in barrels of 15cP drilling mud per ton of clay (4) | 125 | 18-71 |
| Percentage of clay by weight in water to produce a 15cP colloidal suspension (4) | ~5 | ~12 |

(continued)

TABLE 2-1 (continued)

| Parameter | Sodium–Saturated Montmorillonite | Calcium–Saturated Montmorillonite |
|---|---|---|
| Permeability of a 9:3 quartz to clay mixture· (cm/sec) (4) | $2.76 \times 10^{-9}$ | $7.2 \times 10^{-7}$ |
| Permeability of a 7:3 quartz to clay mixture (cm/sec) (4) | $5.0 \times 10^{-10}$ | $3.5 \times 10^{-8}$ |

*Base-exchanged bentonites are calcium bentonites that have been treated with sodium compounds to increase their adsorbed sodium content. They are commonly used in European slurry trenching construction (Boyes 1975).

References:  (1) Baver, Gardner and Gardner 1972, (2) Boyes 1975, (3) Grim 1968 (4) Grim and Guven 1978, (5) Xanthakos 1979, (6) Case 1982.

## Figure 2-2.

# Viscosity and Weight of Mud in Relation to Percentage of Bentonites and Native Clays in Fresh Water

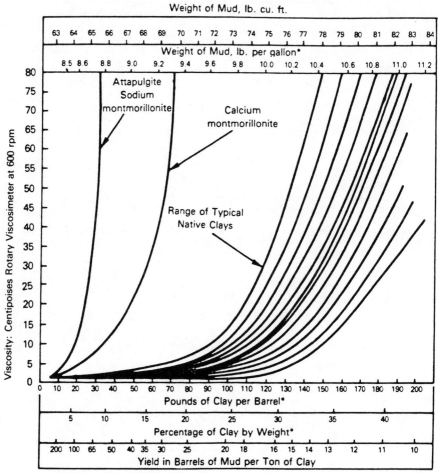

*Clay Specific Gravity Assumed to be 2.50.

c.  Theory of Flocculation and Dispersion

Adsorbed cations also influence the flocculation and dispersion of colloidal clay suspensions.  This is relevant to slurry wall construction in that ions in the groundwater and calcium ions in cement strongly affect slurry properties.

Montmorillonite crystals that are saturated with calcium ions have smaller spheres of influence than sodium-saturated types.  This is thought to occur because the larger divalent calcium ions are held more strongly to the clay, thus the effective net negative charge on each clay particle is lowered, and the size of the diffuse double layer surrounding each clay particle is reduced.  The diffuse double layer is a swarm of cations and water molecules near the surface of the clay particle, surrounded by a layer of anions that are attracted to the cations.  The concentration of the cations decreases as one moves away from the clay surface.  The diffuse double layer acts as a buffer between clay particles (Baver, Gardner and Gardner 1972).  As shown in Figure 2-3, clay faces exhibit a net negative charge, while the edges have a positive charge.  This results in a repulsion between the crystal faces but an attraction between edges and faces.

When sodium is the dominant cation on the clay surface, the diffuse double layer is extensive and the colloids are well dispersed throughout the water.  Very little face-to-face contact occurs.  When calcium is present in sufficient quantities, the double layer is constricted and the water molecule orientation is severely reduced.  Thus, the repulsion between clay crystals is reduced, face-to-face contact can occur, and the particles can form "packets," or "flocs."  (See Figure 2-3.)  The formation of flocs is called flocculation, and this process reduces the amount of swelling that occurs and the viscosity of the solution (Baver, Gardner and Gardner 1972; Boyes 1975).

One of the observable effects of flocculation on slurries and slurry walls is a substantial increase in permeability.  When the zone surrounding each particle is constricted, the amount of swelling is reduced and voids are created.  Through these voids, solution movement can and does occur.  As shown in Table 2-1, the permeability of a mixture of 7 parts quartz sand and 3 parts sodium montmorillonite was measured at $5.0 \times 10^{-10}$ cm/sec, while the same mixture using calcium montmorillonite had a permeability two orders of magnitude higher, or $3.5 \times 10^{-8}$ cm/sec.  In slurries, when flocculation occurs, the flocs can become large enough to begin settling out of the suspension (Boyes 1975).  This can reduce trench stability and interfere with filter cake formation, as discussed earlier in this section.

d.  Theory of Gelation and Thixotropy

One of the most interesting and useful properties of montmorillonite suspensions is thixotropy.  This property is the ability of the colloidal suspension to thicken, or gel upon standing, become less viscous when agitated, yet re-gel when agitation ceases.  It is caused by the formation of

# Figure 2-3.
# Bentonite Particles During Hydration, Gelation, Flocculation, and Dispersion

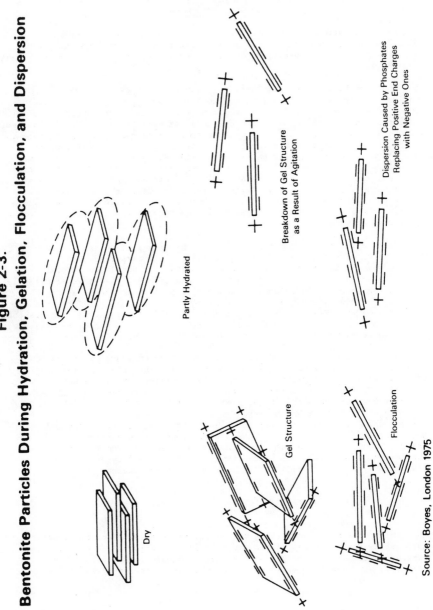

Dry

Partly Hydrated

Gel Structure

Breakdown of Gel Structure as a Result of Agitation

Flocculation

Dispersion Caused by Phosphates Replacing Positive End Charges with Negative Ones

Source: Boyes, London 1975

a "house of cards" structure between positively charged clay particle edges and negatively charged clay faces, as illustrated in Figure 2-3 (Xanthakos 1979). In practice, the gelation of the bentonite slurry provides support for small particles of soil to remain in suspension rather than to sink to the trench bottom (Boyes 1975).

The amount of thixotropy is determined by measuring the gel strength of the slurry. The gel strength is "the stress required to break up the gel structure formed by thixotropic buildup under static conditions" (Boyes 1975). It is measured using a Fann viscometer, as described in Section 4. The difference between the gel strength 10 seconds after agitation and the gel strength after standing for 10 minutes is a measure of the slurry's thixotropy (Xanthakos 1979).

Measurements of 10 minute gel strengths of bentonite slurries can range from about 5 to 20 $lb/ft^2$ and average 10 to 15 $lb/ft^2$ (Xanthakos 1979).

The bentonites used during slurry trench construction behave essentially like the sodium saturated montmorillonites described above. The properties of hydration, flocculation, dispersion and gel strength that are exhibited by the slurries are a result of the interactions of montmorillonite crystals, water molecules, and cations. The ability of a bentonite slurry to perform its functions during slurry trench construction is dependent on these interactions.

### 2.1.3.2   Relative Sodium and Calcium Concentrations

Natural sodium bentonite from Wyoming is commonly used in many of the slurry trenching operations in the United States. These bentonites do not contain pure sodium montmorillonite. One bentonite was reported to contain 60 percent sodium on its exchange complex, with the remaining sites being held by calcium and magnesium. However, the average distribution of cations on Wyoming bentonite is somewhat different. Most of the Wyoming bentonite currently being sold contains an average of 38 to 50 percent sodium, 15 to 35 percent calcium and 10 to 30 percent magnesium (Alther 1983).

High sodium bentonites should be more effective than the low sodium grades in many situations. At sites where a high concentration of calcium salts occurs in the soil or groundwater, or where cement bentonite slurries will be used, higher sodium bentonites are particularly recommended, for the reasons described below. The detrimental influence of the calcium from the cement or the groundwater on the sodium bentonite can be substantial. This is due to the strong attraction between calcium ions and montmorillonite crystals. Because this attraction is so strong, calcium ions can easily displace sodium ions on the clay. The ease of replacement of sodium by calcium increases as the concentration of calcium in the solution and on the clay surface increases. After about 30 percent of the exchange sites on the clay surface become occupied by calcium, the bentonite acts more like calcium montmorillonite than the sodium variety (Grim 1968).

Because there are limited quantities of natural sodium bentonites, some areas are forced to use specially treated calcium bentonites instead. This occurs most frequently in Europe. These calcium bentonites are exposed to sodium-containing materials such as sodium hydroxide to force some of the calcium ions off of the exchange complex of the montmorillonite and then replace them with sodium ions (Grim 1968). Sodium carbonate, which is less expensive and more effective than sodium hydroxide, is also used on some bentonites (Alther 1983). As long as there is less than 30 percent calcium and at least 50 percent sodium on the exchange complex of the montmorillonite, the material will act essentially like a sodium montmorillonite (Grim 1968; Shainberg and Caiserman 1971).

### 2.1.3.3  Bentonite Particle Size

This purely physical parameter can influence the performance of the bentonite in a number of ways. Finely ground bentonite has a larger surface area per unit weight than coarser bentonite because as particle size decreases, surface area per unit weight increases. The increased surface area of the finer particles allows the bentonite to hydrate more readily and form a gel structure more quickly than coarser particles of the same bentonite. Thus the average particle size of the bentonite can affect its performance in the slurry. Typically, the types of bentonite that are recommended for slurry trenching have been pulverized to yield particles small enough so that 80 percent will pass through a number 200 mesh sieve (Federal Bentonite 1981).

## 2.2  Bentonite Slurries

The Wyoming bentonites most commonly used in slurries are mixed at a rate of from 4 to 7 percent bentonite in 93 to 96 percent water (Boyes 1975). This muddy mixture stabilizes the sidewalks of the open trench during excavation. The properties of a well-functioning slurry and the factors that affect bentonite slurry quality are discussed below.

### 2.2.1  Bentonite Slurry Properties

To maintain trench stability while exhibiting suitable flow character-istics, the slurry must have the proper viscosity, gel strength and density. It must form a thin, tough, low-permeability filter cake rapidly and repeatedly. The bentonite slurry supplied to the trench may meet or exceed the quality standards stated in the specifications, however, slurry properties are altered during trench excavation and slurry quality may either improve or degrade during use. Table 2-2 presents data on fresh and in-trench slurries. As shown in this table, the density, viscosity, gel strength, and solids content of the slurry generally increases during excavation, while the overall water content decreases, due to the increased solids content. Brief

TABLE 2-2.

SPECIFIED PROPERTIES OF BENTONITE AND CEMENT BENTONITE SLURRIES

| Parameter | Bentonite Slurry | | Cement-Bentonite Slurry | |
|---|---|---|---|---|
| | Fresh-Hydrated | During Excavation | Fresh-Hydrated | During Excavation |
| Density (g/cm$^3$) (p.c.f.) | 1.01–1.04 (1,2) 65 (3) | 1.10–1.24 (2) 69–85 (4) | 1.03 to 1.4 (8) | |
| Viscosity, apparent (Seconds Marsh) (centipose) | 38–45 (1,5) ~15 | 38–68 (6) | 40–45 (8) ~15 (7) | 38–80 (8) >130 (7) |
| Viscosity, plastic | <20* (7) | | 9 (7) | 30–50 (7) |
| Filtrate Loss, ml | <30 (7) range 15–30 (3) | range 15–70 (6) apparent average 40–60 (6) | 100–300 (3,7) | |
| pH | 7.5 to 12 (6) | 10.5–12 (6) | 12–13 (7) | |
| Water Content, % by weight | ~93–97 (6) | ~78–82 (7) | 76 (7) | 55–70 (7) |
| Bentonite Content, % by weight | 4–7 (6) | ~6 (6) | 6 (7) | 6 (7) |
| Other Ingredients, % by weight | sand~<1*(3) solids ~2 (6) | sand <5* (3) solids 3–16 (6) | cement 18 (7) solids 15–30 (7) | -- 30–45 (7) |
| Gel Strengths 10 seconds, Pascal 10 minutes, Pascal | 7–30 (6) | ~20–40 (6) | 15 (7) 18 (7) | 10 (7) 22 (7) |
| 10 minutes, lb/100 ft$^2$ (24–72 dynes/cm$^2$) | 5–15 (2) | -- | -- | -- |

*Specification for construction of tremie concrete diaphragm walls.

References: (1) Case 1982, (2) Xanthakos 1979, (3) Millet and Perez 1981, (4) US Army Corps of Engineers 1976; (5) Guertin and McTigue 1982b, (6) Boyes 1975, (7) Jefferis 1981a, (8) Ryan 1976.

descriptions of slurry viscosity, thixotropy (gel strength) and density are given below.

### 2.2.1.1  Viscosity

The viscosity of a slurry must be maintained at a level high enough to assist in stabilizing the trench walls, but low enough to avoid interfering with trench excavation (Ryan 1976). Viscosity is a term used to describe a fluid's resistance to flow. It is caused by interparticle attraction (cohesion) and inter-particle friction (Millet & Perez 1981). In bentonite slurries, about 80 percent of the viscosity is due to the attraction between montmorillonite crystal edges and faces. The remaining 20 percent is due to friction (Grim and Guven 1978). Ideally, a fresh bentonite slurry should have a viscosity equivalent to 40 seconds, as measured on a Marsh cone (D'Appolonia 1980).

Marsh cone readings, which are used to measure slurry viscosity, do not really measure viscosity. Instead they measure a series of interrelated properties including density, viscosity, and shear strength (Hutchison et. al., 1975). The Marsh cone viscometer consists of a standard size funnel. To measure slurry viscosity, 1 U.S. quart (946 cm$^3$) of slurry is placed in the funnel. The time taken for this quantity to flow through the funnel is the viscosity in Marsh seconds. This test indicates the response of the slurry to conditions found in the trench. For example, Marsh cone readings less than 40 seconds indicate a slurry that has poor filter cake formation and insufficient trench-supporting ability (D'Appolonia 1980a). Marsh cone readings also indicate the workability of the slurry. If too high, the slurry can become too dense and difficult to work with. If too low, trench wall stability may suffer (Ryan 1976). D'Appolonia (1980a) found that slurry viscosity has a direct influence on filter cake permeability and is one of the most crucial slurry characteristics. The relationship between viscosity and filter cake permeability is shown in Figure 2-4.

### 2.2.1.2  Gel Strength

The gel strength represents the shear strength of the slurry when it is not agitated. It is caused by the edge-to-face linkage of clay crystals in the slurry. Gel strengths are measured using a Fann rotational viscometer, as described in Section 4. Typical values average around 15 lb/ft$^2$ (Xanthakos 1979).

Thixotropy, which is measured as gel strength, is in essence, the shear strength of the slurry. Stated differently, it is the resistance of the solids in the slurry to movement, or shearing (Baver, Gardner and Gardner 1972).

It is evident that viscosity and gel strength are ways of measuring the resistance to movement in liquids and solids, respectively. Because a

### Figure 2-4.

## Relationship between Filter Cake Permeability and Slurry Viscosity

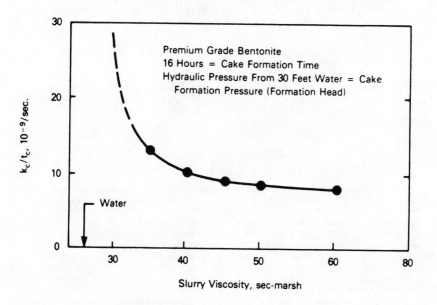

Premium Grade Bentonite
16 Hours = Cake Formation Time
Hydraulic Pressure From 30 Feet Water = Cake
Formation Pressure (Formation Head)

Slurry Viscosity, sec-marsh

Source: D'Appolonia (1980)

bentonite slurry is a thixotropic suspension, it displays properties of both solids and liquids, thus the consideration of both slurry properties is appropriate.

### 2.2.1.3  Density

A fresh slurry of 4-8% bentonite is only slightly denser than water, averaging less than 65 lb/ft$^3$ (1.04 g/cm$^3$) (Case 1982, Xanthakos 1979).  As particles of excavated materials fall into the trench, they become suspended in the slurry and cause the slurry's solids content and density to increase. Densities may increase to 85 lb/ft$^3$ (1.34 g/cm$^3$) or higher when excavating in sandy soils (Shallard 1983).

### 2.2.1.4  Filter Cakes

The filter cakes that are formed on both trench wall are extremely important both during excavation and possibly after backfilling as well.  The formation, function and desirable characteristics of filter cakes are described below.

#### a.  Filter Cake Formation and Function

When trench excavation is initiated, the slurry is pumped into the trench to maintain a slurry level at or near the initial ground level (Millet and Perez 1981).  As the slurry is introduced into the trench, it flows into pores in the strata through which the trench is cut.  Leakage of slurry into these voids continues until the flat clay particles in the slurry begin to accumulate in layers, which grow large enough to bridge the gaps between the soil particles, or until gelation of the slurry within the pores occurs. Figure 2-5 illustrates the relatively rapid initial slurry loss, followed by a reduction in the rate of loss.  This reduction is caused by the formation of a layer of clay particles "plastered" on the trench sides, which reduces lateral liquid flow out of the trench and into the adjacent soil.  This layer is called a filter cake.

The filter cake is a thin glue-like membrane composed of closely packed bentonite particles (Case 1982).  The solids content of the newly formed filter cake ranges from 10 to 50 percent, with higher solids contents found in filter cakes from calcium than from sodium bentonites (Grim and Guven 1978). The filter cake from a slurry containing 5 percent bentonite typically contains 15 percent bentonite (Hutchinson et al 1975).  During active excavation, the filter cake is usually less than 3 millimeters thick.  This thin layer of clay is, however, an effective barrier to water movement as the permeability of the filter cake can be as low as $10^{-9}$ cm/sec (Xanthakos 1979).

## Figure 2-5.

## Fluid Loss During Filter Cake Formation

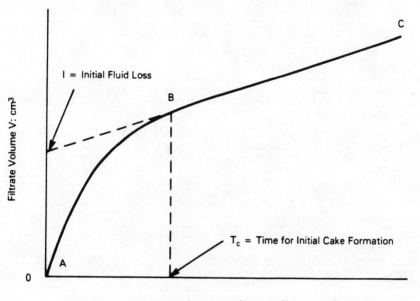

Source: Hutchinson, et al. 1975

Formation of the filter cake is of critical importance in slurry trench construction. This membrane performs numerous functions, including:

- Minimization of slurry loss into surrounding soils

- Stabilization of the soil that is in contact with the slurry by gelling in the soil pores and by plastering the particles against the trench walls

- Providing a plane on each trench wall against which the hydraulic pressure and dead weight of the slurry can act to stabilize the excavation.

b.   Desirable Filter Cake Characteristics

Desirable characteristics of filter cakes include rapid formation and re-formation when necessary, resistance to shearing, and low permeability. Experience has shown that a thin filter cake is an indication of a tough, impermeable membrane, but a thick "flabby" filter cake is likely to allow high fluid losses (Boyes 1975).

Filter cakes must be formed rapidly when the initial soil contact occurs, in order to avoid excessive slurry losses. These membranes must resist mechanical disruption by the backhoe bucket or clamshell during trench excavation. If inadvertently scraped off the trench wall during excavation, the slurry must be of such composition as to allow rapid formation of a new filter cake to avoid possible collapse of the trench.

A high gel strength is desirable in the filter cake because the gel structure contributes to shear strength, and the filter cake must resist shearing forces from both the excavation equipment agitated slurry and the soil comprising the trench wall. In addition, high gel strength indicates rapid formation of a gel structure. When the slurry penetrates soil pores, rapid gelation assists in restricting further slurry flow and thus minimizes slurry losses (Xanthakos 1979).

A final desirable filter cake characteristic is low permeability. The movement of water through the filter cake should be minimized to:

- Avoid wetting and thus softening and lubricating unstable layers that may be present in the soil surrounding the trench (Boyes 1975),

- Avoid increasing pore water pressure, because this increases the total stress on the system and reduces the angle of friction in the soil surrounding the trench (Hutchinson et al. 1975)

- Maintain the slurry level in the trench well above the groundwater level. This sustains the thrust of the slurry on the trench side walls by restricting the pressure losses due to filter cake leakage (Xanthakos 1979).

2.2.1.5  Resistance to Flocculation

In addition to having the proper viscosity, gel strength, density, and filter cake characteristics, a slurry should also have a certain level of flocculation resistance.

As noted earlier, flocculation is undesirable in slurries because as the clay particles form clumps, their effective hydrated diameters are greatly reduced. This increases the size and number of the voids available for water movement, which increases the permeability of the system (Shainberg and Caiserman 1971). Using bentonites that contain a high concentration of sodium or that are chemically treated to resist flocculation can help reduce the likelihood of permeability increases due to flocculation.

Sodium bentonites resist flocculation more effectively than calcium bentonites because the sodium bentonites swell more extensively than the calcium-saturated types. Montmorillonites that have 50 percent of their exchange complex occupied by sodium ions act essentially like pure sodium montmorillonites (Shainberg and Caiserman 1971). However, as the sodium content of the clay decreases, the permeability increases and swelling decreases proportionately (Rowell, Payne and Ahmad 1969). After replacement of sodium by calcium on the exchange complex of the clay begins, it can continue until nearly complete replacement has occurred. In addition, the sodium tends to become more easily displaced as the amount of sodium in the clay decreases (Grim 1968). Thus, a large sodium concentration in the clay is desirable to aid in resistance to flocculation.

2.2.2  Factors Affecting Bentonite Slurry Performance

Numerous factors affect the performance of bentonite slurries. Trench designers should be aware of these factors to maximize performance and minimize problems and unnecessary expenditures. The theoretical aspects of slurry performance are given in this section. The practical applications of these considerations are discussed in Section 5.

Among the factors that affect slurry performance are:

● Filter cake performance

● Gel strength

● Density

● Use of chemical of physical additives.

Each of these factors is described below.

2.2.2.1  Filter Cake Performance

The efficiency of the filter cake in performing its functions depends on numerous factors. These include:

- Characteristics of the slurry
- Characteristics of the strata surrounding the trench
- Time allotted for filter cake formation
- Hydraulic gradient between the slurry and the groundwater
- Presence of contaminants in the spoils or groundwater.

Bentonite quantity and quality strongly affects filter cake functioning. Factors such as the bentonite concentration, the mixing methods used, and the exchangable sodium percentage influence the filter cake thickness, formation time, and permeability.

a.  Bentonite Concentration

Figure 2-6 shows the effect of increasing the bentonite concentration of the slurry on the amount of initial slurry loss. Slurry loss is reduced because the higher bentonite concentration allows greater clay particle interaction. This results in more rapid filter cake formation and higher gel strength in the soil pores that are wetted by the slurry. To minimize slurry loss and consequent trench instability, it is recommended that the bentonite content of the slurry be maintained above 4.5 percent (Hutchinson et al. 1975).

b.  Bentonite Quality

The quality of the bentonite used in slurries greatly influences filter cake formation and performance. Criteria for bentonite quality include sodium content, fineness of grinding, and type and effects of chemical treatments.

The sodium content of the montmorillonite determines the hydraulic conductivity and resistance to flocculation of the filter cake. Montmorillonites containing high sodium contents have been found to swell to a greater degree upon hydration than those containing less sodium. In addition, several researchers have found a strong correlation between the amount of swelling and the hydraulic conductivity of the soil (Rowell, Payne and Ahmad 1969, McNeal 1968). Based on these data, filter cakes from sodium bentonite slurries could be expected to have lower permeabilities than those from calcium bentonites. This hypothesis is supported by tests on clay membranes conducted by Shainberg and Caiserman (1971).

These researchers found that the hydraulic conductivity of the montmorillonite tested was very sensitive to the type of cation adsorbed on the clay. In fact, the hydraulic conductivity of the calcium montmorillonite membrane was 14.2 times greater than that of the sodium montmorillonite.

### Figure 2-6.
### The Effect of Bentonite Concentration on the
### Initial Fluid Loss During Filter Cake Formation

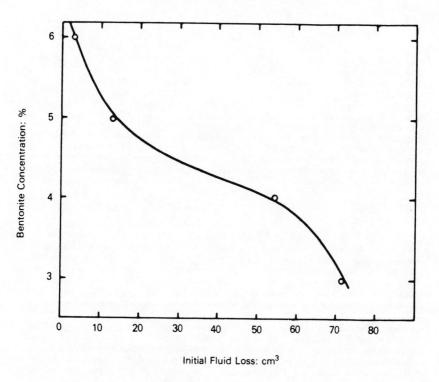

Source: Hutchinson, et al., 1975

Values for the calcium and sodium montmorillonite clay membranes were 9.3 x $10^{-9}$ cm/sec and 0.65 x $10^{-9}$ cm/sec, respectively (Shainberg and Caiserman 1975). These values are similar to the permeabilities reported for filter cakes. In tests of a bentonite slurry in contact with a London clay, for example, the permeability of the filter cake was found to be 2.3 x $10^{-9}$ cm/sec (Xanthakos 1979). The size of the dry bentonite particles affects performance because the smaller particles hydrate more rapidly and have a larger surface area to hydrate and swell than do larger bentonite particles. The grades of bentonite used for slurry wall applications typically have smaller particle sizes than do bentonites used for other applications, such as pond sealing.

c.  Slurry Mixing Methods

The methods used to mix the slurry can also affect the filter cake formation. Bentonite slurries with high shear strengths penetrate a shorter distance into the soil pores before gelation occurs (Xanthakos 1979). Thus high shear strength slurries exhibit faster filter cake formation and less initial slurry loss. Figure 2-7 illustrates the difference in 10 minute gel strengths between slurries mixed by two different methods. In this study, the slurry processed in the high shear mixer initially manifested a higher 10 minute gel strength than the slurry mixed in the anchor stirrer. More importantly, the difference in gel strengths did not diminish during the period of time the two slurries were compared. Even 1,400 minutes (23 hours and 20 minutes) after the initial mixing, the slurry from the high shear mixer had a higher gel strength than the other slurry tested (Hutchinson et al. 1975).

d.  Filter Cake Formation Time

The amount of time allowed for filter cake formation can influence filter cake performance. As shown in Figure 2-5, a certain period of time is required for the initial slurry loss to occur before colloidal packing at the slurry/soil interface produces the filter cake. Studies reported by D'Appolonia (1980) showed that, at any given hydraulic pressure, the filter cake permeability is a function of formation time. According to Xanthakos (1979), the filter cake thickness increases as time passes. Boyes (1975) found that filter cakes formed under quiescent conditions had higher shear strengths than those formed during agitation of the slurry. Because formation time affects filter cake performance so stongly, D'Appolonia (1980a) recommended that 24 hours should elapse between slurry trench excavation and backfilling to allow complete filter cake formation under quiescent conditions.

e.  Strata Characteristics

When the strata surrounding the trench contain numerous large pores, considerable slurry loss can occur before the filter cake can form. In many

## Figure 2-7.
## The Effect of Mixing Techniques and Times on Hydration
## of a 5% Suspension of Ca-Exchanged Bentonite

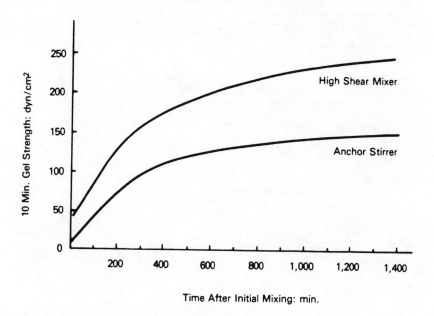

Time After Initial Mixing: min.

Source: Hutchinson, et al. 1975

cases, particles of spoil that were inadvertently mixed with the slurry during excavation can assist in clogging soil pores and can reduce the amount of slurry loss. However, in gravel beds, which allow water movement rates of 1 to 10 cm/sec, the pores are too large to be easily closed (Jefferis 1981a). Thus slurry loss under these conditions continues until rheological blocking occurs (Hutchinson et al 1975).

Rheological blocking is the gradual inhibition of slurry flow due to the increase in slurry shear strength as gelation progresses (Boyes 1975). The effect of this phenomena is a steady but slow decline in fluid loss even in gravel beds, as shown in Figure 2-8. In this figure, the time necessary for filter cake formation in a less permeable stratum is also illustrated. The soil layers containing 0.1 percent sand required rheological blocking coupled with pore space blockage to stop slurry flow. Even so, deep filtration occurred before the filter cake formed. As the permeability of the stratum was reduced by the addition of sand, the time needed for filter cake formation, the amount of slurry lost, and the depth of filtration were reduced (Hutchinson et al 1975).

The time required for filter cake formation varies from less than 30 seconds in fine textured soils, to over 3,600 seconds (6 minutes) in gravel beds. The depth of penetration as shown in Figure 2-8 depends on the permeability of the strata. In strata of very low permeability, slurry loss has been found to be minimal (Xanthakos 1979). One set of tests using a 3.2 percent bentonite slurry in contact with a sandstone having permeability of from $10^{-4}$ to $10^{-8}$ cm/sec showed slurry penetrated into the stone only from 2 to 3 cm (Boyes 1975).

### f. Hydraulic Gradient

Hydraulic gradient also influences filter cake formation and performance (D'Appolonia 1980a). The difference between the hydraulic head of the slurry and that of the groundwater should be as great as possible to improve filter cake characteristics (Guertin and McTigue 1982b). A high hydraulic head in the trench forces the slurry to be packed tightly along the soil/slurry inter-face. This compresses the filter cake and reduces leakage (Hutchinson et al 1975).

### g. Slurry Contamination

Contamination of the slurry can occur due to the presence of salts, cement, extremely basic conditions in the make-up water used. Slurry contamination can decrease filter cake performance. For example, slurry contamination by cement causes portions of the slurry to flocculate. This leads to the formation of relatively thick, permeable, weak filter cakes, high fluid losses and low viscosity in the slurry (Hutchison et al 1975). As the amount of cement is increased, the thixotropic properties of the slurry are inhibited. This leads to lower slurry viscosity, lower gel strength and

## Figure 2-8.
## The Effect of Added Sand on Filtration of a 5% Suspension of a Calcium-exchanged Bentonite through a Fine Gravel Bed

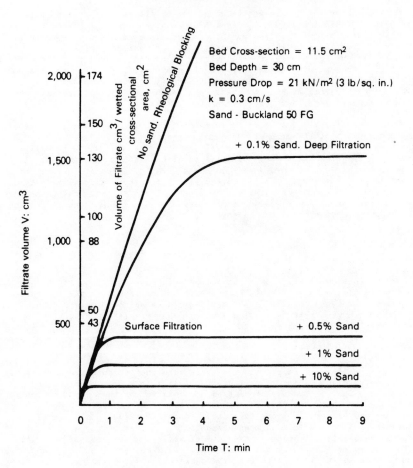

Bed Cross-section = 11.5 cm²
Bed Depth = 30 cm
Pressure Drop = 21 kN/m² (3 lb/sq. in.)
k = 0.3 cm/s
Sand - Buckland 50 FG

+ 0.1% Sand. Deep Filtration

No sand. Rheological Blocking

Surface Filtration

+ 0.5% Sand

+ 1% Sand

+ 10% Sand

Volume of Filtrate cm³ / wetted cross-sectional area, cm²

Filtrate volume V: cm³

Time T: min

Source: Hutchinson, et al. 1975

inhibited filter cake formation (Guertin & McTigue 1982b). These effects also occur in cement bentonite slurries, as is discussed in Section 2.4.1.1. Other contaminants can also influence slurry and slurry wall properties. These are discussed in Section 4.

### 2.2.2.2 Gel Strength

The slurry's gel strength is a measure of its ability to form a gel structure. This gel structure can influence slurry density. The gel strength of the slurry allows the fine particle materials that mix with the slurry during excavation to remain suspended. At a gel strength of 15 lb/ft$^2$, the slurry has the ability to suspend average sized coarse sand particles. These particles are up to approximately 1 mm in diameter. Particles smaller than this, such as fine sands, silts and clays are likely to remain in suspension, while larger particles sink to the trench bottom and form a heavy mixture of slurry, coarse sand, and gravel (Xanthakos 1979).

As the slurry's gel strength increases, the maximum diameter of particles it can support will increase. High gel strength slurries support a large portion of the soil particles that fall into the trench, while low gel strength slurries allow more particles to sink to the trench bottom. As the concentration of suspended solids in the slurry increases, the slurry becomes more dense. Xanthakos (1979) reported slurry density measurements from tests at several slurry trench construction sites. These tests revealed that the sediments that became suspended during excavation increased the slurry density by an average of about 4 to 5.5 percent.

### 2.2.2.3 Density

The density of the slurry can influence the stability of the trench wall. According to Xanthakos (1979), high density slurries resist the pressures exerted on the trench walls by high water tables and low shear strength soils. However, slurries that have a low density do not resist these pressures as effectively as do the higher density slurries. Thus the increase in slurry density that is caused by the slurry's gel structure can contribute directly to trench wall stability.

The heavier soil particles that fall into the trench during excavation do not remain in suspension. Instead, they fall to the trench bottom and accumulate there. The amount of sand accumulation on the trench bottom is dependent on the coarseness of the strata being excavated and other factors, such as the excavation techniques used (Xanthakos 1979). This sand layer does not have a direct effect on trench stability, however it may have an impact on the permeability of the completed cut-off wall, and the ease of backfilling. The density of the slurry taken from the trench bottom (i.e., the sand layer) must be at least 15 pcf less than the backfill. If the slurry is too dense, it will not be displaced properly by the backfill (D'Appolonia 1980b).

### 2.2.2.4  Chemical and Physical Additives

Numerous chemical and physical additives have been used in slurries to improve their viscosity, gel strength, density, or fluid loss rate (Xanthakos 1979). Some of those additives are listed in Table 2-3. It is recommended that the use of any slurry additives be allowed only with the approval of the engineer. Some slurry trench excavation specifications forbid the use of chemically treated bentonites (U.S. Army Corps of Engineers 1975). One problem with the use of chemically treated bentonites is the possibility of enhanced interaction with pollutants. Conversely, certain chemical treatments may render the bentonite less susceptible to chemical attack. Slurry/waste interactions are discussed in Section 4.

## 2.3  Soil-Bentonite Walls

SB walls are excavated under a bentonite slurry in a continuous trench. As excavated materials are removed from the trench, they are mixed with slurry and replaced in the trench a short distance from the active excavation area. Techniques used during slurry trench construction are described in detail in Section 5.

### 2.3.1  SB Wall Properties

A properly designed and constructed SB wall exhibits the following properties:

- Low Permeability
- Resistance to hydraulic pressure and chemical attack
- Low bearing strength and moderate to high plasticity.

#### 2.3.1.1  Low Permeability

Permeabilities of completed soil-bentonite cut-offs have been as low as $5.0 \times 10^{-9}$ cm/sec, although higher permeabilities are more common (Xanthakos 1979). Typical permeabilities of SB walls range from over $10^{-5}$ cm/sec in walls composed primarily of coarse, rather than fine materials, to less than $10^{-8}$ cm/sec in walls containing over 60 percent clay (D'Appolonia 1980b).

TABLE 2-3

COMMON SLURRY MATERIALS AND ADDITIVES

| | |
|---|---|
| Weight materials | Barite (barium sulfate) or soil (sand) |
| Colloid materials | Bentonite (Wyoming, Fulbent, Aquagel, Algerian, Japanese, etc.), basic fresh water slurry constituent<br>Attapulgite, for saltwater slurries<br>Organic polymers and pretreated brands |
| Thinners and dispersing agents | Quebrancho, organic dispersant mixture (tannin)<br>Lignite, mineral lignin<br>Sodium tetraphosphate<br>Sodium humate (sodium humic acid)<br>Ferrochrome lignosulfonate (FCL)<br>Nitrophemin acid chloride<br>Calcium lignosulfonate<br>Reacted caustic, tannin (dry)<br>Reacted caustic, lignite (dry)<br>Sodium acid pyrophosphate<br>Sodium hexametaphosphate |
| Intermediate-sized particles | Clay, silt, and sand |
| Flocculants and polyelectrolytes | Sodium carboxmyethyl cellulose (CMC)<br>Salts<br>Starches<br>Potassium aluminate<br>Aluminum chloride<br>Calcium |
| Fluid-loss-control agents | CMC or other flocculants<br>Pregelatinized starch<br>Sand in small proportions |
| Lost-circulation materials | Graded fibrous or flake materials; shredded cellophane flakes, shredded tree bark, plant fibers, glass, rayon, graded mica, ground walnut shells, rubber trees, perlite, time-setting cement, and many others. |

Reference:  Xanthakos 1979.  Copyright 1979 by McGraw-Hill Books.  Used with Permission.

2.3.1.2  Resistance to Hydraulic Pressure and Contaminants

An SB wall that exhibits an extremely low permeability is not effective in the long run if it cannot withstand the hydraulic gradients induced by its presence or if it disintegrates upon contact with contaminants at the site.

Because of its low permeability, the wall can be used to severely restrict downgradient water movement. This causes the water level on the upgradient side of the wall to rise significantly as compared to the downgradient side. This difference in water levels is termed the hydraulic gradient. A high hydraulic gradient across the wall is likely to develop unless groundwater rerouting is accomplished through the use of upgradient extraction wells, subsurface drains or interceptor trenches (see Section 3). Despite the use of these ancillary measures, the wall should be designed to withstand significant hydraulic gradients. The incorporation of a high concentration of clayey materials into the backfill improves the wall's long-term resistance to hydraulic gradients up to 200 (D'Appolonia 1980b). Wall design is discussed in Section 5.

The wall's resistance to degradation by chemical contaminants is also a primary measure of long term performance. Prior to SB wall construction, extensive testing of the effects of the site's leachate on proposed backfill mixtures should be conducted. In general, clayey backfill mixtures withstand permeation with contaminants more effectively than those that contain less clay (D'Appolonia 1980b).

2.3.1.3  Strength and Plasticity

The strength of SB cut-off walls is not usually of primary concern when designing pollution migration cut-offs. These walls are usually designed to be comparable in strength to the surrounding ground (Jefferis 1981b). If stronger walls are required, coarser material may be added to the backfill, although this practice results in an increase in wall permeability (Millet and Perez 1981). In any case, the strength of a soil-bentonite wall is not usually relevant in hazardous waste applications, except where traffic must pass over the wall. Design of traffic caps is discussed in Section 5.

The response of the SB wall to lateral earth pressures and earth movements is an important factor in the design of pollution migration cut-offs. If the wall is too brittle, shifts in nearby strata caused by overloading the surface by stockpiles or heavy machinery can result in cracking and subsequent leakage of the wall. Fortunately, completed SB cut-off walls behave plastically when stressed. That is, they undergo plastic deformation rather than crack (Guertin and McTigue 1982b). In contrast, CB walls have higher strength than SB walls and can be brittle and thus more easily cracked (Millet and Perez 1981).

2.3.2   Factors Affecting SB Wall Performance

There are numerous factors that can affect the performance of SB Walls. These can be divided into four general groups which are:

- Design criteria
- Backfill composition and characteristics
- Backfill placement methods
- Post-construction conditions at the site.

### 2.3.2.1   Design Criteria

The design criteria that affect SB wall performance include wall width, wall depth, selection of appropriate aquiclude, wall configuration, and use of ancillary measures. These criteria are discussed in Section 5. The factors relating to backfill preparation and post-construction conditions are described below.

### 2.3.2.2   Backfill Composition and Characteristics

To produce a low-permeability, durable cut-off wall, the backfill must contain a high concentration of plastic fines (clays), a minimal amount large-diameter particles, and a suitable concentration of bentonite and water. Contaminants in the soil or water can also affect the wall's performance.

a.   Native Clay and Bentonite Content

A primary requirement for backfill material is that it contain a suitable particle size distribution. For low permeability, this means the backfill must have from 20 to 40 percent fine particles, preferably plastic fines. Fine particles (less than 0.074 mm in diameter or passing a number 200 sieve) exert a significant influence on backfill permeability, as shown in Figure 2-9. At a given bentonite concentration, the backfill permeability will be lower when the backfill material contains a higher proportion of fines. Conversely, increasing the bentonite content of the backfills tested significantly reduced the wall permeability. The bentonite content of the mixed backfill should not fall below 1 percent (D'Appolonia 1980b). Where the strength of the cut-off wall is of primary concern, a higher concentration of coarse and medium sized particles are required. In any case, material over 6 inches in diameter are not considered desirable for use in backfills (Federal Bentonite 1981).

## Figure 2-9.

## Relationship Between Permeability and Quantity of Bentonite Added to SB Backfill

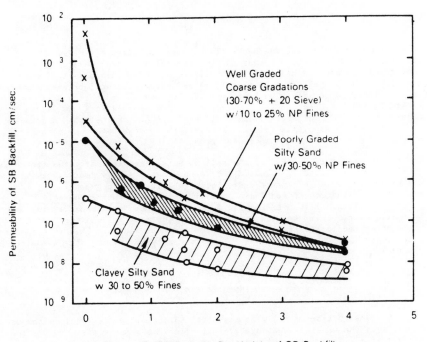

% Bentonite by Dry Weight of SB Backfill

Source: D'Appolonia, 1980

D'Appolonia (1980b) found that plastic fines reduce permeability more effectively than nonplastic fines. This is most likely due to the fact that plastic fines are composed of smaller particles than nonplastic fines. The effect of plastic fines on backfill permeability is shown in Figure 2-10.

Fine particles, particularly clays, contribute to low permeability by assisting in bridging the pores between larger particles and by contributing to the swelling, viscosity, gelation, and cation exchange capacity of the backfill (D'Appolonia 1980b, Boyes 1975). Although these properties find their maximum expression in montmorillonite, other clays exhibit these characteristics to a lesser degree (Grim 1968). Thus the clay content of the backfill has a pronounced effect on SB wall permeability.

### b.    Water Content

The water content of the backfill can also influence the SB wall performance. The amount of water in the backfill should be carefully controlled because the hydraulic conductivity of sodium montmorillonite has been reported to increase dramatically as the water content increases (Low 1976). There is an effective limit on reducing the water content of the backfill, however, because the backfill must slump sufficiently to allow proper placement. The water content of backfills at ideal slumps is from 25 to 35 percent (D'Appolonia 1980a). Even so, the excess water in the backfill has been found to result in increased permeability (Jefferis 1981b).

If the moisture content of the soil material excavated from the trench is over 25 percent initially, the addition of bentonite slurry during backfill mixing results in a very wet backfill that exhibits high permeability. To remedy this situation, D'Appolonia (1980a) suggests spreading the soil material in a thin lift over the backfill mixing area, then broadcasting dry bentonite over the lift at the desired rate. The soil material is then mixed with the dry bentonite prior to the addition of the slurry. This reduces the water content of the backfill while simultaneously increasing the bentonite content.

### c.    Contaminants in Backfill Materials

The construction of a low-permeability SB cut off walls requires the use of soils in the backfill that are free of deleterious materials. To be free of deleterious materials, the proposed soil source must not contain significant amounts of soil organic matter, including plant and animal debris, high calcium materials, including gypsum, chalk and caliche, or high concentrations of soluble salts, including sodium chloride, sodium sulfates or anhydrite.

In addition to the items listed above, other subsurface materials may be detrimental to backfill quality. For example, at some sites where pollution migration cut-offs have been constructed, the soil excavated was contaminated with pollutants. These pollutants may or may not significantly interfere with

## Figure 2-10.
## Effect of Plastic and Non-plastic Fines Content on Soil-Bentonite Backfill Permeability

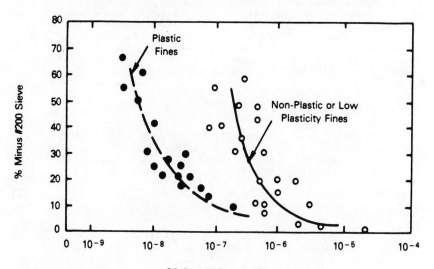

Source: D'Appolonia, 1980

SB Backfill Permeability, cm/sec.

cut-off wall performance. D'Appolonia (1980a) suggested preparing a test mixture to determine compatibility. He further suggested using the contaminated soil if equal in quality to uncontaminated soil, even though the material may decrease the slurry and backfill performance initially. This is because early exposure of the bentonite to the contaminants reduces the permeability changes that occur during subsequent exposure to the contaminants. This approach must be balanced against the fact that contaminant breakthrough may occur earlier.

### 2.3.2.3  Backfill Placement Methods

The mixing and placement of the carefully selected backfill material is of critical importance in the overall performance of the completed wall. The bentonite slurry and soil material must be combined to form a relatively homogenous paste with a consistency similar to that of mortar or concrete. It must flow easily yet stand on a slope of about 10:1, and must be at least 15 pcf (240 kg/m$^3$) denser than the slurry in the trench (D'Appolonia 1980b). The methods used to mix the backfill and the tests used to measure its shear strength, flow characteristics and density are described in Section 5.

### 2.3.2.4  Post-Construction Conditions

Once the backfill has been mixed and placed, the performance of the wall is dependent on the subsurface conditions surrounding the wall. In particular, the hydraulic gradient and the presence of contaminants can influence the wall's ability to function properly.

### a.  Hydraulic Gradient

The difference in hydraulic pressure between the upgradient and downgradient sides of the trench strongly influences the trench's durability as well as its initial permeability. Little data are available on this factor; however, it has been shown that high hydraulic pressures within the trench during filter cake formation result in a lower permeability filter cake. The long-term effect of high hydraulic pressure differentials across the trench on wall permeability is, however, likely to be different (D'Appolonia 1980b). A large difference in hydraulic pressure from one side of the trench to the other is expected to severely tax the integrity of the wall. Methods used to combat high hydraulic gradients include increasing wall thickness and/or using extraction wells or subsurface drains upgradient to assist in equalizing hydraulic pressures near the wall. These are discussed in Section 5.

b.  Presence of Contaminants

The resistance of soil-bentonite cut-off walls to permeation and destruction by various pollutants is the subject of much current research. Bentonite is extremely resistant to degradation from some substances, but others cause rapid dehydration and shrinkage of the montmorillonite particles. SB wall performance can be severely inhibited by contact with incompatible chemical compounds in leachates or wastes.

The wall can be protected from degradation due to chemical incompatability in several ways. First, waste/wall contact can be minimized by using extraction wells or subsurface drains. Second, contaminated soil can be used in the backfill, as described earlier. Third, the concentration of non-montmorillonite clay in the backfill can be maximized.

Non-montmorillonitic native clays are not likely to be as severely affected by chemical contaminants as are bentonites or native montmorillonitic clays. This is because the non-montmorillonitic native clays do not swell as extensively as montmorillonite when they are hydrated. Consequently, if they become dehydrated during chemical interactions, they do not shrink as extensively as montmorillonite does when it becomes dehydrated. When shrinkage is minimized, the associated permeability increase is also minimized. Thus the adverse effects of the chemical interaction can be decreased.

Different types of wastes affect the clay in the backfill in different ways. In addition to dehydration and shrinkage, the clay may be dissolved or its properties can be drastically altered. Data on chemical compatabilities of wastes and SB walls are summarized in Section 4.

The proper design and construction of an SB wall can result in a durable, low permeability cut-off that withstands high hydraulic gradients and permeation with various contaminants. At some sites, the use of SB walls is not appropriate (see Section 5). When SB walls cannot be used CB walls can be installed. These walls are similar to SB walls in that they contain bentonite and form a relatively low permeability cut-off, but they differ in several important ways, as described below.

## 2.4  Cement-Bentonite Slurries

When CB walls are being constructed CB slurries are prepared.  Techniques used to construct CB walls are described in Section 5.

### 2.4.1  CB Slurry Properties

Cement-bentonite slurries normally contain about 6 percent by weight bentonite, 18 percent ordinary Portland cement (o.p.c.) and 76 percent water

(Jefferis 1981b). Typical ranges of CB slurry contents are presented in Table 2-5.

When bentonite slurries are compared to CB slurries, the differences become evident. Table 2-4 illustrates these differences. Most of these differences are due in part to the effects of the calcium from the cement on the sodium montmorillonite in the bentonite. The three most important differences between the properties of CB slurries and bentonite slurries are:

- Physical properties, including viscosity and filter cake formation
- Setting times
- Filter cake permeability.

### 2.4.1.1  Differences in Physical Properties

Because of the calcium in the cement, the properties of the sodium bentonite in CB slurries are permanently altered. For example, the viscosity is higher due to the flocculation of the slurry and the higher solids concentration, 15 to 30 percent in CB slurry, opposed to about 6 percent in bentonite slurries (Millet and Perez 1981, Jefferis 1981b). The results of the filtrate loss test are also higher. This indicates that the time required for filter cake formation is longer and the permeability of the cake formed is higher (Hutchinson et al. 1975; Millet and Perez 1981). A comparison of the properties of bentonite and CB slurries is presented in Table 2-5.

### 2.4.1.2  Differences in Setting Times

The primary difference between CB and SB slurries that is of practical importance in slurry trench construction is the fact that CB slurries begin to harden within 2 to 3 hours after mixing (Case 1982). This necessitates the use of construction techniques different from those used during construction of SB walls, as described below.

CB walls can be constructed either in a series of panels or as a continuous trench that is backfilled with a CB slurry. When CB panels are constructed, alternate panels are excavated under a CB slurry, then allowed to partially set. When they have obtained a sufficient shear strength, the intervening panels are excavated also under a slurry. A portion of the initial panel ends are removed during this second stage to ensure continuity between the initial panels and the intervening ones.

Another result of the rapid setting times of CB slurries as compared to bentonite slurries, is the fact that construction delays can cause problems in set up of CB walls. This is because continued agitation of the CB slurry (that is, more than 24 hours) reduces the ability of the cement in the slurry to set. In fact, 48 hours of agitation can completely prevent setup of the CB wall. This effect can be off-set by the use of blast furnace slag. This

TABLE 2-4

TYPICAL COMPOSITIONS OF CEMENT-BENTONITE SLURRIES

| Constituent | Percentage in Slurry |
|---|---|
| Bentonite | 4-7 |
| Water | 68-88 |
| Cement | |
|   without replacements | 8-25 |
|   when blast furnace slag added, minimums | 1-3 |
|   when fly ash added, minimums | 2-7 |
| Blast furnace slag, maximums, if used | 7-22 |
| Fly ash, maximums, if used | 6-18 |

Reference:  Adapted from Jefferis 1981b.

TABLE 2-5

PROPERTIES OF SOIL-BENTONITE AND CEMENT-
BENTONITE BACKFILLS

| Parameter | Soil-Bentonite Backfill | Cement-Bentonite Backfill |
|---|---|---|
| Density | typically 105-120 p.c.f. (1)<br>1680-1920 kg/m$^3$ (1) | maximum likely 1300 kg/m$^3$ |
| Water Content, % by weight | 25-35(1) | 55-70(2) |
| Bentonite Content, % by weight | 0.5-2 (1) | 6 (2) |
| Other Ingredients, % by weight | Fines 10-20 (3)<br>Fines 20-40 (1) | Cement 18 (2)<br>Solids 30-45 (2) |
| Strength | Plastic. Very little strength (4) normally around 20 p.s.f. unconfined (5) | Ultimate strength Range: 5-55 p.s.i. (3)(7)<br>Normal strength 20-45 p.s.i. (8) |
| Permeability, cm/sec | minimum reported 5.0 x 10$^{-9}$ (6)<br>maximum reported ~1 x 10$^{-5}$ (1) | 1 to 5 x 10$^{-6}$ (2) |

References:

(1) D'Appolonia 1980b, (2) Jefferis 1981b, (3) Millet and Perez 1981,
(4) Guerntin and McTigue 1982b, (5) Ryan 1976, (6) Xanthakos 1979, (7)
Case 1982, (8) Cavelli 1982.

pozzolanic material can replace up to 90 percent of the ordinary Portland cement in the slurry (Jefferis 1981b).

### 2.4.1.3  Differences in Filter Cake Permeability

Although there are some basic differences between the use of bentonite and CB slurries during trench excavation, the critical differences between these two cut-off wall construction techniques appears in the finished cut-off wall.

The most important differences between SB and CB walls with regard to pollution migration cut-offs are that SB walls have much lower permeabilities and higher resistances to certain pollutants than do CB walls (Jefferis 1981b; Xanthakos 1979).  An important factor contributing to the permeability differences can be seen by comparing the permeabilities of filter cakes from each wall type.  For bentonite slurries, filter cake permeabilities can be as low as $10^{-9}$ cm/sec, while permeabilities calculated from filtrate loss tests on CB slurries ranged from about 1 to $4 \times 10^{-6}$ cm/sec (Xanthakos 1979, Jefferis 1981b).  The permeability of a SB wall installed in a dam was tested at $5 \times 10^{-9}$ cm/sec (La Russo 1963).  Samples of an installed CB wall were tested and found to have permeabilities between $10^{-5}$ and $10^{-6}$ cm/sec.  (Jones 1978).  Other important differences between finished CB and SB walls are listed in Table 2-5.

## 2.5  Cement-Bentonite Walls

In contrast to SB walls, CB walls are used where there is a lack of suitable soils or sufficient backfill mixing areas, or there are excessive slopes at the site.  CB walls are also used where strength, rather than low permeability is the primary consideration (Guertin and McTigue 1982b).  The properties of SB and CB walls are compared in Table 2-5.  Appropriate applications of CB walls for pollution migration control are described in Section 5.  Typical compositions of CB slurries were described earlier.  This section describes normal CB wall characteristics and factors affecting the performance of both CB slurries and CB walls.

### 2.5.1  CB Wall Requirements

The requirements for CB wall performance include:

- Strength
- Durability
- Continuity

- Set time
- Permeability.

### 2.5.1.1 Strength

CB wall strength is designed to be slightly greater than that of the surrounding ground, and is typically comparable in strength to stiff clay (Jefferis 1981b, Millet and Perez 1981). Although strengths of CB walls can range from 10 to 1,000 p.s.i., ultimate strengths are generally about 20 to 45 psi and are achieved after 28 days (Xanthakos 1979, Cavalli 1982).

At a hazardous waste site, strength may be required where traffic crosses the wall, or where a weak wall may interfere with the stability of nearby buildings, storage tanks, or bridge foundations or road or rail subgrades.

### 2.5.1.2 Durability

CB walls appear to be quite durable under most conditions, as they can usually withstand compressive strains of several percent without cracking. This is because they are not as brittle as typical concrete walls (Ryan 1976). Moreover, they can withstand relatively high hydraulic gradients. A CB wall only 2 to 3 feet wide can satisfactorily withstand at least 100 feet (30 meters) of hydrostatic head (Millet and Perez 1981). A mixture of 50 $kg/m^3$ bentonite, 70 $kg/m^3$ blast furnace slag, and 30 $kg/m^3$ cement in a CB backfill was reportedly not damaged after 40 days of exposure to a head differential of 200 feet (Jefferis 1981b). Despite the fact that CB walls are normally quite durable, they are not indestructable, as hydrofracturing of CB walls has been reported to occur (Millet and Perez 1981). Also, comparatively little is known of the permanence of CB walls in hostile chemical environments.

### 2.5.1.3 Continuity

Continuity of CB walls is an important factor in construction of cut-offs. Because these walls are sometimes constructed in panels rather than in a continuous trench, there is a possibility for unexcavated portions to remain between the panels. To prevent this, care is taken during the excavation of panels, and the clamshell bucket or backhoe is moved vertically and horizontally throughout each slot at the completion of slot excavation. In addition, when the connecting area between the initial and subsequent panels is excavated, a portion of the set panel is removed to ensure that all intervening soil has been excavated (Guertin and McTigue 1982b). If unexcavated areas are inadvertantly left between panels, leakage can occur.

### 2.5.1.4  Set Time

The time required for CB walls to harden depends on the presence of set time retarders, cement replacements, and water/cement ratios, among other factors.  The speed of set is of interest because of the construction techniques employed.  During CB wall installation, slow setting of panels can delay construction.  This is because alternating panels are excavated, leaving unexcavated areas between each.  After the CB slurries in the first set of panels have set, the areas between them can be excavated.  If the slurries take unduly long to harden, construction can be delayed.  This may occur where fly ash is used as a cement replacement, because a slurry containing fly ash may harden very slowly.  The use of blast furnace slag does not delay CB slurry set up as long as does fly ash (Jefferis 1981b).

### 2.5.1.5  Permeability

The permeability of CB walls is normally about $10^{-6}$ cm/sec (Case 1982).  This can be decreased by adding blast furnace slag or additional bentonite.  Jefferis (1981b) reports that permeability can also be decreased as much as an order of magnitude due to consolidation of the completed wall.

### 2.5.2  Factors Affecting CB Wall Performance

Factors affecting the performance of CB walls include:

- Slurry contents, including bentonite, water, cement, cement replacements

- Mixing methods and speeds.

### 2.5.2.1  Slurry Constituents

The quality and quantity of cement-bentonite slurry constituents can alter the characteristics of the slurry and the completed wall.  Bentonite quality, water quality cement content and the use of cement replacements all affect CB slurry and wall performance.

### a.  Bentonite Content

The low permeability and resistance to chemical attack of CB walls are contributed by the bentonite in the slurry.  Where very low permeability or resistance to aggressive chemicals are required, the bentonite content of the slurry should be increased (Jefferis 1981b).  Increasing the quality of bentonite used in the slurry can also help produce a durable low-permeability CB wall.

An important characteristic of high quality bentonite is its sodium content. Bentonites with higher sodium contents are particularly desirable for use in CB slurries due to the changes in the bentonite slurry caused by the calcium ions in the cement.

When cement is added to a bentonite slurry, several interrelated changes occur. First, calcium ions from the cement begin replacing sodium ions on the exchange complex of the montmorillonite particles. This compresses the diffuse double layer surrounding each clay flake and reduces the net negative charge on the hydrated particles (See Figure 2-1). As the double layer contracts, the pore space between the particles is enlarged, thus increasing the amount of free water in the mixture. Due to the reduction in net negative charges, the mutual repulsion between the clay particles decreases, so the clay flakes come closer together. At this point, the large calcium ions can serve to link clay particles together, causing them to flocculate, or form stacks of particles. These stacks, being much heavier than dispersed clay particles, tend to settle out of the suspension readily. They also have a decreased ability to form a gel structure or a filter cake (Case 1982, Boyes 1975). All of these changes are detrimental to slurry quality.

b.  Water Quality

Water quality can also influence CB slurry characteristics. If water containing calcium ions or dissolved salts is used to mix with the dry bentonite, the cement slurry produced exhibits low viscosity, poor filter cake formation and an increased set time (Guertin and McTigue 1982b). Specifications for water quality include:

- Hardness of <50 ppm (Xanthakos 1979)

- Total dissolved solids content of <500 ppm (U.S. Army Corps of Engineers 1975)

- Organics content of <50 ppm (U.S. Army Corps of Engineers 1975)

- pH of about 7.0 (U.S. Army Corps of Engineers 1975).

Leachate-contaminated water should not be used to mix with the fresh bentonite. If the use of poor quality water cannot be avoided, 10 to 12 percent more bentonite than normal may be required and longer mixing times are recommended (Xanthakos 1979).

c.  Cement Content

The cement content of CB slurries is the chief factor controlling the strength, deformability, and permeability of the finished wall.  Generally, there is a trade-off in CB walls between strength and permeability, for as the cement content is increased, a stronger, more brittle wall is formed (Millet and Perez 1981).  The trade-off is due to the detrimental effects of the cement on the bentonite.  Higher cement contents allow higher wall permeabilities, and, although wall strength can be increased by the addition of coarse materials, these materials also result in increased permeability (Jefferis 1981b).

Due to this trade-off, the ultimate strength of cement bentonite walls is low, normally ranging from 20 to 45 p.s.i. (Cavalli 1982).  The minimum reported strength was 5 p.s.i. in a relatively young wall, and the maximum strength was reported at 55 p.s.i. (Case 1982, Millet and Perez 1981).  The permeability of CB walls is relatively high, usually around $10^{-6}$ cm/sec (Case 1982).  In one completed CB wall tested, the permeability of Shelby Tube samples was on the order of $10^{-5}$ to $10^{-6}$ cm/sec., and the strength was measured at 13 to 15 p.s.i. (Jones 1978).

The ratio by weight of water to cement in the slurry also affects the characteristics of CB walls.  Generally higher ratios produce weaker walls.  Typical water cement ratios range from 3:1 to 11:1.  These are much higher than the ratios found in concrete mixes.  The reason the cement and water do not separate (bleed) to a great extent is the presence of the bentonite in the mixture.  Bentonite absorbs a great deal of water thus minimizing the free water in the slurry.  At the same time, the gel structure of the bentonite particles in the slurry assists in supporting the cement particles and thus reduces settling and prevents excessive bleeding.  A quality CB slurry should show bleed rates of less than 1 percent (Jefferis 1981b).

d.  Cement Replacements

A fourth slurry constituent that can affect CB slurry and wall performance is the use of cement replacements.  Blast furnace slag and fly ash are two of the materials that have been used to replace a portion of the cement used in CB slurries.  Blast furnace slag can be used to replace up to 90 percent of the cement, and fly ash can replace up to 70 percent (Jefferis 1981b).  The resultant cement replacement concentrations are shown in Table 2-4.

When using these replacements, two important slurry properties are altered.  The slurry's set time is extended, allowing the slurry to remain fluid and workable longer.  Thus construction schedules can be extended and the risk of problems caused by delays is reduced.  In addition, the blast furnace slag and fly ash that were described by Jefferis (1981b) did not damage the bentonite as much as cement does.  Thus the viscosity, gel strength, and ability to form filter cakes is less impaired (Jefferis 1981b).

The mechanisms by which the cement replacements slow the setting time and avoid bentonite inhibition are described below.

The fly ash and blast furnace slag require the presence of lime in order to harden.  The lime is not available in the CB slurry until most of the cement particles have fully hydrated.  Since the cement does not fully hydrate upon exposure to water, the blast furnace slag and fly ash delay the setting time.  This delay extends the period of CB workability (Jefferis 1981b).

The use of these cement replacements is less detrimental to the bentonite because blast furnace slag and fly ash do not release calcium ions as rapidly as does cement.  Thus the mass action effect of calcium ions on the exchange complex of the montmorillonite clay is reduced (Jefferis 1981b).

Cement replacements also affect the characteristics of the completed wall.  These effects include:

- Reduction in bleeding rates

- Maintenance of setting ability even though agitated for long periods

- Lowered permeabilities in the completed wall

- Reduced susceptibility to chemical attack.

According to Jefferis (1981b), the bleeding rates of cement-replaced CB slurries are less than those of typical CB slurries.  This effect is most likely due to the fact that blast furnace slag and fly ash do not inhibit bentonite properties as drastically as does cement (Jefferis 1981b).

Another effect of cement replacement is a prolongation of setting time.  When CB slurries are used without cement replacements, they begin to set up within 2 to 3 hours (Case 1982).  If the slurries are agitated to prevent hardening, the ability to set up will be diminished and will be lost altogether if agitation continues for 48 hours.  The addition of blast furnace slag or fly ash to the slurry allow agitation to be continued for up to seven days without substantial loss of setting ability (Jefferis 1981b).

Blast furnace slag can contribute to low permeability in CB walls.  When conventional CB walls or CB walls with fly ash replacement are allowed to set for 7 days, permeabilities of $1$ to $5 \times 10^{-6}$ cm/sec. result.  In contrast, CB walls containing from 2.5 to 7.5 percent blast furnace slag exhibited permeabilities of about $10^{-7}$ cm/sec after 7 days of hardening (Jefferis 1981b).

A final effect of cement replacement on CB walls concerns resistance to chemical attack.  Fly ash replacements can effectively increase a CB wall's chemical resistance, however, blast furnace slag replacements cannot (Jefferis 1981b).

The cement in CB walls is much more susceptible to chemical attack than is bentonite.  For this reason, CB walls are not normally used where exposure to detrimental chemicals is likely.  However if CB walls are required due to site conditions, the addition of protective agents such as fly ash may be desirable.

e.    Chemical Additives

In addition to bentonite, water, cement, and sometimes cement replacements, chemical additives can be mixed into CB slurries to alter their performance.    Several types of additives are used, including deflocculants and setting time retarders.    Deflocculants include chemicals such as sodium hexametaphosphate, oxidants, acids, and peptizing reagents which are added to break up the flocs formed when calcium is added to the slurry (Xanthakos 1979).

Setting time retarders can be added to extend the period of CB slurry workability.    The use of chemical set retarders has several disadvantages. These include the following:

- Compared to the amount needed in normal concrete mixes, the quantity of setting time retarders in CB slurries is much greater, due to the adsorptive effects of the bentonite

- Many chemical retardants lose their effectiveness within 24 hours

- Some may actually accelerate setting after 24 hours

- Some may reduce the strength of the finished wall (Jefferis 1981b).

2.5.2.2   CB Slurry Mixing Methods

The methods used to mix the cement-bentonite slurry also effect the performance characteristics of the slurry.    To obtain optimum slurry properties, it is recommended that first the bentonite be given sufficient time and agitation to hydrate fully, then the slurry be mixed with the cement as rapidly as possible in a high shear mixer.    The reasons for using these techniques are explained below.

If the cement is present in the water to which dry bentonite is added, the slurry will behave as if it were mixed in poor quality water, as described above.    Hydration, swelling, viscosity, and thixotropy will be inhibited (Case 1982, Boyes 1975).    For this reason, the bentonite must be fully hydrated prior to mixing with cement to form a cement-bentonite slurry.

After the slurry and cement are mixed, flash stiffening of the constituents occurs.    If agitated continually for another 5 minutes or so, the mixture becomes fluid again.    The speed of mixing has a pronounced effect on slurry performance.    For example, CB slurries from low shear (i.e., 50 rpm) mixers were compared to slurries from high shear (i.e., 1400 rpm) mixers.    The high shear slurries showed lower bleed rates, a greater sensitivity to drying problems, lower permeabilities when set, and higher unconfined compressive strengths when set than those from the low shear mixers (Jefferis 1981b).

From the discussion above, it is evident that the performance of both the CB slurry and the completed wall are dependent on both the slurry constituents, and the mixing procedures used. Thus, both of these variables should be carefully controlled during design and construction of CB walls.

2.6  Summary

Bentonite slurries can be used to hold open trenches during the construction of soil bentonite and concrete walls. The bentonite used is composed primarily of the clay mineral sodium montmorillonite, whose properties determine the characteristics of the slurry.

The sodium montmorillonite properties that are important during slurry functioning include extensive hydration and swelling, nearly complete dispersion, and thixotropy. These charcteristics allow the slurry to form low permeability filter cakes on the trench walls.

The filter cakes are an important component of the slurry trench, as they minimize slurry loss and groundwater inflow, plaster the soil grains together at the soil/slurry interface, increase the shear strength of the soil into which they flow, and form a plane against which the hydrostatic force of the slurry can act to stabilize the trench walls.

Montmorillonite characteristics also allow the slurry to form a gel structure when agitation is not occurring. This gel structure assists in suspending small particles of spoil inadvertently dropped into the slurry during excavation. The suspended sediments increase the slurry density and viscosity and thus indirectly assist in maintaining trench stability. Chemical additives are used in some slurries to improve the hydration, dispersion, and viscosity of the mixture.

Once the excavation of a slurry trench is complete, the slurry is backfilled using a homogeneous paste composed of soil mixed with bentonite slurry. The characteristics of the soil and slurry used, as well as the water content and placement methods control the permeability of the completed wall.

Cement is added to some bentonite slurries to form a mixture that will harden in time and form a cut-off wall. Because the calcium in the cement interferes with the sodium montmorillonite in the bentonite, properties of cement bentonite slurries differ in some respects from those of bentonite slurries. The most important differences are the facts that CB slurries harden to form a CB wall and that the permeability of CB filter cakes and CB walls is higher than that of bentonite slurries, filter cakes, and completed SB walls.

When CB slurries harden to form CB walls, the relative proportions of cement, water, bentonite, and cement replacements and chemical additives, along with the mixing methods used, control the characteristics of the completed wall.

To determine the suitability of SB or CB walls as a pollution migration cut-off at a particular site, an in-depth site investigation must be conducted. This investigation is described in the following section.

# 3. Slurry Wall Applications

The effectiveness of a pollution control slurry wall is determined, in large part, by its horizontal and vertical configuration as well as the associated remedial measures applied in conjunction with it at a particular site. These are, of course, highly site specific factors. The site conditions that determine both configuration and associated measures include setting, both geologic and geographic waste characteristics, and the nature of the environmental problems caused by the site. Although these factors are site specific, generalizations on applications can be useful in understanding and evaluating a slurry wall alone, and as part of a total remedial effort.

3.1  Configuration

Configuration as used here refers to the vertical and horizontal positioning of a slurry wall with respect to the pollution source location, and the groundwater flow characteristics. Although each slurry wall installation is unique, the vast majority can be described in the terms used in this section.

3.1.2  Vertical Configuration

Vertical configuration refers to the depth of the slurry wall with respect to both geologic formations and the water table. Based on vertical positioning, walls are either "keyed" into a low permeability formation below the aquifer, or placed to only intercept the upper portion of the aquifer. This latter type is commonly referred to as a "hanging" slurry wall.

A description of these two general wall types and their uses follows.

3.1.2.1  Keyed-In Slurry Walls

Keyed-in slurry walls are excavated to a confining layer below it, to contain contaminants that mix with or sink to the bottom of the aquifer. This layer may be a low permeability formation such as a clay or silty clay or may be the underlying bedrock (See Figure 3-1). In either case, the connection

## Figure 3-1.
## Keyed-in Slurry Wall

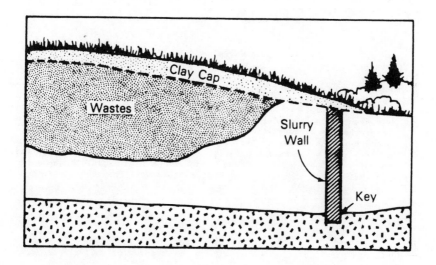

between the wall and the low permeability zone is very important to the overall effectiveness of the wall.

From a construction standpoint, wall key-in can be very straightforward or very complicated. If the low permeability zone is some easily excavated material, such as a clay layer or weathered rock, basic construction quality control should be sufficient to ensure a good key-in (see Section 5). In cases where the low permeability zone is hard bedrock, however, the excavation process may be much more complicated and costly, and may not be necessary. In many cases, a sufficient seal can be formed between the wall and the bedrock by scraping the rock surface clean with the excavation equipment. Depending on the condition of the bedrock, and the anticipated hydraulic head the connection must withstand, the weight of the backfill pressing against bedrock may form a sufficiently tight seal that will meet the designed permeability requirements (D'Appolonia 1982).

### 3.1.2.2  Hanging Slurry Walls

Hanging slurry walls are so called because they are not keyed into a low permeability zone. This configuration is used to control contaminants, such as petroleum products, which do not mix with the groundwater but float on top of it. In such cases, the slurry wall need only extend into the water table to intercept the contaminants (see Figure 3-2). The exact depth of the wall will depend on the thickness of the floating contaminant layer and the historically lowest water table elevation. Other considerations include the extent to which the weight of the contaminant might have depressed the water table, and what effect removal of the contaminants would have on the water table.

### 3.1.3  Horizontal Configuration

Horizontal configuration refers to the positioning of the wall relative to the location of the pollution to be controlled and the direction of groundwater flow (gradient). Based on horizontal configuration, slurry walls may completely surround the pollution source or be placed up or downgradient from it.

These configurations and the type of situations to which each can apply, are described below.

### 3.1.3.1  Circumferential Wall Placement

Circumferential placement refers to placing a slurry wall completely around the wastes contained within a site. Although this requires a greater wall length, thus greater cost, than either upgradient or downgradient placement alone, it does offer some advantages, and is a common practice. A

## Figure 3-2.
## Hanging Slurry Wall

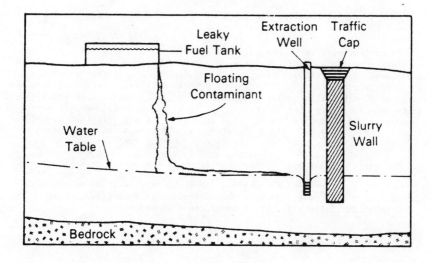

circumferential slurry wall, when used with a surface infiltration barrier (cap), can greatly reduce the amount of leachate generated within a site. If a leachate collection system is used a waste site can be virtually dewatered. This offers the advantages of vastly reduced leachate amounts and can help increase the longevity of the wall by reducing the amount of leachate/wall contact. As can be seen in Figures 3-3 and 3-4, the direction of flow is from the exterior toward the interior. Consequently, leachate/wall contact is minimized while waste containment is maximized. Figure 3-4 illustrates what can be achieved in the way of site dewatering. Walls used in this fashion must be very carefully designed. Because the head differential across the wall is relatively high in these cases, the backfill will be more prone to piping and hydrofracturing than if the head difference were lower. These problems are discussed in Sections 5.8.8 and 5.8.9.

### 3.1.3.2 Upgradient Wall Placement

Upgradient placement refers to the positioning of a wall on the groundwater source side of a waste site. This type of placement can be used, where there is a relatively steep gradient across the site, to divert uncontaminated groundwater around the wastes. In such cases, clean groundwater is prevented from becoming contaminated while leachate generation is reduced. As can be seen by Figures 3-5 and 3-6, a high gradient is required for upgradient placement to be effective. Unless the groundwater can be diverted around the site, and be drained to a lower elevation, it can flow around and return to the same elevation or rise to the surface to overtop the wall.

The use of a wall placed only upgradient of the wastes is limited in the types of situations to which it is applicable. Depending on the actual site setting, and the contaminants involved, an upgradient wall may be keyed in or hanging. In either case, drainage and diversion structures are likely to be needed to successfully alter the flow of clean groundwater.

### 3.1.3.3 Downgradient Wall Placement

Placement of a slurry wall at a site on the side opposite the groundwater source is referred to as downgradient placement. This placement configuration does nothing to limit the amount of groundwater entering the site and so is practical only in situations, such as near drainage divides, where there is a limited amount of groundwater flow from upgradient. Such a situation is illustrated in Figures 3-7 and 3-8. It should be noted that this positioning does not reduce the amount of leachate being generated, but acts as a barrier to contain the leachate so it can be recovered for treatment or use. Although this placement may be used as a keyed-in wall for miscible or sinking contaminants, it is most often used to contain and recover floating contaminants. In either case, compatibility between the wastes and the wall backfill is important because contact between the two would be difficult to avoid. In addition, care must be taken in designing a downgradient wall installation to

## Figure 3-3.
## Plan of Circumferential Wall Placement

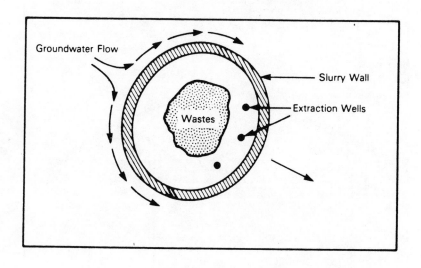

## Figure 3-4.
## Cut-away Cross-section of Circumferential Wall Placement

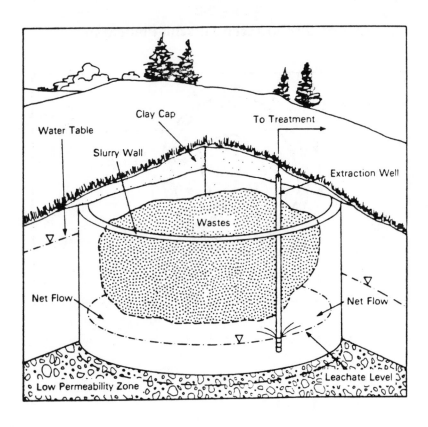

**Figure 3-5.**
**Plan of Upgradient Placement with Drain**

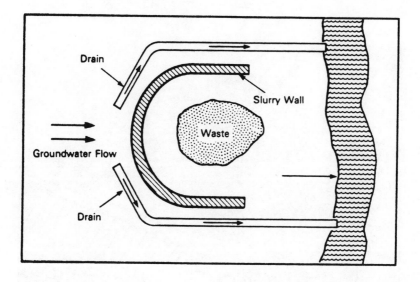

## Figure 3-6.
## Cut-away Cross-section of
## Upgradient Placement with Drain

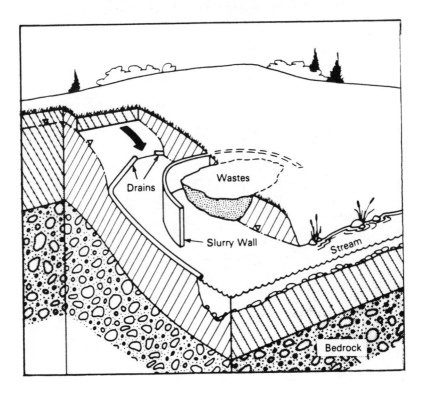

# Figure 3-7.
## Plan of Downgradient Placement

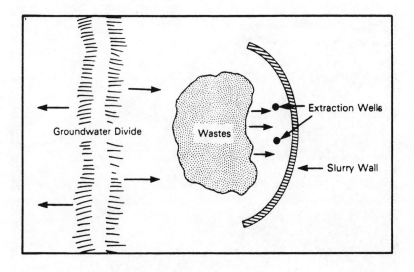

## Figure 3-8.
## Cut-away Cross-section of Downgradient Placement

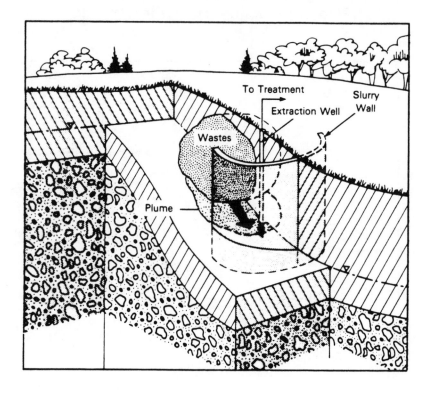

ensure the build up in head behind the wall does not result in overtopping of the wall by the contaminated groundwater.

The above discussion centers on slurry walls used to control the groundwater regime in the vicinity of pollution sources. However, slurry walls, especially soil-bentonite walls, are also used for the control of methane and other landfill gases (Lager 1982). It has been shown that both the water table and fine, moist soils can be effective barriers to gas migration (Moore 1977). This implies that for gas control, the slurry wall may be either keyed-in or hanging, whichever is shallower. A gas control slurry wall will be placed opposite the waste site in the direction or directions of gas migration, and so could be placed on only one side, or completely surrounding the site. It should be noted that to be truly effective in controlling the gas migration, venting, and particularly forced venting of the gases is recommended (Rovers, Tremblay, & Mooij 1977).

In summary, slurry walls can be applied to a pollution problem in a variety of ways. Table 3-1 shows the possible combinations and outlines their typical uses. It should be remembered that the effectiveness of the completed slurry wall which is a passive measure, will be dependent not only on its configuration and proper construction, but on the other remedial measures used in connection with it, in particular, active methods of handling groundwater, e.g., wells or drains.

3.2  Associated Remedial Measures and Practices

The effectiveness of slurry cut-off trenches can be dramatically increased by incorporating additional remedial measures into the overall plan addressing the problem. Some of these measures are:

- Groundwater pumping

- Surface and subsurface collection

- Surface sealing

- Grouting, sheet piling or synthetic membrane installation.

These measures affect the hydrologic environment at a site, and can result in a more efficient and effective control program. The following sections discuss additional control measures, giving a description, and mentioning installation considerations when they are used with slurry walls. More detailed discussions of each technology can be found in the EPA "Handbook for Remedial Action at Waste Disposal Sites", EPA-625/6-82-006, June 1982.

3.2.1  Groundwater Pumping

Groundwater pumping involves the installation of a series of wells or wellpoints located such that the cones of depression formed while pumping each

TABLE 3-1.
SUMMARY OF SLURRY WALL CONFIGURATIONS

| Vertical Configuration | Horizontal Configuration | | |
|---|---|---|---|
| | Circumferential | Upgradient | Downgradient |
| Keyed-in | Most common and expensive use<br><br>Most complete containment<br><br>Vastly reduced leachate generation | Not common<br><br>Used to divert groundwater around site in steep gradient situations.<br><br>Can reduce leachate generation<br><br>Compatibility not critical | Used to capture miscible or sinking contaminants for treatment or use<br><br>Inflow not restricted, may raise water table<br><br>Compatibility very important |
| Hanging | Used for floating contaminates moving in more than one direction (such as on a groundwater divide) | Very rare<br><br>May temporarily lower water table behind it<br><br>Can stagnate leachate but not halt flow | Used to capture floating contaminants for treatment or use<br><br>Inflow not restricted, may raise water table<br><br>Compatibility very important |

will intersect.  The result is a locally depressed water table in the area being pumped.  Pumped groundwater can be treated, if contaminated, and reinjected.

There are several ways in which this measure can be applied in concert with slurry walls.  In a situation where a wall is containing a contaminant plume, pumping can remove trapped, contaminated groundwater.  This reduces the concentration of contaminant in contact with the wall.  This may be important if there exists a possibility of wall degradation due to chemical attack, or if the recovered contaminants are of some value.

In another situation where a wall is diverting groundwater flow away from a waste disposal site, pumping can reduce the hydrostatic pressure exerted against the wall.  This reduces the rate of flow through the wall, since Darcy's law states that the rate of flow is dependent on hydraulic gradient across the wall.  This may be important in situations where a large head difference is anticipated across the wall.  Reducing the head difference also reduces the possibility of wall failure through piping.

Using cut-off walls and pumping concurrently has several advantages. First, the reliability of the wall is improved by reducing the probability of chemical attack or piping.  In many instances, pumping systems are used to protect the wall by keeping leachate away from it.  Second, since the slurry wall is creating a low permeability boundary, the rate of pumping needed to lower the water table elevation or remove contaminants is reduced.

When a well is pumped, the elevation of the water table is lowered in a cone-shaped manner (see Figure 3-9).  This effect is known as drawdown.  In order to lower the water table over a wide area, the drawdown "cones" for several wells must intersect (see Figure 3-10).

Drawdown is affected by the following factors:

- Pumping rate

- Permeability and thickness of water bearing zone

- Manner of groundwater recharge

- Presence of boundaries

- Length of pumping time.

The calculation of drawdown is one of the most important exercises in design-ing and installing well points or extraction wells.  The location of wells or well points, the depth of the screen, and pumping rate are all variables determined by the desired amount of drawdown.  Extensive geohydrologic testing of a site is usually required for satisfactory solution of the equations.

## Figure 3-9.
## Shape of Drawdown "Cone"

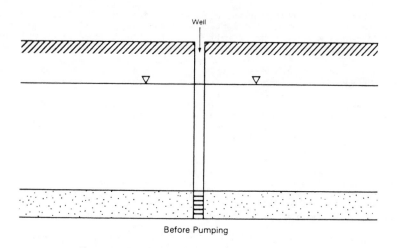

Before Pumping

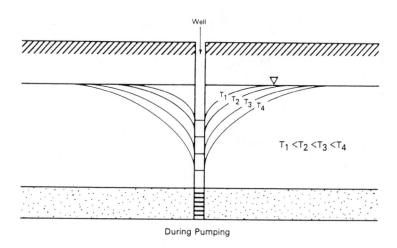

During Pumping

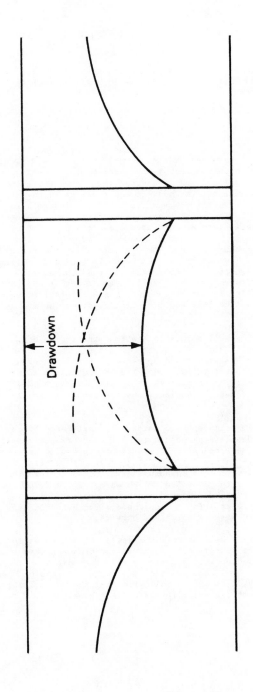

Figure 3-10.
Intersection of Drawdown Cone of Two Adjacent Wells

3.2.1.1  Pumping Systems

There are two types of pumping techniques used for dewatering:  well points and extraction wells.  While similar, each technique has special applications.

a.  Well Points

Well points are made to be driven in place, jet placed by water, or installed in open holes.  They consist of a slotted screen, reinforced and pointed at one end, and connected to a riser pipe or casing of the same or smaller diameter.  The most common practice is to water jet to the desired depth, flush out fines, and leave the coarser material to collect around the well point.  The point can then be driven into coarser material.  Once in place, the well points are connected to a header pipe (see Figure 3-11).

Well points can be from 1.4 inches in diameter up to 6 inches in diameter.  The size of a well point is generally determined from experience, and is a function of the permeability of the aquifer.  Fine-grained materials (e.g., silts and clays) usually require smaller well points.  Well points are not installed to depths greater than 20-25 ft for groundwater pumping purposes due to the fact that suction pumping is ineffective at depths greater than 20-25 ft.

Spacing well points is based on the radius of influence of each well and the composite effects required to achieve the desired drawdown.  Once theoretical drawdowns and spacing are developed using equations, a few well points can be installed and tested to determine actual values, since equations assume idealized conditions.  Adjustments can be made, which usually require minor decreases in spacing, thus achieving the desired decline in water table elevation.

The location of well points is complicated by the presence of the cut-off wall of much less permeability than the surrounding material.  The less permeable zone has a great impact on the cone of depression formed by well points (see Figure 3-12).  Drawdown is much greater near the wall, because rate of flow is less through the wall than through the surrounding matrix.  This reduces the area from which water can be drawn during pumping, resulting in a faster rate of drawdown near the wall.  This is useful since it requires less pumping capacity to achieve desired drawdown near a slurry wall than it does in the absence of such a barrier.

Locating well points in relation to slurry walls is dependent upon whether the slurry wall is upgradient or downgradient of a contamination source.  Well points associated with upgradient walls can be used to dewater behind the wall once it is in place, or they can be used to reduce the water table upgradient of the wall, reducing the hydraulic gradient across the wall.  These situations are illustrated in Figures 3-13, 3-14, and 3-15.

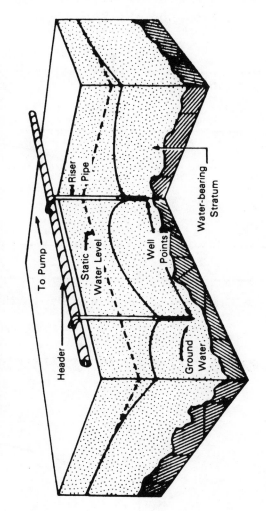

**Figure 3-11.**
**Schematic of a Well Point Dewatering System**

## Figure 3-12.

## The Effect of Drawdown in the Absence and Presence of a Slurry Wall

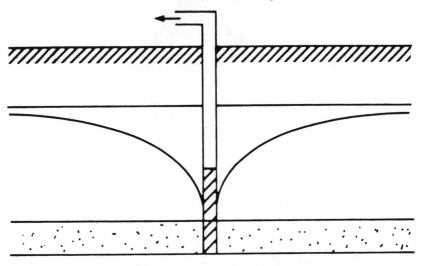

**A. Drawdown in Absence of Slurry Wall**

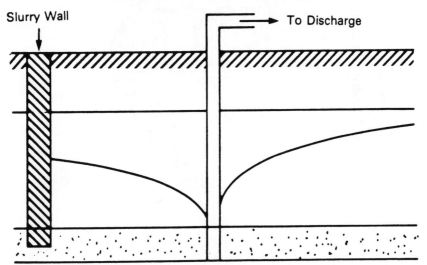

**B. Drawdown in Presence of Slurry Wall**

# Figure 3-13.
# Well Point Located Behind an Upgradient Slurry Wall
# Cut-Away View

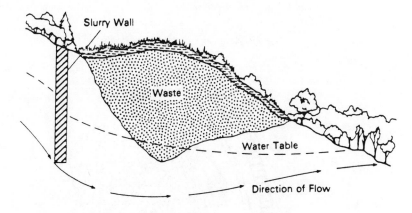

## A. Before Well Points Are Pumped

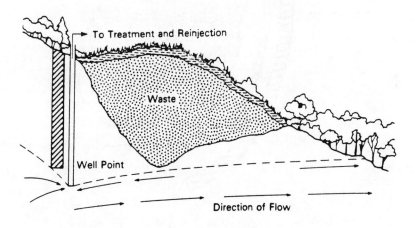

## B. After Pumping

## Figure 3-14.
## Well Points Located Behind an Upgradient Slurry Wall,
## Plan View

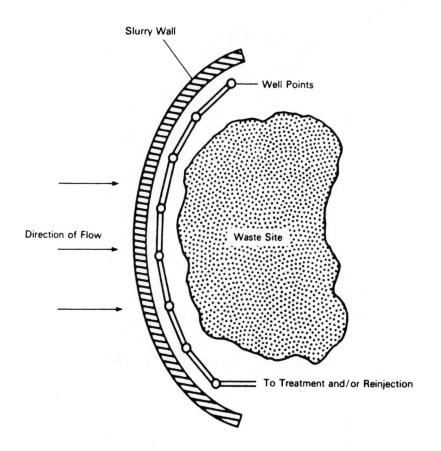

C. Map View of Slurry Wall and Well Point System

## Figure 3-15.

## Well Points Located Before an Upgradient Slurry Wall

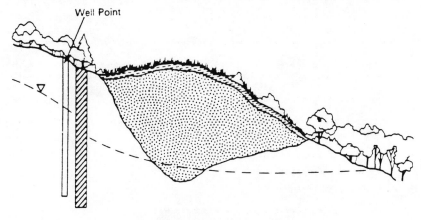

A. Before Pumping

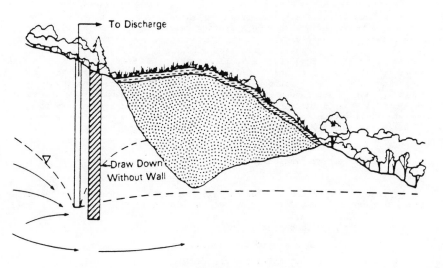

B. After Pumping

Well points associated with downgradient walls are commonly used to remove contaminated groundwater trapped by the wall. Installation can be such that the concentration of contaminants in groundwater near the wall is substantially reduced, lowering the possibility of chemical attack and removing the contaminant from the subsurface environment.

Groundwater pumped from this type of system must be treated before being reinjected. Treatment systems are discussed in a following section.

The depth and design of the well points is dependent upon whether the contaminant plume is heavier or lighter than water. Installation of well points downgradient of a site can result in reducing or virtually eliminating the flow of groundwater through the slurry wall.

Water pumped from the well points can be reintroduced into the subsurface environment by one of several means. These include:

- Reinjection wells or well points
- Surface spraying
- Recharge trenches.

Reinjection wells or well points are simply wells or well points where recovered or treated water is pumped back into the aquifer. Spraying refers to recharge using large area sprayers, much like irrigators used in arid farmland. Trenches are simply excavated ditches where water is allowed to infiltrate into the subsurface.

Of the three methods, a recharge trench is the most cost-effective. Water is pumped into the trench and infiltrates into the subsurface. The trench can be dug with a backhoe and often requires little or no maintenance. Maintenance, when necessary involves removing from the trench materials that may be clogging it, such as accumulated wind blown material or bacteria and fungus. The trench results in a local elevation in the water table, but since water is infiltrating at its own rate, as opposed to reinjection, the impact is not as severe. Reinjection wells or well points are more costly to install, incur costs through operation and maintenance, and may result in a substantial rise in the local water table. Sprayers are also costly to operate and maintain, and site considerations (such as a need for large areas of well-drained soil) may prohibit their use.

b.  Extraction/Injection Wells

Extraction wells are similar to well points in that they lower the water table by pumping. They differ from well points in several ways. Wells are:

- Able to go much deeper
- Not limited to unconfined aquifers
- Capable of almost unlimited capacity.

Extraction/Injection wells are installed using one of several drilling techniques, depending upon the conditions existing at a site. In installing these wells, a hole is drilled to the desired depth; the hole being of a diameter larger than that of the well. The well consists of a screen much like that used in a well point though usually longer, topped by a riser pipe to the surface. Appropriate size material, e.g., gravel or sand, is added to fill the annulus between the well and the drill hole. Usually, grout or some other sealant is used to isolate the formation being pumped from other formations.

The wells themselves must be of sufficient diameter to house a submersible pump and to accommodate expected flow. Casings and screens must be sufficient to withstand pressures developed during pumping.

In selecting a location for extraction/injection wells drawdown cones and radii of influence must again be calculated. In using extraction wells, larger capacities can result in larger radii of influence, reducing the number of wells needed. Wells can be placed either upgradient or downgradient of a slurry wall, much like well points, and will affect the water table in much the same way. Extraction wells are suitable for use in conjunction with slurry cut-off walls if the depth is beyond the effective range of well points or if high capacities are required.

c. Skimmer Systems

Skimmer systems have applicability in situations where contaminants are lighter than water and form layers on top of the water table. Systems have been developed that rely on a series of pumps and probes which lower the water table and pump the floating contaminants. The probes detect the concentration of contaminants being pumped, and automatically shut down or start-up the system when certain trigger concentrations are reached. These systems have been used successfully to recover oil or petroleum products which have made their way to the water table (see Figure 3-16). Proponents of these systems claim that they are so sensitive that recovered material is virtually 100% free of water, and can be re-used as is, without additional processing (Oil Recovery Systems, Inc. 1982).

Skimmer systems are made up of three major components. They are:

● Submersible pump to create a cone of depression

● Probe assembly to prevent the submersible pump from pumping contaminants

● Recovery unit, which uses its own probe system and pumps high concentrations of contaminants.

Installation and operation of the system is relatively straightforward. A well is drilled which intersects the contaminated layer and water table. The well is cased using a perforated casing allowing the passage of both contaminant and water. A submersible pump lowers the water table, causing the contaminants to migrate to the recovery well. A probe which differentiates

# Figure 3-16.
## Skimmer Systems

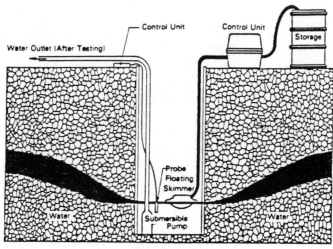

A. Floating

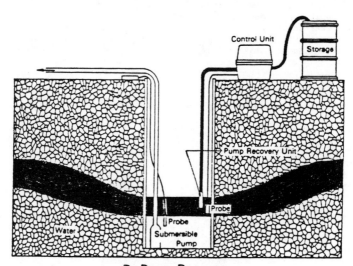

B. Pump Recovery

Source: Oil Recovery Systems Inc. (Undated)

between water and the contaminant is located above the submersible pump and automatically shuts the pump down when contaminants are detected. The recovery unit, also with a probe, pumps the contaminant layer and shuts off when concentrations fall below a certain level. Contaminants are stored in a tank for final disposition, and the pumped water can be reinjected after testing and treatment.

There are two types of recovery units; one which "floats" on top of the contaminant layer, and one which pumps from within the layer. The floating systems require larger diameter wells, usually over 18" in diameter. The pump system can be used in smaller diameter wells but usually not less than 6 inches in diameter. The pump recovery units have a higher pumping rate than the floating units, and can be used at greater depths. New units are available which contain filters to further concentrate the contaminant during recovery.

Skimming recovery systems can be used in concert with cut-off walls to effectively remove floating contaminants trapped by a wall. The wall can prevent further migration of the contaminant, causing a build-up of the material at the well. Either type of recovery unit can then be used to recover the "ponded" material.

### 3.2.1.2  Groundwater Treatment

The type of treatment system used depends on the contaminants present. Treatment systems may be relatively simple or quite complex. If publicly owned treatment works (POTW's) are near, they may be used to treat water but preliminary on-site treatment may be necessary in order to meet certain limits set by the POTW. Using an existing facility will substantially reduce the cost of treatment. If the water must be reinjected, more complete on-site treatment may be necessary prior to reinjection. In any case, treatment systems must be designed to meet site-specific situations. Treatability studies should be conducted to determine effectiveness of the treatment system options. Mobile labs and treatment modules are available to perform on-site studies and treat groundwater.

### 3.2.2  Collectors and Drainage Systems

Collectors and drainage systems can be used in conjunction with slurry walls to control surface and subsurface waters. Surface water control measures, for example, can be used at a slurry wall site to prevent water from infiltrating into the disposal area. In combination, surface water controls and a slurry wall can often serve together to curtail leachate generation. Surface trenches can be used as recharge points during the dewatering of a slurry wall site. There are numerous types of surface water collectors among which are the following:

- Dikes and berms
- Ditches, diversions, waterways
- Terraces and benches.

Subsurface drainage systems are designed to intercept and collect shallow subsurface water flow. In conjunction with a slurry wall, as with surface water controls, these systems can intercept water before it reaches the disposal area, thus controlling leachate generation. The interception and re-direction of groundwater in the vicinity of a slurry wall may also serve to relieve water pressure on the wall itself. The basic components of a subsurface water drainage or collection system are listed below:

- Gravel trenches or permanent drains
- Drain filter material
- Basin, sump or pit.

The design and use of surface and subsurface water control measures is always dependent upon site specific conditions. For a more complete discussion of these technologies and their applications, see U.S. EPA (1982).

### 3.2.3  Surface Sealing

Surface sealing, or capping, is the process by which surface areas are covered to minimize surface water infiltration, control erosion, and contain contaminated wastes and volatiles. A variety of low permeability cover materials and sealing techniques are available for such purposes.

Surface sealing can be particularly important in conjunction with slurry walls because one of the major routes of infiltration is vertically along the wall itself and this could seriously alter the effectiveness of a wall. To prevent infiltration, a surface cap can be installed which is below grade sloping upward away from the trench. This cap should be added after the slurry trench has been backfilled, and should consist of low permeability clay or other suitable material. If the area in which the trench lies is expected to accommodate traffic, especially if the wall is an initial step in a larger remedial action project, the surface cap must be constructed to distribute weight and avoid placing a stress directly upon the wall. To accomplish this, a special "traffic cap" can be installed. This cap also is V shaped sloping up and away from the trench, but is backfilled with alternating layers of clay, gravel, and geotextiles. The geotextiles can be anchored with soil away from the trench to provide additional strength.

There is a variety of materials available for surface sealing purposes. Fine-grained soils such as clays and silty clays have low permeabilities and are therefore best suited for capping because they resist infiltration and percolation of water. Very often different soil types can be blended together to broaden the grain size distribution and minimize the infiltration capacity of the soil cover. Chemical stabilizers, cements, lime, or fly ash can also be added to cover soils to create stronger and less permeable surface sealants. Finally, synthetic membrane liners and asphalt mixtures can also be used as surface sealants.

### 3.2.4 Ancillary Measures

A site requiring remedial action, is seldom the ideal setting for any one remedial technique and in the case of slurry cut-off walls there are several additional measures that can be used to reinforce the integrity of the wall. These techniques include grouting, sheet piling and the use of synthetic membrane liners. The following section will describe these three techniques and discuss how they can be used in conjunction with slurry cut-off wall installations.

#### 3.2.4.1 Grouting

Grouting is the practice of pressure injecting a fluid material into soil, rock or concrete so as to decrease the soil/rock permeability and/or strengthen the formation. Three major types of grouting techniques are practiced in the construction industry:

- Area Grouting - Low pressure blanket or area grouting performed to seal and consolidate soils near the surface

- High-Pressure Grouting - Grouting at depth to seal fissures or small void spaces

- Contact Grouting - Injection of a slurry at the outer surface of an excavation to seal possible passages for water flow.

The latter two are the more commonly used techniques when grouting is necessary as part of a slurry cut-off wall installation. One of the principle elements in the design of a cut-off wall is the connection between the wall and the underlying aquiclude. Keying a cut-off trench into the existing aquiclude requires depth enough to penetrate any weathered zones, pervious lenses, desiccation cracks or any other geological features that might allow seepage under the cut-off wall. In many situations trench excavation can be accomplished using standard excavation equipment, however, excavating into rock can pose problems. Even in a situation where the rock mass is jointed or fractured, it is often next to impossible to excavate without using percussion tools or heavier machinery that can further fracture the rock mass (D'Appolonia 1980). If the trench construction equipment on-site includes a crane, no additional equipment would be needed other than a chisel and clamshell which are suspended from the end of the crane. Use of heavier equipment can often be quite costly and time consuming. Consideration must also be taken for the area surrounding the site in a decision to use heavy machinery. Often there is a problem with either site access or physical constraints on the site itself and heavy equipment is impractical. In many cases, as an alternative to using heavier and more expensive equipment and attempting to advance the cut-off into the rock, the decision is made to grout the interface between the cut-off wall and the rock (Figure 3-17). This can be accomplished by using either one of two grouting techniques. The aquiclude can be sealed during trench excavation, prior to wall installation by the contact grouting method or the wall-aquiclude contact can be reinforced after the wall has been emplaced. The latter case entails the use of high-pressure grouting.

Bottom key grouting is one application of grout injection associated with slurry cut-off wall installations. Additional practices include grouting one or both ends of the completed wall to some existing structure on site and, area grouting of soil material along sections of a constructed wall that need extra reinforcement.

It is sometimes practical to utilize structures already existing on-site as part of a pollutant containment solution. An example of such a pre-existing structure might be a flood protection wall or dike. If a remedial action project required the construction of a slurry cut-off wall on the river side of a dike to prevent contaminant migration into the surface waters, it might be possible to contain the contaminant plume using the dike as part of the containment wall by grouting the wall-dike contact at one or both ends (Figure 3-18). There are, of course, many factors not discussed here that must be considered before arriving at such a decision, such as the permeability of the dike material, depth of the contaminant plume, or direction of groundwater flow. It might be necessary, for example, to grout only the downstream end of the cut-off wall depending upon the areal groundwater flow pattern and contaminant movement.

Area grouting of soil or loose material along a slurry cut-off wall might be necessary to retard erosional processes along the length of the wall. A situation in which this type of grouting technique could be applied, might be where a wall has been installed along a steep slope. Erosion rates can be significantly reduced by grouting loose material surrounding the wall.

Grouting materials fall into three groups: cement, bituminous, and chemical. Some specific grout mixtures include Portland cement, sand-cement, clay-cement, clay-bentonite, bituminous emulsions, sodium silicate, and acrylamide. The applicability of each material is based on grain size or fissure size, and the anticipated area of grout penetration. The subsurface environment must be investigated thoroughly prior to the design of a grouting program. Initially, it must be determined with tests whether or not a site is, in fact, groutable. Areas of extremely low permeability or great variability may not be groutable. Other tests and investigations will provide the necessary hydrogeologic information in order to choose the best-suited grout or grouts.

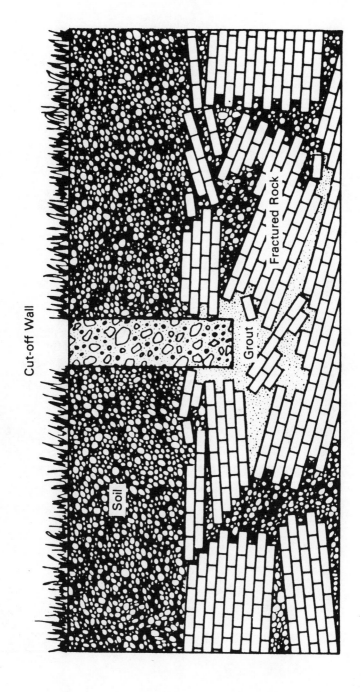

Figure 3-17.
Bottom Key Grouting

Cut-off Wall

Soil

Grout

Fractured Rock

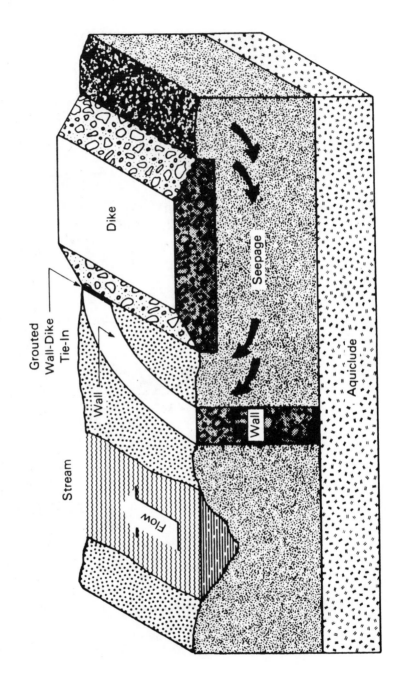

Figure 3-18.
Cut-off Wall-Dike Contact

3.2.4.2  Sheet Piles

Sheet piles are typically used to brace trenches and other excavations, or to support retaining walls and bulkheads (U.S. EPA 1982). Their main utility is to hold earth materials in place. The use of sheet piling in conjunction with slurry cut-off walls is yet another alternative remedial measure, in which it can be used as an erosion control. Examples of this type of sheet pile utilization, however, have not been identified in the reviewed literature. The following is a discussion of sheet piles and their most common applications, in addition to possible applications in adjunct with cut-off walls.

Sheet piles can be fabricated from three materials; wood, precast concrete, and steel (U.S. EPA 1982). Wood is generally an ineffective water barrier and because slurry cut-off walls are generally constructed at sites where leachate or groundwater containment is the objective, it would not be advisable to use wooden structures. Concrete sheet piles are used primarily in situations that require a great amount of strength, such as is needed during dam construction. Sheet piling strength, in this degree, most likely would not be a requirement in a leachate containment remedial project. Steel sheet piling, in a case where sheet piling was chosen to be an additional remedial measure, would be, in comparison, the most effective in terms of both cost and potential for groundwater cut-off.

Steel sheet pilings are installed by driving the interlocking piles into the ground with a pneumatic or steamdriven pile driver. In some cases, the piles are pushed into pre-dug trenches (U.S. EPA 1982). The lengths of piles range between 4 and 40 feet and their widths range between 15 and 20 inches. Many steel pile manufacturers offer their own shape of piling and often their own form of interlock. Steel sheet piling can be used in conjunction with a slurry cut-off wall as an erosion control or resistance mechanism. In slurry cut-off wall projects where contaminant containment is of utmost importance, and sheet piles are to be used as erosion controls in a location where there may be leachate or groundwater build up, it is crucial that the piles are as well locked as possible to minimize seepage through the interlocks. For this reason, the pilings should be assembled at their edge interlocks before they are driven into the ground. When initially placed in the ground, sheet piling is permeable. The edge interlocks, which are necessarily loose to facilitate placement, allow water passage. With time, however, soil particles are washed into the pile seams and water cut-off is effected to a greater extent (U.S. EPA 1982). The time required for sealing to take place depends on the rate of groundwater flow and the soil texture involved. In very coarse, sandy soils, the wall may never seal. Additionally, steel sheet piles should not be considered for use in extremely rocky soils. Even if enough force can be exerted to drive the piles around or through cobbles and boulders, the damage to the piles might render them ineffective.

### 3.2.4.3  Synthetic Membrane Liners

Synthetic membrane liners can also be used in conjunction with slurry cut-off walls and comprise the third group of associated remedial measures. In certain situations, it may be possible to reinforce the integrity of the cut-off wall with the addition of a synthetic liner. The liner materials are available in a variety of compositions with relatively well known chemical compatibilities.

Placement of a synthetic liner into the ground as a vertical barrier is a relatively difficult procedure. The liner is suspended vertically in and along one side of a slurry filled trench and the trench is then backfilled. Placement of a liner within a cut-off wall does have disadvantages. The liner material is extremely heavy and is stored and purchased on large rolls. Frequently, suspending the liner vertically in the trench is next to impossible because of the size and weight of the sheet. Also, once the liner is successfully placed in the trench, there is always the possibility that a bottom corner of the liner will be uplifted during the backfilling process (Villaume 1982). If this were to happen, water might be permitted to flow around the barrier. Careful inspection should be enforced during the installation process.

A possible way of overcoming problems that might arise due to the weight and bulk of the liner material itself, would be to install the liner in smaller sections. However, care must be taken to ensure that there is sufficient overlap of the sections so as not to permit water seepage. In conclusion, the use of liners as secondary containment measures can reinforce the integrity of the wall and create additional protection against possible seepage due to chemical attack on the backfill material.

### 3.3  Summary

The effectiveness of a slurry wall, with respect to both costs and technical performance, is determined in large part by the configuration employed. This configuration is determined by the specific remedial goals of a specific site. For most uncontrolled hazardous waste sites, a circular, keyed-in slurry wall offers the most complete containment. Nonetheless, slurry walls installed for hazardous materials containment are nearly always used in conjunction with some other remedial techniques. These range from relatively simple measures such as surface sealing, to complex groundwater extraction and treatment systems. Effective use of slurry walls for waste site remediation is dependent on the selection of the most appropriate configurations and materials, and on the selection of the other remedial measures employed with it.

# 4. Site Investigation and Characterization

The data from a site investigation are used by a design firm to formulate specifications for the remedial measures to be implemented at the site. These specifications are then used by the firms installing the slurry cut-off wall and other remedial measures. Because all later actions are dependent on the quality and completeness of the site investigation, the effectiveness of the entire remedial action is directly determined by the thoroughness of the site investigation.

This section discusses the types of data that should be acquired during the site investigation, possible data sources to be researched, and methods used to conduct field and laboratory analyses. The physical constraints imposed by the site's surficial features are discussed, followed by a description of subsurface site investigative procedures. Finally, information is presented on the procedures used to characterize wastes and leachates and their effect on wall quality and durability.

## 4.1 Physical Constraints

There are a number of physical considerations regarding both the site and the working area that affect the applicability of slurry wall types and the techniques used for their construction. Table 4-1 summarizes the various physical constraints that may be encountered and must be resolved. These constraints include:

- Topography

- Vegetation density

- Land drainage patterns

- Availability of water

- Location of utility crossings

- Proximity of property lines, major residential areas and transportation routes

89

TABLE 4-1.

TYPES OF PHYSICAL CONSTRAINTS AND THEIR EFFECTS
ON SLURRY WALL CONSTRUCTION

| Physical Constraints | Possible Affected Areas | Approach Required |
|---|---|---|
| Topography: Irregular contours Steeply sloping terrain | • Necessary equipment <br> • Site access and work space <br> • Type of wall selected | • Selection of equipment capable of operating in site specific terrain <br> • Extensive site preparatory work – leveling of areas for site entry and work space <br> • Use of CB wall in panels or diaphragm wall |
| Site Access and Work Space: Site congestion/ traffic Steep terrain Dense vegetation Lack of head room Insufficient space for mixing | • Extent of site preparation and pre-construction <br> • Type of equipment selected <br> • Type of wall selected <br> • Wall construction process | • Special equipment needs; construction of access road; leveling of working area; clearing of dense vegetation <br> • Amount of head room affects type of equipment selected or needed to relocate obstruction <br> • Amount of work space affects wall type selected; SB wall requires space for mixing; CB wall requires less area for operations, but it is more expensive; SB can be mixed away from trench but this approach may mean CB is cheaper for the site |

(continued)

Table 4-1. (continued)

| Physical Constraints | Possible Affected Areas | Approach Required |
|---|---|---|
| Site Access and Work Space: (continued) | | • Extra time needed for site preparation and construction |
| | | • Appropriate easement clearances |
| Utilities: Abandoned sewers, Pipelines, Leakage from water mains, sewers, Power/telephone cables | • Equipment selection | • Special equipment necessary for excavation around piping and sewer lines; or need for manual excavation |
| | • Construction process (operations) | |
| | • Problem control methods | • Sequence of trench segment excavation may change if utility discovered; excavate other areas first |
| | • Sudden slurry loss and possible trench collapse if unanticipated pervious zone, i.e., sewer piping is encountered and ruptured | • Watermain or sewer leakage may cause slurry contamination and loss of trench stability; a control plan necessary at outset of project |
| | | • Sudden slurry loss requires immediate placement of solid materials (soil, debris) into trench |
| Cultural Features: Old foundations, Nearby structures, Overhead structures | • Equipment selection | • Foundation penetration to isolate site |
| | • Construction process (operations) | • Excavation around foundations, or incorporate foundation into wall; if foundation support needed CB or diagraphm may be required |
| | • Problem control methods | (continued) |

Table 4-1. (continued)

| Physical Constraints | Possible Affected Areas | Approach Required |
|---|---|---|
| Cultural Features: (continued) | • Headroom | • Special equipment needed if breaking old foundations<br>• Tall equipment, e.g., cranes, may be restricted<br>• More time may be necessary for operations<br>• Experienced problem control personnel necessary |
| Other: Availability of water Time of year; water table fluctuations, temperature Subsurface geology; large subsurface boulders Type of wall backfill | • Equipment selection<br>• Slurry mixing<br>• Time needed and available for project completion<br><br>• Site preparation<br>• Problem control methods | • Equipment selection for boulder destruction or excavation<br>• Site may need de-watering system if water table is high or is expected to rise<br>• SB backfill cannot be mixed in sub-freezing temperatures<br>• CB will not set in certain temperature ranges<br>• Experienced problem control-personnel necessary<br>• Transport of water to site if none available |

References: (1) Ryan 1980a, (2) U.S. Army Corps of Engineers 1978, (3) Xanthakos 1979, (4) Wetzel 1982, (5) Tamaro 1980, (6) Ryan 1980b, (7) Namy 1980.

- Site accessibility

- Other man-made features.

### 4.1.1  Topography

Topographic features that should be noted during on site investigation include the steepness of the slopes on the site, the types of land drainage patterns present, and the proximity of the site to major bodies of water. These features can be discerned from topographic maps but should also be noted during site investigations.

### 4.1.2  Vegetation Density

Areas having extremely dense vegetation should be expected to require extra site preparation prior to field investigations or construction activities.  Dense vegetation can inhibit access and hide important surficial features such as small outcrops or erosion gullies.  Surveying of the proposed trench line and location of the bore holes is also delayed by dense vegetation.

### 4.1.3  Land Drainage Patterns

As noted previously, land drainage patterns at the site can be preliminarily assessed using topographic maps.  Additional information on the presence of erosion gullies, heads of drainageways, and anomolous features must be obtained during site visits.  Because surficial land drainage patterns directly affect subsurface water movement, this site feature should be carefully assessed.

### 4.1.4  Availability of Water

A great deal of water is necessary during slurry cut-off wall installation.  The source amount, quality of the water available should be ascertained during the site investigation.

### 4.1.5  Location of Utility Crossings

If water electric, gas, telephone, sewer or other utility lines cross the site, the exact locations should be determined and marked so that they are disturbed as little as possible during the site investigation and subsequent trench excavation.  If these lines cross the excavation site, provisions for re-routing must be made.

In addition data on the availability of water, sewer, electricity and telephone service should be noted.

### 4.1.6 Proximity to Property Lines

The location of the site relative to property lines, major residential areas, and transportation routes is an important element to be considered during the site investigation. If existing structures are very close to the site, the effects of trench excavation on structural stability must be assessed, and provisions made for interim structural support. Residential structures require special provisions, such as noise control and fencing of the site. Major transportation routes transecting the site must be re-routed. If the site characteristics make it necessary to consider installing the slurry cut-off wall close to property lines, permission of nearby property owners for access road use or land disturbance may be necessary. These factors should be noted in the site investigation report.

### 4.1.7 Site Accessibility

In remote areas or extremely congested locations, site access may be a problem. Remote areas may require the construction of roads or bridges and bringing water and other utilities to the site. Construction in congested environments may be complicated by access roads, such as driveways or alleys, or overhanging obstructions, such as signboards or utility lines. In these areas, equipment mobility may be seriously hampered.

### 4.1.8 Presence of Other Man-Made Features

Certain man-made features can seriously affect the design and installation of slurry cut-off walls. These features should be thoroughly investigated during the site characterization. Included in this category of physical site constraints are: mines, dams, irrigation ditches and tunnels. The location, size and other characteristics of these man-made features should be determined during the site investigation.

Some of the slurry walls installed to date have been placed in sites having a number of interesting site constraints. Two examples of the procedures used are given below.

During excavation dewatering at a large industrial plant, Ryan (1980b) reported that the following constraints were identified for this site:

- Concrete foundations under site

- Tight access conditions throughout site.

In addition to these constraints, the owner needed to maintain access across the site, the foundations had to be penetrated to isolate the site and its wastes, and it was hoped that the old foundations could be used as much as possible as part of the wall. The final solution to this site involved the following:

- Constructing an open-cut along the foundation alignment
- Using a hydraulic ram to break the old foundations
- Filling the opencut.

After these procedures were accomplished, the slurry trench was excavated to its design depth and a CB slurry was installed.

At another site, an SB slurry trench was to be installed around a waste lagoon. The installation took place on top of a dike which was 20 feet wide. The base of the backhoe was 14 feet wide so there was no problem using the backhoe for excavating the trench. A bulldozer was normally used to mix and place the backfill, however, since the bulldozer could not work in the limited area on top of the dike, a crane with a clamshell bucket was used for backfill mixing instead (Wetzel 1982).

## 4.2 Subsurface Investigations

As an initial step in obtaining information on the subsurface conditions existing at a site, all available sources of hydrogeologic data should be gathered. These include: geologic and topographic maps, hydrogeologic reports, aerial photographs, well drilling logs, and soil surveys. By reviewing published and other historical data, a preliminary characterization of the site can be made concerning the subsurface environment. Table 4-2 summarizes the principal sources of available geotechnical data.

A description of the hydrogeologic framework of an area should include a discussion of the following factors:

- Structural attitude and distribution of bedrock and overlying strata

- Chemical and physical properties of these strata including mineralogy, and permeability

- Weathering of these strata including the degree of alteration, the pattern and depth of weathering and any evidence of incompetent rock

- Groundwater regime, including water table depths, aquifer types, flow gradients and groundwater quality

- Soil characteristics including soil type and distribution, particle size distribution and permeability.

TABLE 4-2.

PRINCIPAL SOURCES OF AVAILABLE GEOTECHNICAL DATA

Published Data

1. U.S.G.S. Surficial Geology Maps
2. U.S.G.S. Bedrock Geology Maps
3. U.S.G.S. Hydrological Atlases
4. U.S.G.S. Basic Data Reports
5. State and County Geologic and Hydrologic maps and reports.
6. National and Local Technical Journals, Magazines and Conference Proceedings
7. U.S.S.C.S. Soil Maps

Unpublished Data

1. Local test boring and well drilling firms
2. Local and State highway departments
3. Local water departments
4. State well permit records
5. State and Local transportation departments
6. State and Federal Environmental Agencies
7. State and Federal Mining Agencies
8. Army Corps of Engineers
9. Local consulting, construction and mining companies
10. Geologists, hydroleogists, and engineers at local universities
11. Historical records
12. Interviews

Notes: U.S.G.S. - United States Geological Survey
       U.S.S.C.S. - United States Soil Conservation
                    Service

Reference: Guertin and McTigue 1982c.

Through the examination and analysis of this information specific data gaps can be identified and programs of further exploration can be planned and implemented to broaden or add to existing knowledge of site conditions.

There are three major issues involved in slurry wall design and construction that require an accurate and detailed hydrogeologic assessment. They include (1) the type of excavation equipment to be used (2) the depth to which the trench and subsequent wall will extend, and (3) the extent to which soils found onsite can be used in the backfill. These three issues must be continuously considered throughout the subsurface investigation in order to develop an appropriate and adequate slurry wall design for a particular situation. The design of a slurry wall project should progress in stages as investigations proceed and more detailed subsurface information is gathered and analyzed (Guertin and McTigue 1982c).

The following sections discuss the geologic, hydrologic and soil data necessary for the proper design and construction of a slurry wall.

4.2.1  Geology

The types of geologic information needed to properly design and construct a slurry wall include: rock depth, rock locations, location of structural discontinuities and the degree to which weathering in each rock type has occurred.

The existing rock types and the nature of the weathered zone will often determine the type of equipment used during excavation of the trench (Goldberg 1979). The depth to which a trench must be excavated will also play a major role in determining the type of equipment necessary at a particular site. The types of excavation equipment used during slurry trench excavation are described in Section 5.

The existence of an impervious geologic formation at a particular site into which a slurry wall can be keyed is the geologic characteristic that most strongly influences the vertical extent of a slurry wall. The depth to such an aquiclude frequently determines the excavation depth of the trench. Trench excavation for a keyed-in wall must extend into the aquiclude at all points along the trench length in order to avoid seepage zones that can easily breach the cutoff (Namy 1980). The elevation of the aquiclude's surface, however, is not necessarily constant. For this reason, the contour of the aquicludes surface must be carefully mapped.

The distance that the cut-off wall must penetrate into the aquiclude is determined by the composition and geochemistry of the impervious layer. If the aquiclude is a competent impervious bedrock, a minor penetration may be satisfactory. In contrast, an excavation that is carried into a clay formation may employ deeper penetration into the aquiclude as a safety factor (Millet and Perez 1981). It should be noted that although the presence of an aquiclude is an important consideration in the design of a slurry wall, there are cases in which it is unnecessary to key into an impervious layer, such as a scenario involving floating organic wastes, e.g., coal tar residuals. In this case it is only necessary to extend the wall to some specified depth below the base of the waste column.

Structural discontinuities and anomalous subsurface conditions that might interfere with either the wall continuity as it is being excavated or the tie-in with the aquiclude should be identified and methods for dealing with the discontinuities should be developed prior to excavation activities. Even if there is an acute awareness of potential problems, complications can arise and possible solutions for closures of pervious areas (called windows) in the wall should be evaluated.

The site-specific data needed to evaluate an area for the purposes of design and construction are seldom available solely from published sources. Thus the determination of the character and condition of the existing rock must be made through site investigative techniques, such as:

- Test borings
- Test pit excavations
- Rock coring
- Geophysical surveys
- Laboratory analyses.

Detailed descriptions of these techniques and the types of data that can be collected through their use can be found in ASCE (1976) and Ash et al (1974).

### 4.2.2  Hydrology

In addition to understanding the areal geology, an understanding of the groundwater system and its interactions with surface water is necessary prior to designing a slurry wall system for installation at a site. A detailed description of the groundwater regime is needed to more clearly define pollutant migration at a site. Only with a thorough understanding of potential plume configurations can the optimum slurry wall system be selected and implemented. Evaluations must also be made to determine the necessity for site dewatering during construction and if so, what the effects might be to surrounding land and structures. The types of hydrologic information that are typically required to design and construct an effective slurry wall are:

- Determination of boundary conditions, e.g., hydraulic head distributions, recharge and discharge zones, locations and types of boundaries

- Determination of material constants, e.g., hydraulic conductivity, porosity, transmissivity, area extent and thickness of geologic units, location of geologic units (accomplished during geologic investigation)

- Analysis of ground and surface water quality, e.g., background water quality, waste constituent concentrations, boundary conditions of wastes.

As with the initial stages of a geological investigation, preliminary data needed for determining the hydraulic system at a site can be obtained from numerous published and unpublished sources (see Table 4-2). Those sources most applicable to the hydrologic investigation are:

- Federal and state Geologic Surveys (USGS)

- Soil Conservation Service (SCS)

- Environmental Protection Agency (EPA)

- Local Water Control Boards (i.e., state and county)

- Drillers logs

- Operators plans and permits.

These data could include reports on the local geology, surface and groundwater quantity and quality, hydraulic properties of materials, and location of groundwater users. Based on the amount and quality of information obtained from these sources, it may be necessary to perform an additional on-site data collection program. This program could be very simple, where existing local wells are sampled for water quality and yield. An on-site data collection program may also be very complex, if new wells are drilled, geologic materials are sampled, pump tests are performed, and water quality and quantity samples are taken and analyzed. The level of effort spent in field collection programs should be adequate to fill the needed knowledge gaps so that a working slurry wall can be designed at a minimum cost.

Discussions of the various methods and testing techniques available for the accurate definition of the groundwater regime at a site can be found in numerous references, however, a recommended source of information is Guertin and McTigue (1982c).

In addition to the investigation of the movement and distribution of existing groundwater, it is equally important to study groundwater quality. Water quality has important influences on selection of the bentonite slurry and backfill, on the selected equipment and on the environmental concerns relative to disposal of uncontaminated groundwater from extraction wells (Guertin and McTigue 1982c). Depending upon the suspected or known waste types at a site, laboratory analyses of groundwater and/or surface water samples, will involve tests for different chemical constituents. The testing conducted relies entirely on site specific conditions. These issues are discussed in Section 4.3.

Using the data obtained for a site, numerous hydrogeologic and slurry wall design specifications can be produced. These could include the development of:

- Potentiometric surface maps and flow nets for the hydrologic system

- Geologic cross-sections with water table levels

- Depth and extent required for slurry wall

- Type of slurry wall that can be constructed based on contaminant compatibility and intended use.

For each site where a pollution migration cut off wall is to be constructed, a detailed hydrologic analysis must be performed to ensure success. Failure to perform this analysis could result in walls which allow contaminants to migrate past them (i.e., either under or around), walls that deteriorate because of contaminat interaction or walls that are over designed causing increased costs.

### 4.2.3  Soils and Overburden

Examination of the soil conditions existing at a site is another important part of the subsurface investigation. Soil information, in addition to being required for excavation and construction planning purposes, is needed primarily for the backfill design. The design of the backfill is probably the most important factor in the design of a slurry wall system (Case 1982). The backfill composition that is selected for a particular slurry wall site will consist of a designated percentage of small sized particles called fines. The desired particle size distribution of the backfill is determined during the design stages of the wall (Case 1982). It is, therefore, necessary to evaluate the presence of fines in the area of excavation. If sufficient fines are not available on-site, then a borrow source must be identified and plans for transportation of the material to the site should be incorporated into the construction contract. Additional soil parameters that should be measured during a site soil survey for the purpose of designing the backfill material are the following:

- Soil water content
- Permeability
- Horizontal and vertical distribution
- Chemical properties (e.g. organic content)
- Gradation (discussed above as percent of fines).

If suitable soils are not available nearby, a decision may be made to use alternative backfill.

Though maps and aerial photographs of an area may provide useful soil information, a slurry wall construction project should have on-site subsurface soil explorations conducted to obtain the necessary detailed information on soil types. This information is typically obtained through the use of the same investigative measures used to obtain hydrogeologic information. These include soil borings, test pits, and geophysical investigative methods followed by laboratory analyses of the samples collected. When properly correlated, the data obtained by utilizing these techniques, can be used to accurately define the type and extent of the soil strata underlying a site area. Two references are recommended as sources of information regarding soil investigative techniques.    They are McCarthy (1977), and Ash et al (1974).

There are two points with respect to site investigation and characterization that require reiteration. The first point involves the measures used to examine site conditions. It is important that the subsurface investigations involve both direct and indirect methods of exploration, particularly where conditions are suspected to be complex. Neither of the two types of techniques are solely capable of providing all of the information required to adequately describe the subsurface environment of a site area. Their use in conjunction with one another, however, can provide the detail and level of certainty necessary to properly characterize a site.

The second point is directed towards slurry wall application and effectiveness in a particular situation. The more thoroughly a site is characterized by investigation, i.e., the more detailed information available on surface and subsurface conditions, the more effectively a slurry wall may be designed and employed to control a pollution problem. Even the most experienced professionals cannot properly design and construct a slurry wall without having a thorough understanding of the situation at hand.

4.3  Wastes and Leachates

The presence of organic or inorganic compounds in the groundwater can have a detrimental effect on the bentonite slurry used during wall construction as well as on the ability of the finished wall to restrict pollutant migration. These chemicals can affect the physical/chemical properties of the bentonite and the backfill material, leading to failure of the wall either during construction or during its operational lifetime. Thus, before a slurry wall is considered as an appropriate remedial action at a site, the effects of the leachate on the bentonite slurry and the finished wall must be determined. A compatability testing program is necessary to provide the information needed to properly select the type of bentonite and backfill material that should be used in the slurry wall construction.

The following sections outline the effect that chemicals have on bentonite and backfill material, and laboratory tests that can be used to establish the potential effectiveness of the slurry wall.

4.3.1  Effects of Groundwater Contaminants on SB Walls


Different chemicals can affect the physical/chemical properties of the bentonite and backfill material, leading to:

- Flocculation of the slurry
- Reduction of the bentonite's swelling capacity
- Structural damage of the bentonite or backfill material.

These changes can in turn lead to failure of the trench during excavation and/or increase the permeability of the finished cut-off wall. These potential adverse effects on the performance of slurry walls are discussed further in the following sections.


4.3.1.1  Effects of Groundwater Contamination on Bentonite Slurries


Contaminated groundwater can come in contact with the bentonite slurry during trench excavation or if it is used to hydrate the bentonite. The major problems presented by the contaminants is flocculation of the slurry and/or a reduction in swelling capacity of the bentonite, leading to poor filter cake formation and potential collapse of the trench (Alther [no date], Xanthakos 1979). This is caused usually by the presence of high concentrations of electrolytes, such as sodium, calcium, and heavy metals, in the groundwater (Matrecon 1980, Alther [no date]). These ions can produce several changes in the betonite/water system that will lead to flocculation or reduced hydration of the bentonite.

Monovalent sodium ions on the surface of the bentonite can be readily exchanged with multivalent ions, such as calcium or other metal ions, contained in the leachate. The replacing multivalent ions will have a smaller radius of hydration than the sodium ion, thus reducing the dimension of the double layer (see Section 2). This will in turn greatly reduce the swelling capacity of the bentonite. (Alther [no date], D'Appolonia and Ryan, 1979). Thus the bentonite will not fully hydrate, and can settle out of suspension (Alther [no date]). Ions in solution can also compete for available water with the clay surface, causing a decrease in the thickness of the water shell around the clay particle (Matrecon, 1980). This can also impede the full swelling potential of the bentonite (Metrecon 1980, Hughes 1975).

These mechanisms will cause a compression of the double layer of water molecules surrounding each clay particle. This results in a decrease in the repulsive interactions between clay particles that can lead to an increased potential for particle aggregation resulting in flocculation of the bentonite suspension (Weber 1972).

4.3.1.2  Effects of Groundwater Contaminants on the Permeability of
         Cut-off Walls

Recent studies have shown the effects of a variety of inorganic and
organic compounds on SB slurry walls (D'Appolonia and Ryan 1979, D'Appolonia
1980a).  As Table 4-3 illustrates, slurry walls can withstand the attack of a
number of chemicals commonly found in leachates.  The soil bentonite mixtures
utilized in these studies contained from 30 to 40 percent fines.  The results
of a large number of permeability tests utilizing a wide range of pollutants
indicated that a well graded soil bentonite mixture containing more than 30
percent fines and about 1 percent bentonite will show only a small increase in
permeability when leached with many common contaminants (D'Appolonia 1980a).

The commercial brands of bentonite used in preparing the slurry or
backfill does not seem to have a significant effect on the ability of the
bentonite to withstand the effects of leachate or permeability.  Table 4-4
illustrates the effects of several different types of chemicals on the
permeability of four brands of commercially available bentonite hydrated with
fresh water.  For the brands of bentonite tested, there was not a significant
difference between their ability to withstand the effects of various chemicals
(D'Appolonia 1980a).

Increase in the permeability of the finished SB slurry wall can be caused
by chemical and physical changes in the structure of the bentonite and
backfill material.  These changes, caused by the compounds contained in the
leachate, can affect the swelling potential of the bentonite as well as alter
the structure of the bentonite and backfill material.

Numerous organic and inorganic compounds can, through a variety of
mechanisms, cause bentonite clay particles to shrink or swell.  All of these
mechanisms affect the quantity of water contained within the interspatial
layers of the clay structure.  Inorganic salts can, as discussed above, reduce
the double layer of partially bound water surrounding the hydrated bentonite,
thus reducing the effective size of the clay particles.  (D'Appolonia and Ryan
1979).  Upon disassociation, organic bases can be sorbed into the internal
surfaces of clay particles thus affecting the interlayer spacings (Anderson
and Brown 1981).  Neutral-nonpolar and neutral-polar compounds can replace the
water contained in the clay particle interlayers, thus affecting the size of
the bentonite particle (Anderson and Brown 1981).  This can lead to increased
permeability of the finished slurry wall, possibly resulting in breaching of
the wall.  For example, a decrease in the amount that hydrated bentonite has
swelled increases the amount of pore space in the backfill, thus increasing
the permeability of the wall.  In the worst case, a large reduction in the
effective particle size can result in the physical erosion of the soil/
bentonite matrix under the seepage pressure (D'Appolonia and Ryan 1979).  This
can lead to piping failure of the wall.  The probability of this type of
failure occurring can be reduced, if the backfill material contains at least
20 percent plastic fines (D'Appolonia 1980b).

TABLE 4-3.

SOIL BENTONITE PERMEABILITY INCREASES
DUE TO LEACHING WITH VARIOUS POLLUTANTS

| Pollutant | Backfill[0] |
|---|---|
| $Ca^{++}$ or $Mg^{++}$ @ 1000 PPM | N |
| $Ca^{++}$ or $Mg^{++}$ @ 10,000 PPM | M |
| $NH_4NO_3$ @ 10,000 PPM | M |
| Acid (pH>1) | N |
| Strong Acid (pH<1) | M/H* |
| Base (pH<11) | N/M |
| Strong Base (pH>11) | M/H* |
| HCL (1%) | N |
| $H_2SO_4$ (1%) | N |
| HCL (5%) | M/H* |
| NaOH (1%) | M |
| CaOH (1%) | M |
| NaOH (5%) | M/H* |
| Benzene | N |
| Phenol Solution | N |
| Sea Water | N/M |
| Brine (SG=1.2) | M |
| Acid Mine Drainage ($FeSO_4$ pH ~3) | N |
| Lignin (in $Ca^{++}$ solution) | N |
| Organic residues from pesticide manufacture | N |
| Alcohol | M/H |

N – No significant effect; permeability increase by about a factor of 2 or less at steady state.

M – Moderate effect; permeability increase by factor of 2 to 5 at steady state.

H – Permeability increase by factor of 5 to 10.

* – Significant dissolution likely.

[0] – Silty or clayey sand, 30 to 40% fines.

Reference: (1) D'Appolonia (1980a), (2) D'Appolonia and Ryan 1979.

TABLE 4-4.

INCREASE IN THE PERMEABILITY OF FOUR BRANDS
OF BENTONITE CAUSED BY LEACHING WITH VARIOUS POLLUTANTS

| Permeant | Final Permeability/Initial Permeability | | | |
| --- | --- | --- | --- | --- |
| | Slurry Ben 125 | National Premium Brand | Saline Seal 100 | Dowell M179 |
| Lignin in $Ca^{++}$ solution | 1.9 | 1.5 | 2.5 | 1.4 |
| NaCl based salt solution (conductivity 170,000) | 2.7 | 1.8 | 2.7 | N/A |
| Ammonium nitrate (10,000 ppm) | 1.8 | N/A | 2.8 | N/A |
| Acid mine drainage (pH ~3) | N/A | 1.5 | 1.3 | N/A |
| Calcium and magnesium salt solution (10,000 ppm) | 2.9 | 3.2 | 3.2 | N/A |

N/A:  Data not available.

Reference:  D'Appolonia 1980a.

Strong organic and inorganic acids and bases can dissolve or alter the bentonite or soil portion of the backfill material, leading to large permeability increases (D'Appolonia and Ryan, 1979, Alther [no date]).  Aluminum and silica, two of the major components of bentonite, are readily dissolved by strong acids or bases, respectively.  (Matrecon 1980).  Strong bases, though, usually produce a greater increase in permeability than acids due to the dissolution of silica (D'Appolonia and Ryan 1979).  Laboratory studies have shown that a well graded soil-bentonite backfill containing more than 20 percent plastic fines and about 1 percent bentonite shows only a small increase in permeability when exposed to a solution in the pH range of 2 to 11 (D'Appolonia and Ryan 1979).

While a properly designed slurry wall can withstand the effects of many chemicals, it is essential to know the long term effects that the compounds found in the groundwater will have on the permeability of the wall.  Thus it is essential to test any pollutant with the actual backfill material that is going to be used.  (D'Appolonia and Ryan 1979).  The following sections address testing methods which can be used to determine the impact of leachate on SB slurry walls.

### 4.3.2  Compatibility Testing

To test the compatibility of compounds contained in the groundwater with the material used in the construction of slurry walls, a series of laboratory tests should be performed.  Since there are, as yet, no standard tests and testing procedures established for determining the compatibility of chemicals with slurry walls; the types of tests and their associated testing procedures can vary widely between laboratories.  Through discussions with both private and public laboratories and a review of the literature, several quantitative testing methods were identified as being applicable.  These include:

- Viscosity test
- Filter-press test
- Permeability test
- Examination of Bentonite Mineralogy.

In performing any of these tests, representative samples of the leachate and backfill material must be collected.  Procedures for groundwater and soil sample collection can be found in several publications, such as U.S. EPA (1981).

### 4.3.2.1  Viscosity Test

The viscosity of the bentonite slurry can be an important factor in determining the effect of the compounds contained in the groundwater on the slurry.  Groundwater contaminants can change both the viscosity and gel

strength of a bentonite slurry. Thus by testing the changes in slurry
viscosity caused by the addition of leachate, the effects can be established
and potential remedial responses can be sought.

One device that is recommended by the American Petroleum Institute (API)
for testing slurry viscosity is the direct indicating viscometer, as
illustrated in Figure 4-1. By utilizing this device the plastic viscosity,
yield point, and apparent viscosity can be easily determined. The procedures
for performing this test and the required calculations are outlined in API
(1982).

### 4.3.2.2  Filter-Press Test

The standard filter-press test that is commonly used to evaluate drilling
mud has been utilized to indicate the effects of leachate on slurry and filter
cake performance. In the filter press test, bentonite slurry is introduced
into a high pressure filter apparatus, as in Figure 4-2. A pressure is
applied to the filter apparatus, and the resulting filtrate is collected
(Xanthakos 1979; API 1982). The quantity of filtrate should be within
established limits. By introducing a representative quantity of leachate into
the bentonite slurry before the test is performed, the short-term effects on
fluid loss can be established. If there are any detrimental effects, the
fluid loss will be outside the bounds of the established limits. The
procedures and apparatus needed in order to conduct this test are outlined in
API (1982).

### 4.3.2.3  Examination of Bentonite Mineralogy

An examination of the mineralogy of the bentonite backfill before and
after it has been exposed to the leachate in the permeameter test could be
used to determine short-term chemical effects on the clay structure. By
utilizing standard laboratory tests, such as X-ray diffraction the effects of
the leachate on the clay structure can be determined. This can provide an
indication of the long-term stability of the bentonite backfill.

### 4.3.2.4  Permeability

The effect of leachate on the permeability of a soil/bentonite cut-off
wall can be ascertained by several standard soil testing procedures. By
comparing the permeability of a soil/bentonite mixture when it is permeated
with leachate to that obtained when it is permeated with water, a determination can be made of the leachate's potential affect on the permeability of
the SB cut-off wall.

Laboratory procedures for performing permeability tests can be divided
into several general categories depending on how the level of liquid used in

## Figure 4-1.
## Rotational Viscometer

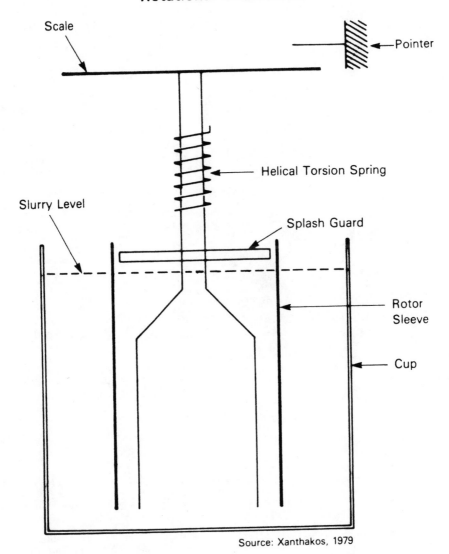

Source: Xanthakos, 1979

# Figure 4-2.

# Filter-Press Test Apparatus

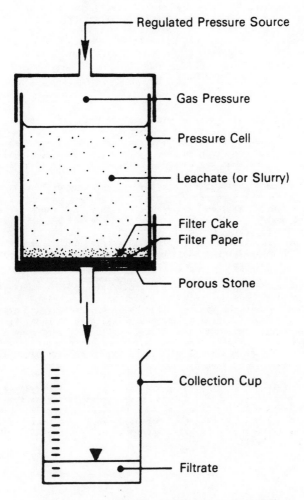

Source: D'Appolonia & Ryan 1979

the apparatus is maintained during the course of the test, e.g., constant or falling head permeability tests, and the type of apparatus used to contain the soil/bentonite sample, e.g., fixed wall or triaxial permeameters.

Any of the established permeability testing procedures can be utilized, such as those outlined in OCE (1970). While all permeability tests can potentially be affected by a number of problems, the evaluation of the results of a particular permeameter test hinges not so much on the type of equipment utilized but the test and quality control procedures followed during the study. Data currently available show that the use of fixed wall or triaxial type devices does not affect the results of the permeability tests on slurry trench cut off wall backfill materials (Ayres 1982). Thus more attention needs to be paid to the test procedures than the type of equipment used.

## 4.4    Summary

Both the feasibility of a slurry wall for remediation at a particular waste site, and the degree of success with which it is used, are dependent on thorough investigation and characterization efforts. These efforts define and delineate those site-specific factors affecting wall design specifications, ease of installation, and the overall performance of the final cut-off.

There are many physical factors that in some way would constrain the use of a slurry wall at a given site. Most of these factors would not preclude the use of a slurry wall, but would require additional engineering and construction measures to overcome. Investigation and characterization of physical site constraints would reveal and define the need for such pre-trenching activities as site grading, or rerouting of fences, utilities or roads. All of these factors could have an impact on construction costs and so must be well characterized.

A thorough investigation and characterization of the sub-surface conditions at a site is essential to slurry wall feasibility, design and construction. A detailed delineation of a site's geology and hydrology will help define the proposed slurry wall depth, and ease of excavation, and indicate potential construction problems. Soils and overburden characterizations will also reveal potential excavation and construction problems, but are most important for determining the suitability of on-site materials for use as backfill material in a SB wall.

The importance of a complete characterization of site wastes and leachate should not be underestimated. Several waste types have been shown to be destructive to both SB and CB walls and could seriously affect their integrity. Permeability testing of proposed backfill materials, with actual site leachate is currently the most accurate method for predicting the longevity of the wall.

   The site investigation and characterization efforts are essential in developing a wall design suited to controlling that site's contamination. They also play a major role in identifying those factors that pose problems for wall installation and developing methods for dealing with them.

# 5. Design and Construction

This section addresses the design and construction procedures that are used to install a soil bentonite or cement bentonite wall. Each step, from the pre-design stage to the clean up of the site is described.

First, site specific factors that should be evaluated prior to slurry wall design are discussed. These factors affect the feasibility and conceptual design of slurry wall use at a particular site, and the relative applicability of the two slurry wall types.

Next, slurry wall design types and components are described. This description illustrates the various portions of a design package and the types of data that typically are contained in each.

Slurry wall construction requirements, including materials, quality control, equipment, methods, and dimensional parameters are listed in the third part of this section.

Following this a brief discussion of preconstruction steps is given. In addition to evaluating the site and producing the design, the bid package must be prepared and bids evaluated before the construction contract can be awarded.

Once the contract is awarded, wall construction can begin. The techniques used during construction of soil bentonite walls are described in detail. CB and diaphragm walls are also discussed. The final portion of this section addresses problems associated with slurry trench construction. Typical solutions to these problems are also discussed.

## 5.1 Design Procedures and Considerations

The process of designing a slurry wall requires assessment of site specific data and consideration of numerous design variables, to determine the feasibility of a slurry wall and to select the most appropriate wall type for use at the site. This section describes these processes.

### 5.1.1  Feasibility Determination

Using the data from the site investigations, the designer must determine the feasibility and applicability of installing a slurry wall at the site. Factors to consider include:

- Potential waste incompatibility

- Anticipated hydraulic gradients and maximum allowable permeability in the completed wall

- Aquiclude characteristics - depth, permeability, continuity, and hardness

- Wall placement relative to wastes and leachates

- Costs and time considerations.

#### 5.1.1.1  Waste Compatibility

Waste and leachate compatibility with proposed slurry wall backfill mixtures can be determined using the laboratory tests described in Section 4. Where long-term permeability is crucial, clay mineralogy and geochemical testing is advisable. These tests provide an indication of which proposed backfill mixtures show the greatest resistance to long and short term permeation by the pollutants at the site.

#### 5.1.1.2  Permeability and Hydraulic Gradient

Data on the anticipated hydraulic pressures on either side of the wall indicate the range of hydraulic gradients to which the wall may be exposed. When projected permeabilities and wall areas are known, the rate of subsurface movement through the wall, can be determined using Darcy's law. Darcy's law states that

$$q = kia$$

where q is the volume of water flowing through the wall, k is the coefficient of permeability of the wall, i is the hydraulic gradient, and a is the cross-sectional wall area (Mitchell 1976).

To illustrate how Darcy's law can be used to estimate a slurry wall's effects on groundwater flow at a hypothetical site, consider the following hypothetical situation: a proposed slurry wall is designed to be 164 feet (50 meters) long, 82 feet (25 meters) deep, and 3.2 feet (1 meter) thick. The hydraulic gradient at the site is estimated at 2, and the wall's permeability is designed to be less than $2.12 \times 10^{-3}$ gpd/ft$^2$ ($1 \times 10^{-7}$ cm/sec). According

to Darcy's law, the amount of water that will move through the wall is 57 gpd
(0.216 $m^3$/day. Before the slurry wall was installed, the permeability of the
same area was about 2.12 gpd/$ft^2$ (1 x $10^{-4}$ cm/sec), a low permeability for
undisturbed soils. The amount of water flowing through the area each day
prior to slurry wall installation was 57,000 gpd (216 $m^3$/day. Thus, this
particular slurry wall would reduce the volume of water flow through this area
by 99.9 percent. In areas having higher initial permeabilities, the effect of
the slurry wall would be even greater.

### 5.1.1.3  Aquiclude Characteristics

Another factor to consider when evaluating the feasibility of a slurry
wall is the aquiclude at the site. Ideally, it should also be thick,
impermeable, and unfractured, and should be soft enough for a backhoe or
clamshell to excavate a 1- to 3-foot key-in to prevent seepage under the
slurry wall. In areas where aquicludes are very hard, slurry walls will be
more expensive to install or the aquiclude wall union less certain. Where the
aquiclude is thin, discontinuous, or fractured, slurry walls can be expected
to be less efficient in pollution migration control due to seepage through the
aquiclude and other remedial measures may be called for.

### 5.1.1.4  Wall Configuration and Size

An early assessment of possible wall locations and configurations can
indicate the overall amount of wall exposure to wastes and leachates, the
types and placements of auxiliary measures and the actual length and depth of
wall required. These factors, along with an estimate of the necessary wall
durability, can assist designers in projecting the cost of the construction
effort. Detailed data on wall applications and configurations are presented
in Section 3.

### 5.1.1.5  Cost and Time Factors

The need for rapid response at some sites necessitates an evaluation of
the construction time required. According to Miller (1979) soil bentonite
slurry walls are normally installed at a rate of 25 to 100 linear feet per
day. Thus, the wall described previously could be installed in 2 to 7 days,
assuming the work is accomplished in a nonhazardous environment. Hazardous
conditions can more than double on site work time.

### 5.1.2  Selection of Slurry Wall Type

If it is determined that a slurry wall is feasible, the type of wall
(SB or CB) that is required should be established. To decide whether a

soil-bentonite or cement-bentonite cut-off wall should be installed at a particular site, several factors need to be considered. The following factors affect the suitability of SB or CB walls:

- Required permeability and hydraulic pressure
- Leachate characteristics
- Availability of backfill material
- Required wall strength
- Aquiclude depth
- Site terrain
- Cost.

### 5.1.2.1  Permeability and Hydraulic Gradient

Where low permeability is required, SB walls are used, and the wall width is determined by the hydraulic head across the trench. Case (1982) recommends that the trench should "have a width of 0.5 feet to 0.75 feet per 10 feet of hydrostatic head on the wall. Thus, for a 100 foot head loss, wall thickness should range from 5 to 7.5 feet." In comparison, a CB wall only 2 to 3 feet thick will stand up to the same hydrostatic force (i.e., 100 feet). Deeper walls are generally wider then shallower ones because larger excavation equipment is used for deep walls and this equipment generally digs a wider trench (Millet and Perez 1981). Generally, CB walls are designed to be narrower than SB walls due to the greater shear strength and the higher cost of cement bentonite walls (Millet and Perez 1981, Ryan 1976).

### 5.1.2.2  Leachate Characteristics

SB walls exhibit a lower permeability and a greater resistance to chemical attack, particularly to acids, than CB walls. For this reason, SB walls are favored for use as pollution migration cut-offs (Jefferis 1981b and Xanthakos 1979).

Where floating rather than sinking contaminants are encountered, the slurry wall does not have to be extended down into the aquiclude. Instead, a "hanging" wall is installed. These walls are usually soil bentonite types.

### 5.1.2.3  Availability of Backfill Material

In some sites, the material excavated from the trench is contaminated due to contact with polluted groundwater. This contaminated soil may be unsuitable for use in the backfill. Samples of this material should be mixed with bentonite slurry and tested to determine the effects of the contaminants on the SB wall permeability. Testing of SB wall/leachate compatibility is discussed in Section 4. In some cases, the contaminants will increase the permeability of the completed wall, but the increase may be less than the increase that could be caused by the sudden exposure of the wall to the polluted groundwater. At these sites, it may be advisable to use the contaminated material in the backfill, providing the gradation is adequate (D'Appolonia 1980b). If, however, the contaminated soil is discovered to be inappropriate for use as backfill material, a suitable borrow area should be found. Where no such borrow area is available nearby, CB walls may be more appropriate.

### 5.1.2.4  Wall Strength

Generally, CB walls are used where heavy vertical loadings are anticipated and large lateral earth movements are not expected. This is because CB walls have a higher shear strength and lower compressibility than SB walls. CB walls are, however, more likely to crack than relatively plastic SB walls (Millet and Perez 1981). If the wall must be extended beneath roads, rail tracks or in close proximity to existing foundations, CB walls can be used. In addition, CB walls can be used in localized areas requiring strength and tied into SB walls for the rest of the trench distance.

### 5.1.2.5  Aquiclude Depth

CB walls are more expensive than SB walls due to the cost of the cement. For this reason, CB walls are not generally used where the aquiclude is deep, or where very long cut-off walls are required (Ryan 1977).

### 5.1.2.6  Site Terrain

At sites where slopes are steep and the areas for backfill mixing are limited or non-existent, and low permeability is not critical, CB walls may be preferred. In general, SB walls are limited to areas where the maximum slope along the trench line is on the order of 2 percent or less. At many sites, hills can be leveled and depressions backfilled with compacted soil prior to trench construction. The lack of sufficient backfill mixing areas can be overcome by hauling trench spoils to a central backfill mixing area, then hauling mixed backfill back to the trench. Pug mills can also be used for backfill mixing. These operations -- site leveling use of pug mills and central backfill mixing -- result in slower construction rates and higher costs.

In contrast to SB walls, CB walls can be constructed in areas of steeper terrain by utilizing the CB panel construction technique described later in this section.

5.1.2.7  Cost

As mentioned earlier, a CB wall is typically more expensive than a SB
wall of the same volume due to the cost of the cement.  Where thick or deep
walls are planned, CB walls will, in most cases, be more expensive than SB
walls.  Where wall thickness can be minimized and very low permeability is not
essential, CB walls be can considered.

After the type of slurry wall has been selected, the preparation of the
design can begin.

5.2  Specification Types and Design Components

The objective of the design phase is to produce accurate specifications
for wall construction.  Normally, the design of a slurry wall for pollution
migration control involves producing either a performance type specification
or a materials and methods specification.

5.2.1  Differences in Specification Types

Performance specifications consist of the performance standards which
spell out what the owner or engineer expects to receive in exchange for
payment.  These specifications stipulate the results desired by the owner and
leave the achievement of the results the responsibility of the contractor.
This type of specification provides the widest latitude to the contractor but
still maintains the quality desired for the end product.  Historically,
performance specifications allow innovation on the part of the contractor to
achieve results at reasonable costs.

The most commonly used measure of slurry wall performance is the
permeability of the completed cut-off.  Often, the maximum permeability is
specified at $10^{-7}$ cm/sec (Lager 1982).  Materials requirements are also
specified.  Most design engineers and bentonite producers use performance type
specifications.

The materials and methods type of specifications, which are normally used
for major construction projects are typically very long because requirements
for both materials and methods are spelled out in great detail.  Although this
type of specification is applicable for slurry trench installations, the
general consensus of design and construction firms with much slurry trenching
experience is that construction costs are typically increased without
improving the quality of the installation if materials and methods types of
specifications are used.

In some situations, this specification type may be favored over
performance specifications.  For example, where there are not qualified
bidders for a project or where special structural considerations are involved,

a materials and methods type specification may be necessary.  For this reason, components of both design and performance specifications are described below.

### 5.2.2  Components of Design

In slurry wall designs, the following items are typically addressed:

- Scope of work
- Construction qualifications
- Construction requirements of the trench and slurry wall
- Materials
- Equipment and facilities
- Performance
- Clean up
- Quality Control and Documentation
- Measurement and Payment.

Each of these items are briefly described below.

#### 5.2.2.1  Scope of Work

This section describes in general terms what the contractors will be required to accomplish including material quantities and performance period.

#### 5.2.2.2  Construction Qualifications

This should describe the prior experience required of the contractor and his personnel on site.  This could be expressed in terms of a specific number of similar jobs, in years of experience in slurry trench construction, or both.  This requirement is not always stipulated.

#### 5.2.2.3  Construction Requirements of the Trench and Wall

Among the items included in this section are the width and depth of the trench, the aquiclude to be penetrated, and the depth of penetration, the location, continuity, verticality, and permeability of the completed wall. The two most important design considerations, which are the selection of the aquiclude and the design of the backfill, must also be described (D'Appolonia 1980a).

### 5.2.2.4 Materials

This section should specify the material standards to be maintained during construction. It usually covers water quality, bentonite type, slurry quality, backfill characteristics, and additives, if any. Each of these materials should be separately addressed to ensure compliance with design requirements for the particular site.

### 5.2.2.5 Equipment

This section should be used to ensure that the contractor has the proper equipment on site to perform the following:

- Trench Excavation
- Slurry Mixing
- Slurry Placement
- Backfill Mixing
- Backfill Placement
- Site Clean-up.

### 5.2.2.6 Methods

This section describes the acceptable methods of slurry mixing, trench wall stabilization, trench excavation, backfill mixing, backfill placement and clay cap construction. The design engineer must ensure that the slurry is properly hydrated prior to use, that the slurry is pumped into the trench at the start of excavation, and that sufficient slurry is kept in the trench to maintain trench wall stability.

The trench for an SB or CB wall must be excavated so that it is continuous to the required depth along the specified line of excavation. Unexcavated areas within the trench are prohibited, as these interfere with wall integrity. To ensure continuity in CB panel walls, sufficient overlap between adjacent panels must be required (Geo-Con, Inc. 1979).

The consistency of SB backfill material (as measured by slump) must be specified in order to maintain the desired flow properties during backfill placement. The required backfill properties are described in Section 5.3.2.5. The method of backfill placement should also be addressed in order to avoid entrapping pockets of slurry or pervious materials during backfilling that interfere with wall performance. After completion of the trench backfilling process, the trench must be protected from desiccation by means of a clay cap. Techniques for construction of this cap must be described, particularly if the cap is designed to withstand traffic loads.

This section should also include the acceptable methods for controlling problem areas such as slurry flocculation, loss of slurry in the excavation, maintenance of slurry density and premature gelation of the slurry. Some of these methods are described in Section 5.7.

The specifications should describe the condition of the site as it is left by the contractor. This could address the fate of waste slurry, filling of hydration ponds, and site grading and revegetation.

### 5.2.2.7  Quality Control and Documentation

The contractor should be required to perform testing to include documentation and in some instances certification during the construction. Tests and certifications should cover both the excavation and the materials used. In many cases, the owner/engineer will establish QA/QC procedures independent of the slurry wall contractor.

### 5.2.2.8  Drawings

The design should include sufficient data for the bidders to estimate the volume of earth to be excavated and the relative difficulty of excavation. Specifically, the drawings should show:

- Any earth-moving required before actual trench construction can begin

- A plan view of slurry trench with areas for slurry preparation and equipment

- A cross section of the trench to show depth and location of any utility or road crossings

- Soil boring, locations, and depths.

A plan view of the site will show trench location, location of slurry hydration ponds, water sources and water storage tanks, and slurry storage areas. If the spoil from the trench cannot be used for backfill, borrow areas may be located, and the designated borrow areas shown on the plan. In this situation, the location of spoil disposal may also be delineated.

The cross section of the trench will show depth of excavation and variation in the trench depth, water table elevation, and soil strata. In addition, any crossings, such as utilities, process piping, wastewater piping, are shown.

Soil borings and their location will give field inspectors and construction personnel some idea of the expected difficulty of excavation in a given area.

5.2.2.9  Measurement and Payment

Slurry trench cut-off wall specifications typically conclude with
sections concerning measurement and payment.  This section defines acceptance
criteria and payment method.

These brief descriptions of slurry wall specification types and design
components illustrate their role in the overall slurry wall installation
process.

## 5.3  Slurry Wall Requirements

The specifications for a slurry wall must present a logical flow of
design criteria.  The first step in developing criteria for cut-off walls
using slurry trench method is to define objectives.  The objective in most
hazardous waste applications will be to design a system that inhibits groundwater flow to a specific degree, for a specified period.

The design factors affecting the effectiveness and durability of
completed CB and SB walls are:

- Wall location
- Wall depth
- Wall width
- Wall continuity and verticality
- Connection to surface structure
- Material quality
- Methods and procedures used.

The slurry wall design should specify the location length and grade of
the finished wall as well as the wall depth and width.  Other requirements,
such as permeability, continuity and verticality should also be stated.

### 5.3.1  Location

This is shown on drawings attached to the specifications.  The design
includes instructions to construct the wall along the lines and grades shown
on the drawings.  Factors affecting slurry wall locations relative to waste
locations and hydrogeologic conditions are described in Section 3.

5.3.2  Depth

Slurry wall depth is controlled by the depth to the aquiclude.  The
selection of the aquiclude is one of the most important items in the slurry
wall design.  Although several relatively impervious zones may be encountered,
the aquiclude used as a cut-off wall foundation should be continuous,
relatively free of fractures and other pervious zones, and within the reach of
currently available excavation equipment.  Selection of a suitable aquiclude
is based on the data obtained during site investigations, as described in
Section 4.  Usually the cut-off wall is extended 2 to 3 feet into the
aquiclude past the zone of "pervious lenses, weathered zones, desiccation
cracks or other geological features that might permit seepage under the
cut-off" (D'Appolonia 1980a).  If the acquiclude to be penetrated is of
questionable integrity in the excavation area, the base of the cut-off can be
grouted to seal pervious zones beneath the wall (D'Appolonia [unpublished]).
In the case of a hanging slurry wall, the depth of the seasonally lowest water
table determines wall depth.

5.3.3  Width and Permeability

In addition to wall location and depth, the wall width and permeability
are stipulated in materials and methods specifications.

Design width depends on several factors, including:

- The required cut-off effectiveness
- Head loss across the wall
- The hydraulic gradient
- The size of the available excavating equipment.

The permeability of the completed cut-off is usually stated in
performance specifications.  For adequate pollution control, it is necessary
to maintain a wall permeability of $1 \times 10^{-7}$ cm/sec or less (D'Appolonia
1980a).  This permeability is achievable using SB walls with high fines
contents.  Cement bentonite walls usually have higher permeabilities; on the
order of $1 \times 10^{-6}$ cm/sec (Jefferis 1981b).

The relationship between required wall thickness and hydraulic gradient
is given in Section 5.1.2.6.  Data on equipment sizes and excavation depths
are presented in Section 5.3.7.

5.3.4  Continuity and Verticality

The continuity and verticality of the completed wall can significantly
affect wall performance and must be carefully specified.  Soil bentonite or CB

trench walls are excavated in a continuous trench, and continuity is tested by passing the backhoe bucket or clamshell vertically and horizontally along each segment before it is backfilled. When a circumferential slurry wall is constructed, a segment of the earliest-backfilled trench is reexcavated to ensure complete continuity.

In CB panel walls, each panel is excavated under a CB slurry then allowed to set before excavation of the intervening panels is begun. The overlap at each panel joint is dependent on wall depth and the type of equipment used. A minimum of 3 feet of each end of each partially set CB panel is excavated when the intervening panel is excavated. The intervening panel is allowed to harden and that particular wall segment is then complete (Geo-Con, Inc. 1979).

Soil bentonite walls are usually not required to be strictly vertical, as these walls are seldom, if ever, used in a load-bearing capacity as part of a structure. Verticality can affect wall continuity, particularly at corners. If one wall is vertical but the other slants outward at the base, a large unexcavated area may exist in the corners. For this reason, some specifications call for nearly vertical walls, or a 5-foot overlap at wall corners (U.S. Army Corps of Engineers 1975). Good field quality control will insure a nearly vertical wall and good continuity.

5.3.5 Surface Protection

Another requirement of completed soil bentonite walls that they be protected from consolidation and compaction as well as from erosion. The completed wall must not be allowed to consolidate unevenly and thus form deep cracks, or to consolidate enough to form a seepage path or a depression at the ground surface that follows the original trench excavation (Millet and Perez 1981). Consolidation is a function of backfill gradation and water content, and the ratio of trench width to depth. In most cases, it can be predicted in advance and so not cause unforeseen problems. Wider walls have been found to consolidate more than narrow ones, and excessive fines content is said to result in a greater degree of consolidation. In trenches wider than 8 feet, having a depth from 50 to 90 feet, consolidation was reported to average 1 to 6 inches (Xanthakos 1979). One 3-foot wide wall backfilled with material containing an average of about 60 percent fines consolidated about 6-8 inches over the course of about 6 months. The surface of the SB wall was dry and cracks less than 1 inch wide and a few inches deep were evident prior to placement of a clay cap (Coneybear 1982).

To protect the surface of finished SB walls, clay caps are often installed (Millet and Perez 1981). These can be designed to support traffic by interspersing geotextiles (construction fabric) between a series of clay lifts and by covering the surface with gravel (Zoratto 1982). As consolidation occurs during the first few months after trench construction, additional clay layers may be added (U.S. Army Corps of Engineers 1975).

5.3.6  Materials, Quality Control, and Documentation Requirements

The types of materials that are acceptable during slurry trench construction are often specified in great detail.  Quality requirements for the following items are commonly listed:

- Dry bentonite
- Water
- Fresh slurry
- In-trench slurry
- Backfill materials
- Mixed backfill.

Table 5-1 presents a materials quality control program for soil bentonite walls.  The types, frequencies and results of the tests are specified. Additional requirements are described below.

5.3.6.1  Dry Bentonite

The quality of the dry bentonite should be tested frequently, for example by checking the pH, viscosity and fluid loss of a slurry made from the bentonite.  Certification of compliance with the material specification from the bentonite manufacturer must be obtained.  Other criteria for dry bentonite include physical and chemical purity and dry fineness (percent passing a number 200 mesh sieve).

Another bentonite quality criteria is the type of additives allowed. Additives are reportedly present in most, if not all, commercial "natural" sodium bentonite sold in the U.S. (D'Appolonia and Ryan 1979).  Among the types of additives used in bentonite are peptizers, bulking agents, softening agents, dispersants, retarders and plugging or bridging agents (Corps of Engineers 1975; IMC., [no date]).  Some of these are listed in Table 2-3. Although some specifications categorically prohibit the use of additives, others require the engineer's prior approval and manufacturer's certification of compliance with stated characteristics before the additives can be used (U.S. Army Corps of Engineers 1976; Geo-Con Inc. 1979).  Specifications requiring approval of additives usually refer to additives other than those allowed in "natural" bentonites.

5.3.6.2  Clay

At some sites, the use of native clay materials has been attempted. There are several drawbacks to the use of other clays in the slurry during trench construction.  The primary ones are the difficulty in meeting slurry

TABLE 5-1.

MATERIALS QUALITY CONTROL PROGRAM FOR SB WALLS

| Quality Control Item | Subject | Standard Name | Type of Test | Frequency | Specified Values |
|---|---|---|---|---|---|
| | Water | - | -pH<br>-Total Hardness | Per water source or-as changes occur | As required to properly hydrate bentonite with approved additives.<br>Determined by slurry viscosity and gel strength tests. |
| | Additives | - | Manufacturer certificate of compliance with stated characteristics | | As approved by Engineer |
| Materials | Bentonite | API Std 13 Standard Procedure for Testing Drilling Fluids | Manufacturer certificate of compliance | | Premium grade sodium cation montmorillonite |
| | Backfill Soils | - | Selected soils obtained from a borrow area approved by the Engineer<br>Roll to 1/8" thread | | 65 to 100% 3/8" Sieve<br>35 to 85% passing #20 Sieve<br>15 to 35% passing #200 Sieve |
| Slurry | Prepared for Placement into the Trench | API Std 13 Standard Procedure for Testing Drilling Fluids | - Unit Weight<br>- Viscosity<br>- Filtrate Loss | 1 set per shift or per batch (pond) | Unit Weight    1.03 gm/cc<br>V — 15 centipose of<br>— 40 sec-Marsh @ 68°<br>Loss — 15 cc to 25 cc in 30 min<br>— @ 100 psi |
| | In Trench | API Std 13BI Standard Procedure for Testing Drilling Fluids | - pH<br>- Unit Weight | 1 set per shift at point of trenching | pH — 8<br>unit weight = 1.03 - 1.36 gm/cc |
| | | | - Slump | 1 set per 200 cu yds | Slump 2 to 6 inches |
| Backfill Mix | At Trench | ASTM C 143 Slump Cone Test | - Gradation | | 65 to 100% passing 2/8" Sieve<br>35 to 85% passing #20 Sieve<br>15 to 35% passing #200 Sieve |

Reference: Federal Bentonite 1981.

specifications and controlling slurry quality (Boyes 1975). As Table 5-2 shows, a 6 percent solution of commercial montmorillonite gives a viscosity of 15 centipoise (cP). To obtain an equivalent slurry using typical native clays, a solution containing about 25 to 36 percent clay would be necessary unless they are very high in montmorillonite (Grim and Guven 1978). At this clay content, the slurry would be denser than is desirable for trenching slurries: dense slurries are detrimental because thay may not be displaced properly by the backfill.

Like montmorillonite, native clays are composed of very small particles that will pass through a 200 mesh sieve. Most native clays are found mixed with larger-sized particles such as silt, sand, and gravel. These larger particles are difficult to separate from the clay. The amount of clay in the native deposits normally will vary both horizontally and vertically. Because of this variation, it will be difficult to control the clay concentration in slurries made from native clays. A third problem with non-montmorillonitic native clays is that they are much less thixotropic than montmorillonite. They may take days to develop a gel structure rather than minutes (Boyes 1975). For these reasons, typical clays do not perform as well or as consistently in slurries as montmorillonite; therefore, the use of non-montmorillonitic clays is not recommended for most applications.

### 5.3.6.3 Water

Water quality must be tested for each water source used. Tests include pH, total hardness and content of suspected deleterious substances (U.S. Army Corps of Engineers 1976). Reported water quality requirements include:

- Hardness of < 50 ppm

- Total dissolved solids content of < 500 ppm

- Organics content of < 50 ppm

- Other deleterious substances (i.e., oil or leachate) < 50 ppm

- pH of about 7.0 (Xanthakos 1979, U.S. Army Corps of Engineers 1975).

### 5.3.6.4 Fresh Slurry

The fresh hydrated bentonite slurry should have a minimum viscosity of 40 seconds Marsh, a unit weight of about 65 p.c.f.) a pH of from 7 to 10, a bentonite content of from 4 to 8 percent (Case 1982, Xanthakos 1979, Boyes 1975 and Alther 1982). The factors affecting bentonite and slurry quality are discussed in Section 2. Common slurry properties and the tests used to measure them are presented in Table 5-3.

One test that is often conducted on fresh slurries is the filtrate (or fluid) loss test (API 1982). This test is supposed to simulate formation of the filter cake (Millet and Perez 1981). The filtrate test involves measuring

TABLE 5-2.
COMPARISON OF SELECTED PROPERTIES OF CLAYS

| Parameter | Montmorillonite | Kaolinite | Illite | Other Clays or Sheet Silicates |
|---|---|---|---|---|
| Amount of water the dry clay can absorb, % of dry weight (1) | 200-300% (1) | -- | -- | 100% |
| Volume change due to hydration under similar conditions | 2-11 $cm^3$/g (2) | | | vermiculite >montmorillonite >beidellite >kaolinite >halloysite (2) |
| Hydration rate | Water sorption continues for about 1 week (2) | -- | -- | water sorption for most colloidal clays is complete in 1 to 3 days (2) |
| Particle shape | thin, flat, irregular plates (3) | irregular, flat six-sided shapes (2) | -- | attapulgite-fibrous, sepiolite-fibrous, most others irregular and flat (3) |
| Theoretical Specific surface area, $m^2$/g | 700-800 (2) | 5-20 (2) | 100-200 (2) | vermiculite 300-500 (3) |
| Cation Exchange Capacity, meq/100g | 60-150 (3) | 3-15 (2) | 10-40 (2) | vermiculite 100-150 (2) attapulgite/sepiolite 3-15 (3) |
| Liquid Limit (%) | 150-700 (4,5) | 29-75 (4) | 59-90 (4) | attapulgite 160-230 (6) |
| Plastic Limit (%) | 65-97 (4) | 26-35 (4) | 34-43 (4) | attapulgite 100-120 (6) |

(continued)

TABLE 5-2.  (continued)

| Parameter | Montmorillonite | Kaolinite | Illite | Other Clays or Sheet Silicates |
|---|---|---|---|---|
| Shrinkage Limit (%) | 8.5-15 (6) | 25-29 (6) | 15-17 (6) | -- |
| Percentage of clay by weight in water to produce a 15 cP colloidal suspension | ~5.5-12 (4) | -- | -- | ~25-36 for typical native clays (4) attapulgite-same as montimorillonite (4) |
| Density of charge meq/m$^2$ x 10$^{-3}$ (2) | 1.1-1.9 | 6-7.5 | 1.0-2.0 | vermiculite 3.0-3.3 |
| Layer thickness in Å (6) | expansive >10 air dry 15 | 7.15 | 10 | vermiculite 14 muscovite 10 biotite 10 halloysite 10 |
| Particle density, g/cm$^3$ (2) | 2.5 Wyoming bentonite (5) 2.2 Japanese bentonite (5) | -- | -- | mica 2.8-3.2 (2) |

References:  (1) Case 1982, (2) Baver, Gardner and Gardner 1972, (3) Grim 1968, (4) Grim and Guven 1978, (5) Xanthakos 1979, (6) Mitchell 1976.

TABLE 5-3.
COMMON SLURRY PROPERTIES AND TESTING METHODS

| Property | Definition | Current test method |
|---|---|---|
| Concentration | lb bentonite/100 lb water<br>kg bentonite/100 kg water<br>lb bentonite/ft$^3$ water | |
| Density | Mass of given volume of slurry | Mud Balance |
| Plastic viscosity apparent viscosity, yield stress | For a slurry behaving as a Bingham body, the flow law is<br>$\quad T = yT_0 + N_P D$<br>where $T$ = shear stress<br>$\quad T_0$ = yield stress<br>$\quad N_P$ = plastic viscosity<br>$\quad D$ = rate of shear<br>$\quad TD$ = apparent viscosity | Fann V-G viscometer |
| Marsh cone gelation | Time for 946 cm$^3$ (1 U.S. quart) or 1500-cm volume to drain from a standard cone or time for 500 cm$^3$ of the 500-cm$^3$ volume to drain from cone (Japan) | Marsh funnel viscometer |
| Initial gel strength | Minimum shear stress to produce flow; designated as $T_8$ | Rotational viscometer |
| 10-min gel strengh | Shear strength obtained by allowing 10 min to elapse between stirring and reading | Rotational viscometer |
| pH | Logarithm of reciprocal of hydrogen-ion concentration | pH electrometer; pH papers usually not reliable |
| Filtration or fluid loss | Volume of fluid lost in given time from fixed volume of slurry when filtered at given pressure through standard filter | Filter-press test (but this procedure does not permit exact estimation); stagnation-gradient test more appropriate |
| Filter cake | Thickness and strength of filter cake for standard or actual conditions | Thickness measured in fluid-loss test, strength estimated from triaxial tests |
| Sand content | Percentage of sand greater than 200-mesh in suspension | API standard sand-content test using a sand-screen set |

the amount of water lost from a 15cP slurry through filter paper when
subjected to a pressure of 100 p.s.i. for 30 minutes (Grim and Guven 1978).
Some controversy exists as to whether or not this test accurately reflects the
ability of the slurry to form a filter cake.

Despite the fact that the test may serve as a useful indicator, the
filtrate loss test has several innate flaws, including the facts that the
filter paper used has very little similarity to the strata at the slurry/soil
interface, and that the pressures used are not representative of in-place
pressures found in slurry trenches (Hutchison et al. 1975).

In addition, there is little if any relationship between the results of
the standard API filtrate loss test and the permeabilities of filter cakes
from the same slurry (D'Appolonia 1980b). Thus the filtrate loss test is
regarded by some persons involved in slurry trench construction as
inappropriate for slurry specification (D'Appolonia 1980b, Millet and Perez
1980).

### 5.3.6.5  In-Trench Slurry

The requirements for the in-trench slurry are few and simple. The
in-trench slurry becomes denser due to the suspension of soil particles in the
slurry. For the in-trench slurry, two measurements are important. A slurry
sample taken from the trench bottom near the toe of the backfill should be at
least 15 p.c.f. less dense than the backfill material, and must be capable of
passing a Marsh funnel. This is to allow complete and rapid displacement of
the slurry during backfilling (D'Appolonia 1980b).

### 5.3.6.6  Backfill Materials

The gradation of the soil material used for the backfill must be tested.
For a low permeability cut-off, at least 20 to 60 percent fines should be
presented (D'Appolonia 1980). Although plastic fines yield lower
permeability, non-plastic fines will show a greater ability to withstand
chemical attack. Larger particles, such as cobbles or clay lumps greater than
5 inches across should be prohibited (IMC [no date]).

### 5.3.6.7  Mixed Backfill

Once the backfill material has been selected, it must be mixed with the
slurry in the proper proportions so that it has the following characteristics:

- A bentonite content of 1 to 2 percent
- A moisture content of 25 to 35 percent
- A fines content of 20 to 60 percent.

In addition, the mixed backfill should have a:

- Slump from 2 to 7 inches on the ASTM C143-74 "Slump of Portland Concrete" Test

- Density at least 15 pcf greater than that of the slurry in the trench

- Shear strength low enough to allow ready flow, and preferably lower than that of the filter cake.

     a.  Slump

A typical backfill used in a pollution migration cut-off wall has a water content between 25 and 35 percent, a bentonite content ranging from 0.5 to 2 percent and a fines content of from 20 to 40 percent. The soil excavated from the trench typically has an initial moisture content of from about 10 to 20 percent (D'Appolonia 1980b). This moisture aids in mixing the slurry with the backfill by softening the materials (Coneybear 1982). When the backfill is mixed in these proportions, the backfill forms a thick paste that will flow easily (D'Appolonia 1980b). The slump of the backfill, which is an expression of its propensity to flow, is of great practical importance during backfilling operations.

If the backfill slumps too much, a very flat backfill slope occurs. This interferes with the efficiency of excavation. Conversely, backfill with too little slump allows voids and honeycombs to form and may cause entrapment of pervious materials, leading to the formation of high permeability "windows" in the finished wall (Millet and Perez 1981).

When the backfill folds over and traps pockets of slurry, another problem results. The slurry does not become mixed with the backfill. Instead, it gradually rises to the top of the trench, due to its lower density. This may lead to wall weakness in the areas where the slurry pockets were initially.

To avoid the problems listed above, a slump of 2 to 7 inches is usually specified (Case 1982). Figure 5-1 shows a cross-sectional view of a completed trench, showing the successive layers of a well placed backfill.

     b.  Density

Backfill densities typically range from 105 to 120 p.c.f. At these densities, the backfill easily displaces the slurry in the trench (D'Appolonia 1980). Even so, samples of the slurry taken from the trench bottom should be tested for density prior to initiation of backfilling operations.

## Figure 5. 1.
## Typical Backfill Profile in Trench with Irregular Bottom

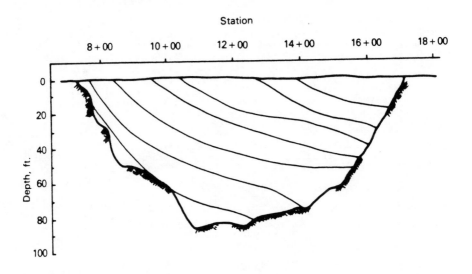

Source: D'Appolonia 1980

c.   Shear Strength

The shear strength of the backfill must be high enough to allow it to stand on a 5:1 to 10:1 slope (Millet and Perez 1981).  Preferably its shear strength is lower than the shear strength of the filter cake to avoid disrupting it.  Data on the relative shear strengths of the backfill and the filter cake were not located.  However, Boyes (1975) stated that the shear strength of bentonite filter cakes is greater than that of concrete emplaced in slurry trenches during concrete panel wall construction, and that the shear strength of one filter cake was measured at 0.00051 $N/m^2$.

The fate of the filter cake during backfilling has been the subject of controversy.  Some people involved in slurry trench construction feel that the filter cakes on both of the trench walls remain intact not only during backfilling but also during subsequent permeation with groundwater. D'Appolonia (1980b) suggested that the downstream filter cake may degrade under the influence of high hydraulic gradients across the trench.  The bentonite particles may then be forced into the soil pores if the soil permeability is high enough.  Jefferis (1981a) proposed that the upstream filter cake would be more likely to decompose and be forced into the cut-off wall.  This is because the hydraulic pressure on the upstream side of the wall is so much higher than the pressure on the downstream side.  Experimental evidence cited by D'Appolonia (1980b) indicates that, as long as the backfill contains at least 15 to 20 percent fines, this will not occur.

5.3.7  Equipment

Appropriate equipment must be available to accomplish the following tasks associated with slurry wall construction:

- Slurry mixing

- Slurry supply to the trench

- Slurry density control

- Trench excavation and aquiclude key-in

- Backfill mixing

- Backfill placement

- Hauling of backfill or spoils, if necessary.

The type and size of this equipment is job dependent and is usually selected by the contractor rather than specified.

### 5.3.7.1  Slurry Mixing

The slurry mixing and placement equipment must be capable of supplying adequate quantities of slurry during excavation.  For slurry mixing, hydration and control, the following equipment and facilities are needed:

- Mixing apparatus such as a venturi (flash) mixer or a paddle (high vortex) mixer

- Pumps, valves, pipes, hoses, fittings and small tools

- Slurry hydration and storage ponds (or paddle mixer for small jobs)

- Slurry cleaning equipment, including airlift pumps, valves, pipes, and desanders, or mudshakers, if sand removal is desired.

### 5.3.7.2  Trench Excavation

For trench excavation, it is important to ensure the equipment used can maintain a continuous excavation line to the total depth required.  Table 5-4 lists types of excavation equipment commonly used for slurry trenching.  If the aquiclude is composed of a hard type of rock, the backhoe or clamshell may not be able to rip it out.  In this type of situation, the slurry wall can be terminated at the top of the rock layer or special equipment such as drills or chisels may be used for key-in.  If rock fractures are noted during key-in excavation, grouting may be necessary.

### 5.3.7.3  Backfill Mixing

Bulldozers or graders are commonly used for backfill mixing, although mechanical batchers or pugmills may be employed at sites where backfill mixing areas are not available.  When a single centralized backfill mixing area is planned, sufficient flat area must be set aside for this operation.

### 5.3.7.4  Backfill Placement

Backfill placement equipment normally consists of a bulldozer that slowly slides the mixed backfill into the trench at a point slightly in advance of the peviously-placed backfill.  (Backfill placement methods are described in detail in Section 5.4.6.)  Clamshells are also used at some sites.  At sites where the trench spoils are unsuitable for backfill mixing, soils from a borrow area, along with bentonite slurry, must be hauled to the trench.  To assist in placement of mixed backfill from trucks a metal trough-like device can be used to direct it into the trench at the proper point.  The trough is

TABLE 5-4.
EXCAVATION EQUIPMENT USED FOR SLURRY TRENCH CONSTRUCTION

| Type | Trench Width (feet) | Trench Depth (feet) | Comments |
|------|---------------------|---------------------|----------|
| Standard backhoe | 1-5 (1) | 50 (2) | Most rapid and least costly excavation method (1) |
| Modified backhoe | 2-5 (1,3) | 80 (2) | Uses an extended dipper stick, modified engine & counterweighted frame; is also rapid and relatively low cost (1) |
| Clamshell | 1-5 (3) | >150 (3) | Attached to a kelly bar or crane; needs $\geq$ 18 ton crane; can be mechanical or hydraulic (3) |
| Dragline | 4-10 | >120 | Primarily used for wide, deep SB trenches (4) |
| Rotary drill, percussion drill or large chisel | - | - | Used to break up boulders and to key into hard rock aquicludes. Can slow construction and result in irregular trench walls (3) |

References: (1) Case 1982, (2) D'Appolonia 1980, (3) Guertin and McTigue 1982, and (4) Shallard 1983.

advanced to coincide with the advancing backfill placement area (Zoratto 1982).

### 5.3.8  Facilities

The facilities necessary for slurry wall construction include a trailer or small building for supervisory operations and quality control procedures. Necessary testing equipment includes a Fann viscometer, mud balance, moisture tester (or sample cans, a balance and an oven), pH meter, sieves, Marsh funnel, and slump testing equipment (Xanthakos 1979, Zoratto 1982).

### 5.3.9  Methods

In a materials and methods specification, the methods to be followed during each stage of construction are spelled out in great detail. This section lists the steps that are typically described in the specifications. Discussions of each step are given in Section 5.4. The steps for which methods are described include:

- Slurry mixing and hydration
- Trench excavation
- Backfill mixing
- Backfill placement
- Protective capping construction
- Site clean up.

### 5.3.10  Safety Procedures

At non-hazardous sites, safety procedures for slurry wall construction are very similar to those for most other construction sites. The personnel involved in trench construction at hazardous waste sites must, however, be protected from exposure to contaminants from the trench spoils, the wastes or leachates and the area surrounding the excavation. Hard hats, as well as rubber boots, gloves, and protective coveralls may be required. Where volatile toxins are suspected, air-supplied respirators may be necessary. Personnel required to use safety equipment include equipment operators, inspectors, QA/QC personnel and all other personnel near the trench.

5.4   Preconstruction Activities

Preconstruction activities typically follow a chronology that includes:

- Designing the installation
- Estimating the costs
- Assembling the bid package and advertising
- Evaluating proposals
- Awarding the construction contract.

### 5.4.1  Slurry Wall Design

The design of a slurry wasl requires consideration of numerous site-specific conditions, as described earlier.  The data that are gathered during the design phase are carefully evaluated and organized to produce the slurry wall specifications and plans, along with drawings of the site and the proposed slurry wall.  These documents are used by the owner or engineer and by potential contractors to estimate the complexity and cost of the slurry wall construction.  The two types of slurry wall design specifications most frequently encountered are described in Section 5.2.  The procedures and considerations involved in slurry wall design were detailed in Section 5.1.

### 5.4.2  Cost Estimates

The designer must develop a cost estimate for slurry trench installation that can be compared with bids received from potential construction contractors.  Although a rough figure of $3-5/square foot of soil bentonite wall is generally accepted, it is not specific enough for sites where special problems are anticipated.  To prepare a cost estimate, detailed information on costs and cost variation between sites is necessary.  These data are presented in Section 7.

### 5.4.3  Bid Package Preparation

The bid package consists of a number of documents that will make up the eventual contract.  Components of the bid package are typically the following, which are the same topics covered for most construction contracts:

- Invitation to bid
- Instructions to bidders
- Contractor's bid sheets or proposal

- The agreement between owner and contractor
- Performance bonds and insurance
- General and special conditions of the contract
- Specifications (general and special technical requirements)
- Plans and drawings (Jessup and Jessup 1963).

The bid package should give bidders enough information, both technical and contractual, to prepare and submit bids which accurately reflect the effort that will be required to complete a quality, cost effective slurry wall.

The bid package is.usually sent to prospective contractors who have responded to an advertisement. In some cases, only pre-qualified firms are invited to bid. Bids are then submitted by those interested firms for evaluation.

5.4.4  Bid Evaluation and Contract Award

Public works financed by Federal, State, or local funds are usually required to be awarded to the lowest responsible bidder, as determined by the opening and reading aloud of sealed bids at a specifically designated time (Jessup and Jessup 1963). Therefore, much emphasis is placed on bid prices.

After proposal evaluation, and bid examination have been completed, the most qualified firm submitting the lowest bid is determined. The construction contract is then awarded to the firm selected in the bidding process.

5.5  Soil Bentonite Wall Construction

Following award of the construction contract, the selected firm will proceed with construction of the slurry wall. The major activities include:

- Preconstruction Assessment and mobilization
- Site preparation
- Slurry preparation and control
- Slurry mixing and hydration
- Slurry placement
- Backfill preparation
- Backfill placement
- Site cleanup and demobilization.

Discussions of these activities follow.

### 5.5.1  Preconstruction Assessment and Mobilization

Three major activities occur during the mobilization phase of slurry trench construction.  These are:

● Layout site plan

● Determine the equipment, type, amounts of materials, and facilities required

● Determine number and source of personnel required.

#### 5.5.1.1  Plan Layout

A preliminary layout is prepared based on drawings supplied by the engineer.  Once the preliminary layout is developed, a close examination of the proposed construction site must be performed in order to ensure that all details of the plan are practical.  After the onsite examination, a final layout of the worksite can be prepared.  A diagram of a typical slurry wall construction site is shown in Figure 5-2.

#### 5.5.1.2  Equipment Requirements

The specifications and drawings, test boring records, subsurface exploration reports, and records of utility lines are the first sources of information for determining equipment, materials and facilities needs.  In addition, an on-site inspection may be required to gain the detailed understanding needed for planning the construction activities.

The major work elements and equipment and facilities typically associated with each work element are:

● Excavation
  - hydraulic backhoe
  - mechanically operated clamshell
  - hydraulically operated kelly-mounted clamshell

● Slurry preparation and control
  - high speed colloidal batch mixer for small projects
  - flash mixer for large projects
  - pumps, valves, pipes and tools
  - hydration ponds
  - desanders, hydrocylones or screens

● Slurry placement
  - pumps
  - placement hoses and piping

## Figure 5-2.
## Typical Slurry Wall Construction Site

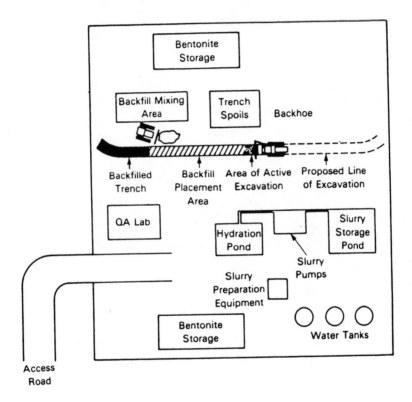

- Backfill preparation
  - dozer or grader

- Backfill placement
  - dozer
  - mechanically operated clamshell
  - trucks and trough

- Supervision and quality assurance
  - shed or trailer
  - Marsh funnel
  - mud balance
  - standard sieves.

Numerous factors influence the types of equipment required as well as the final plan layout and the relative difficulty of construction activities. Some of these factors, along with their potential effects on slurry trench construction operations are listed in Table 4-1.

Determining the correct equipment applications for a particular project is based upon construction requirements and the constraints imposed by the job site. For example, choice of excavation equipment depends upon the depth of the slurry wall and the soil in which the wall is placed. The maximum excavation depth for a standard backhoe is about 50 feet, but larger, extended models are available to reach up to 80 feet in depth (D'Appolonia 1980a). Both clamshell excavation systems will reach depths more than 150 feet, with the hydraulic model sometimes preferred in more difficult digging conditions (Guertin and McTigue 1982c) (See Table 5-4).

Consideration must also be given to site access and obstructions. Access roads might limit the size of equipment that can be brought to the site, while obstructions at the site might preclude the use of some types of equipment.

### 5.5.1.3  Personnel Requirements

When determining the sources of personnel for use at slurry trench construction site, two choices face the construction firm. The firm can send their own equipment and personnel to the construction site or they can rent equipment and hire personnel locally. Most firms will use varying combinations of each approach. For larger jobs and critical small jobs, it is frequently more efficient to send equipment and personnel directly from the construction firm. Small jobs can often be handled effectively by using only specialized company-owned equipment, such as a extended backhoe arm, accompanied by supervisory personnel. Other equipment such as bulldozers, cranes, clamshells, and large backhoes can be rented near the job site. Laborers and certain equipment operators can be hired locally for the specific job. However, there are no set rules, and each construction contractor will tailor his approach on a site-by-site basis.

Slurry trench construction contractors are best able to judge appropriate equipment and personnel needed at the job site. However, site owners and their representatives should be aware of the approach to be taken by the construction contractor, and should be satisfied that appropriate equipment and personnel are available at the job site.

### 5.5.2  Pre-Excavation Site Preparation

Once site planning has been completed, necessary permits and clearances have been obtained, and required utility, water and other services have been arranged, preparation of the construction site can proceed. The work site can then be cleared if necessary, security fences erected, utility and water hook-ups made, equipment and facilities brought in and set-up, and construction materials delivered. At this time, work can proceed to move or remove obstructions if necessary.

### 5.5.3  Slurry Preparation and Control

Before excavation begins, the slurry must be prepared. To do this, bentonite and water quality must be tested, hydration ponds must be constructed, lines laid, pumps placed, and the mixing area prepared. The slurry is then mixed in a venturi of paddle mixer and allowed to hydrate fully prior to placement in the trench for SB slurry trench cut-off construction or mixing with cement for CB cut-off construction.

#### 5.5.3.1  Testing Bentonite and Water

Bentonite quality is critical to the quality of the slurry. Bentonite is usually shipped to the job site accompanied by laboratory test results showing that it meets quality criteria. These criteria include physical and chemical purity, pH, gel strength, dry fineness (percent passing the number 200 sieve) and filtrate loss. At the job site, these criteria are checked frequently, such as by testing every truckload of bentonite delivered. It is important for the site owner to require field testing of delivered bentonite, because deliveries are occasionally rejected by field testing. At a minimum, testing of pH, viscosity and fluid loss should be conducted in the field for bentonite delivered to the site. (Quality control tests are described in Section 5.3.2.5.)

Slurry quality decreases significantly if the quality of make-up water is poor. Make-up water should be relatively low in hardness, near neutral or slightly higher pH and low in dissolved salts. Water suitable for drinking is not necessarily suitable for mixing with bentonite. Water of inadequate quality will result in higher bentonite consumption and a lumpy slurry that is difficult to mix and that contains above average amounts of free water. In some instances, poor quality water can be chemically treated to make it suitable for mixing (Ryan 1977).

### 5.5.3.2  Slurry Mixing and Hydration

Two types of mixing systems are most frequently used. These are batch mixing and flash mixing. In the batch system, specified quantities of water and bentonite are placed in a tank and are mixed at high speeds with a circulation pump or paddle mixer. Mixing continues until hydration is complete and the batch is ready for use in the trench. Hydration is usually complete in a matter of minutes for the two to five cubic yard batch produced by this system. Because of the low output of the batch system, its use is limited to small jobs.

The second type of mixing system is the flash or venturi mixer. For this system, bentonite is fed at a predetermined rate into a metered water stream as it is forced through a nozzle at a constant rate. The slurry is subjected to high shear mixing for only a fraction of a second, which is not always adequate for hydration. Therefore, the slurry is often stored until hydration is complete. This is determined by periodically measuring the Marsh Funnel viscosity.

When Marsh Funnel viscosity readings stabilize, hydration is considered complete. Flash mixing is a process that can be operated at high production rates. Because a majority of cut-off walls require continuous production of large amounts of slurry, flash mixing is the more common of the two mixing methods (Ryan 1977).

The type of mixing system used has been found to affect the quality of the slurry produced. High shear (or high speed batch mixers) produce slurries with higher gel strengths (Xanthakos 1979). Section 2 discusses the influence of gel strength on slurry quality.

The grade of bentonite dictates the percent needed for a given slurry and hydration time. For example, a grade 90 (bbl/ton) bentonite may have to be mixed at a 6.3 percent concentration, while a grade 125 would require 4.5 percent concentration for an equivalent slurry. Hydration times for higher grades are likewise lower, which may result in higher slurry production rates for a given slurry preparation facility (Ryan 1977). However, the higher cost of the higher grade bentonites requires that the selection of bentonite grade to be made on a site by site basis. Frequently a mud balance test is run on slurry from the hydration pond as a quality control check of the bentonite content. Viscosity and pH are also checked frequently (Cavalli 1982).

### 5.5.4  Slurry Placement

From the hydration pond, slurry is pumped on an as needed basis to the open slurry trench. Slurry level in the trench must be maintained at least several feet above the water table and normally within a foot or two of ground level. This slurry level is maintained to provide the hydrostatic pressure necessary to hold open the trench.

Once a slurry trench installation is underway, backfill and excavation are being performed simultaneously, with a minimum amount of trench remaining open under the slurry. Figure 5-3 illustrates the excavation and backfill placement operations. The amount of trench remaining open at any one time depends on the properties of the backfill material and the characteristics of the excavation equipment, which are discussed in the following sections. Samples removed from the trench for QC checks must be representative, that is they should not be taken only from the top surface of the slurry but should be taken at various depths in the trench. Characteristics of the slurry, while geared toward keeping the trench open during excavation and backfilling, must also allow displacement by the backfill material. That is the reason for maximum as well as minimum values for parameters such as density, viscosity, and sand content. Those requirements are listed in Table 5-1. During the excavation operation, some of the spoil becomes incorporated in the slurry. This increases slurry density and sand content. A high sand content indicates a high density and a likelihood of problems with eventual displacement of the slurry by the backfill (D'Appolonia and Ryan 1979).

### 5.5.5  Trench Excavation

Excavation of a slurry trench proceeds much as any trench excavation except that only the portion of the trench above slurry level can be visually inspected for continuity.

Trench excavation is usually accomplished with appropriately sized backhoes with adequate boom length and bucket capacity. Frequently, boom lengths are extended by construction contractors to meet the needs of the trench installation. Counterweights are often required to offset the movement created by the long boom lifting a full bucket from the trench. The backhoe is the favored means of excavating a slurry trench because it is much faster than other equipment, such as the crane and clamshell. However, boom lengths are currently limited to 70 to 90 feet. For greater depths, the crane and clamshell are normally used. Drag lines have been used in the past, but have been used rarely for recent installations (D'Appolonia 1982).

Trench continuity is critical to a successful installation. For checking continuity of slurry trenches, several approaches have been used. All of them may be employed at a given site to insure that the trenching is continuous from the ground surface to the aquiclude key-in.

The field inspector should have boring logs and a cross-sectional drawing of the trench so that visual inspection of excavated material and degree of extension of the backhoe boom will indicate approximate depth and whether the aquiclude has been reached. Soil boring data can also be used to quantify the aquiclude key-in. By watching excavated material for a change in color or

## Figure 5-3.
## Cross-section of Slurry Trench, Showing Excavation and Backfilling Operations

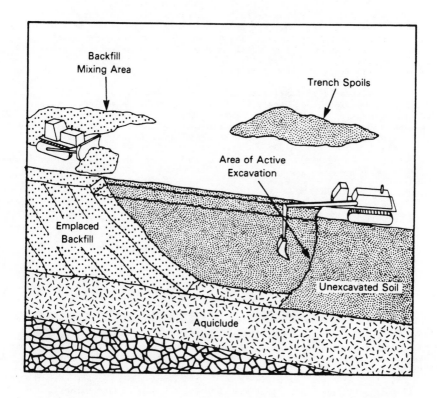

texture, construction personnel can determine when the subsurface layer which is to be keyed into is reached.

Sounding of depth with a weighted line or a rod should be performed frequently to ensure an even trench bottom and to detect any irregularities. Finished trench depths should be recorded for preparation of a drawing showing trench cross section.

### 5.5.6 Backfill Preparation

Standard practice during backfill preparation for soil bentonite walls is to use excavated material mixed with slurry from the trench for backfill. In this case, the slurry provides moisture necessary for backfill mixing. When trench spoils are used, the material excavated from the trench is usually placed nearby, slurry is added and a bulldozer is used to track and blade the material until it is thoroughly mixed.

A relatively level working surface is needed for backfill mixing. At sites that are too steep, backfill mixing areas can be excavated. These should be at least as wide as the width of the excavating equipment track. Where no backfill mixing areas are available, batch mixers or pugmills can be used, although these are slower than using a bulldozer for backfill mixing.

A number of quality control checks are necessary for backfill preparation activities. These include tests of the:

- Fines content
- Slump
- Wet density
- Presence of contaminants.

### 5.5.6.1 Fines Content

A key parameter in the design of a backfill is the sieve analysis and particularly the amount of fines. The content of fines in the backfill is directly related to the permeability of the finished SB wall and its ability to withstand chemical attack. A standard practice is to perform permeability testing in the pre-construction phase to define the range of acceptable grain size distributions that will provide the design permeability. During construction, frequent grain size distributions and less frequent permeability testing is performed on the backfill material to ensure that the design permeability requirements will be met by the completed slurry trench. Grain size distributions can be performed in a field laboratory and are much less expensive to run than permeability tests, which are usually run in a laboratory.

### 5.5.6.2  Slump

Slump cone testing should be performed frequently on backfill material after mixing to make sure the backfill is wet enough to slump in the trench without trapping pockets of slurry yet dry enough to displace the slurry easily.  High slump also indicates a gentler slope of backfill in the trench, which would require keeping more of the trench open.  A slump of 2 to 6 inches is adequate (D'Appolonia 1980).  Additional information on the slump of the backfill and its effect on the finished wall can be found in Section 2.

### 5.5.6.3  Wet Density

Mud balance testing should be performed frequently on the backfill before it is placed in the trench.  Mud balance tests indicate the wet density of the backfill.  This shows for certain that the backfill will or will not readily displace the slurry.  The wet backfill sample used for the mud balance test can be dried and reweighed to determine the water content.  A very high water content can result in excess water infiltration into the trench walls and excess settlement of the backfill.  The separation of water from an excessively wet backfill can also dilute the slurry in the trench.

### 5.5.7  Backfill Placement

Once trench excavation has proceeded for a distance that will not result in backfill material being re-excavated, backfill placement can begin.  First, samples of slurry at the base of the trench are collected and tested for wet density.  The slurry should be at least 15 pcf less dense than the backfill mixture (D'Appolonia 1980b).  If the slurry is too dense, it will not be displaced properly during backfill placement.  The dense slurry or coarse material on the trench bottom must be removed via airlift pumps, a clamshell bucket or other method.  This slurry can be used for backfill mixing or it can be desanded via desanders, hydrocyclones or screens, and returned to the trench.

To place the initial layer of backfill, a clamshell is often used.  The backfill must not be allowed to drop freely through the slurry, as this may cause segregation of the backfill particles or entrapment of slurry pockets within the backfill.  For this reason, the clamshell lowers the initial grabfull of backfill to the trench bottom.  The next grabfull is placed on top of the first, and so on until the backfill is visible at the ground surface.  Thereafter, the backfill is pushed into the trench by bulldozers or graders.  The point of trench backfilling progresses towards the area of active excavation (D'Appolonia and Ryan 1979).  Figure 5-2 illustrates this process.

The slope of the emplaced backfill is normally 5 to 10:1.  The distance to be maintained between the toe of the backfill and the area of active excavation varies greatly, depending on soil types and backfill slopes.

Ideally this distance is kept to a minimum to avert trench stability problems (D'Appolonia 1980b). Some specifications have set the distance at from 30 to 200 feet (U.S. Army Corps of Engineers 1975, Ryan 1976).

Sounding the placed backfill should be conducted to show the slope at which the backfill is coming to rest, and to indicate possible problems with trench wall collapse and entrapment of pockets of slurry. Depths should be recorded and plotted on a cross sectional drawing of the trench. Trench excavation and backfilling progress can also be recorded in this manner.

When a slurry wall is constructed to entirely surround a waste site, the excavation must end with enough overlap to ensure that all material designated for excavation is removed. The inspector must determine that the backhoe bucket is removing backfill materials from the full trench depth to verify that the trench is continuous for its entire length.

### 5.5.8  Capping

To protect the finished SB wall, either a dessication cap or a traffic cap is applied to the slurry wall surface.

Once backfill has been completed, cracking is soon observed on the top of the slurry wall unless it stays wet. To complete the installation, the top i to 3 feet of wall is removed to eliminate the cracks and a high quality backfill material replaces it. The material used is usually required to have a high clay content and to be compacted in lifts over the trench. This forms a low permeability cap to protect the cut-off wall from excessive dessication (U.S. Army Corps of Engineers 1976). This is followed by topsoil and seeding or a gravel layer to prevent water and wind erosion.

Where traffic over the wall is anticipated, a traffic cap can be constructed to reduce the load on the completed cut-off. To do this, lifts of compacted clay are interspersed with geotextile layers. Gravel can be used over the final geotextile layer at the surface. At one facility where a soil bentonite cut-off wall was close to a heavily traveled gravel road, the cap consisted of an 18-inch thick compacted clay lift topped by a geotextile sheet. This was overlain by another 18-inch thick compacted clay layer topped by another geotextile sheet. Inches of gravel were placed over the final sheet of geotextile to distribute the weight and bear the load of the vehicles (Coneybear 1982).

### 5.5.9  Clean Up Activities

After wall construction is complete, the excess slurry and mixed backfill must be disposed of in a manner that avoids erosion and disruption of sewer lines. The slurry should not be allowed to enter sanitary or storm sewer lines due to the potential for pipe blockage from the slurry. It also should not be left as a thick layer on the soil surface, as this may result in excessive ponding of surface water. One method of slurry disposal would be to mix the slurry with dry coarse soil to produce as dry a mixture as possible. This material could then be either buried or spread in a thin layer over disturbed areas, then fertilized and seeded. Any contaminated soil from the excavation must be disposed of in accordance with site requirements. All disturbed areas should be stabilized and site maintenance procedures, as outlined in Section 6, should be instituted.

There are a number of differences in construction activities that vary with construction materials. The following is a brief summary of cement bentonite and diaphragm wall construction techniques.

## 5.6  Cement Bentonite Wall Construction

The discussion that was presented above is an outline of a soil bentonite (SB) cut-off wall construction. Modifications to the construction specifications are necessary when constructing a cement-bentonite (CB) cut-off wall. These modifications include:

- The requirements for backfill materials are eliminated.

- A description of the standards for cement and cement storage is added in the materials section.

- A description of the CB slurry requirements and the cement/water (C/W) ratio to be maintained for desired compressive strength is added to the materials section.

- The methods to be used for tie in of adjacent CB panels (if used) are addressed in the performance section.

- Under the Quality Control section, a requirement is added for the manufacturer's certification of the cement and the testing of cement/ water ratio for each batch of mix is required.

Cement bentonite (CB) slurry walls involve the use of a slurry consisting of water, bentonite and cement. The advantages of CB walls are that backfill material is not needed and they exhibit some structural strength. In addition, by excavating a section (panel) at a time, a CB wall can be installed on a site with more extreme topography.

Two types of CB walls are being used. The in-place method involves simply excavating under a CB slurry and leaving the slurry in place. The slurry eventually sets to provide some structural strength. For the replacement method, excavation takes place under a bentonite slurry. Once excavation of the section of wall is complete, the bentonite slurry is pumped out of the trench and the CB slurry is pumped in and allowed to set. The replacement method is used only when setting of the CB slurry could possibly occur while excavation is being completed.

Cement bentonite slurries begin to set within 2 to 3 hours after the cement and slurry are mixed. If the slurries are agitated for over 48 hours, they lose their ability to set (Jefferis 1981b). For this reason, when it appears that the excavation of a single CB panel will take longer than a day or so to complete, cement retarders are added to the slurry or the replacement method is used. Examples of this situation would be very deep excavations, when rock is encountered in the excavation, or when keying the trench into bedrock.

Quality control procedures for CB walls are identical to those for soil bentonite walls. However, composition of the CB slurry is more critical, therefore care must be taken when weighing and mixing components of the slurry. This is because the calcium in the cement causes an irreversible decrease in slurry quality, as described in Section 2. Table 5-5 shows typical materials quality control standards for cement-bentonite cut-off walls.

## 5.7  Diaphragm Wall Construction

Construction of diaphragm walls also involves the use of bentonite or CB slurries, although these walls are not normally used for pollution migration cut-offs, except where high strength is required. Diaphragm walls are composed of either precast concrete panels or cast-in-place concrete sections. Unlike SB and CB walls, these walls develop a great deal of strength over time and can be used as structural components. A brief description of the techniques used for construction of diaphragm walls is given below.

Precast concrete panel walls are cast offsite in segments from 1 to 3 feet thick, from 10 to 20 feet wide and from 30 to 50 feet long. The panels are lowered into a trench containing bentonite slurry and secured in place. Due to their dimensional limitations, concrete panel walls are usually only employed where depths of 50 feet or less are required (Guertin and McTigue 1982b). An exception to this general rule occurs where a CB slurry is used in the trench. The panel is lowered into the trench and secured, and the CB slurry that remains in place is allowed to set up around the panel. Using this technique, the trench can be extended lower than 50 feet, and the panel suspended in the CB slurry. The CB slurry then forms a cut-off both below and on either side of the diaphragm panel. The CB slurry also forms the joints between the panels (Jefferis 1981b).

Cast-in-place concrete walls are constructed by excavating a short trench (or slot) under a bentonite slurry. When the slot is completed, the slurry is desanded if necessary to reduce its density and to avoid problems with sand accumulations on the reinforcing bars (Guertin and McTigue 1982b). The maximum recommended slurry density is 75 p.c.f. and the maximum recommended sand content is 5 percent (Millet and Perez 1981).

The reinforcing bars are lowered into place, then the concrete is tremied into place, using a funnel-like apparatus that directs the concrete to the trench bottom. The apparatus is raised as the concrete level rises. Slurry

TABLE 5-5.

MATERIALS QUALITY CONTROL PROGRAM FOR CEMENT/BENTONITE WALLS

| | Subject | Standard | Type of Test | Frequency | Specified Values |
|---|---|---|---|---|---|
| | Water | — | - pH<br>- Total Hardness (Ca & Mg) | Per water source or as changes occur | As required to properly hydrate bentonite with approved additives. Determined by slurry viscosity and gel strength tests. |
| Materials | Bentonite | API STD 13A | Manufacturer certificate of compliance | | Unaltered sodium cation montmorillonite |
| | Cement | ASTM C 150 | Manufacturer certificate of compliance | | Portland, Type 1 (Type V or Type II for certain applications) |
| Bentonite Slurry | Prior to Addition of Cement | API STD 13B | - Viscosity | 1 set per shift or per batch (pond) | $V > 34$ sec-Marsh @ 68°<br>$pH \geq 8$ |
| C-B Slurry | Upon introduction in the trench | API STD 13B<br>API STD 10B | - C/W Ratio<br>- Viscosity | Each Batch<br>5 per shift | $C/W = 0.20$<br>$V = 40$ to 50 sec-Marsh |

Reference: Federal Bentonite 1981.

is pumped out as the concrete is tremied in. The slurry is then filtered and used in the next panel. This process is illustrated in Figure 5-4. A cast-in-place wall, when set, is composed of a concrete panel sandwiched between two bentonite filter cakes.

These walls are not normally used for pollution migration control due to their susceptibility to leakage through panel connections, their high permeability relative to SB walls and their greater expense. In addition, relatively minor earth movement can cause leakages through panel connections, cracking of the relatively brittle concrete, and differential settlement of the panels (Guertin and McTigue 1982b).

5.8   Potential Problems During and After Construction

There are several mechanisms or processes that can affect the construction or functioning of slurry walls and cause construction delays, trench collapse or wall leakage. These are usually the result of either excavation and installation procedures, or unforseen subsurface conditions.

Wall disruption may occur during excavation and installation and requiring re-excavation of the slurry trench. Once the wall is in place, improper construction techniques or adverse physical and chemical processes can affect the integrity of the wall and its impermeability. The following discussion focuses on the various problems that may be encountered and methods used to overcome them. Types of problems include:

- Unstable soils
- High water tables
- Hard rock in excavations
- Sudden slurry losses
- Slurry flocculation
- Trench collapse
- Inadequate backfill placement
- Cracking
- Chemical disruption.

5.8.1   Unstable Soil

At some sites, the surface soils are too soft to support heavy construction equipment. A work platform can be constructed of compacted soil along with the proposed line of trench excavation. The construction equipment can maneuver on this platform and the trench can be excavated directly through it.

# Figure 5-4.
# Schematic of Conventional Cast-in-Place Diaphragm Wall

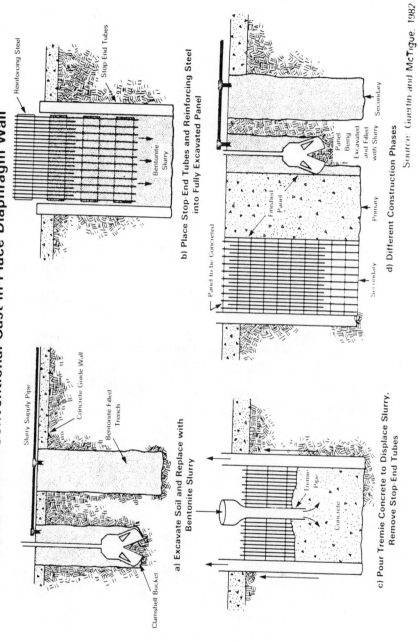

a) Excavate Soil and Replace with Bentonite Slurry

b) Place Stop-End Tubes and Reinforcing Steel into Fully Excavated Panel

c) Pour Tremie Concrete to Displace Slurry. Remove Stop-End Tubes

d) Different Construction Phases

Source: Guertin and McTigue. 1982

5.8.2  High Water Table

A work platform can also be used to maintain sufficient hydraulic head in the slurry trench to offset high groundwater pressures (Namy 1980). The slurry level must be maintained at least several feet above groundwater levels, as described earlier.

When groundwater levels suddenly rise close to the surface, the trench may collapse unless measures are quickly taken. The U.S. Army Corps of Engineers (1976), recommends in their specifications that, should this occur, the contractor should stop excavating and begin backfilling any open trench sections as rapidly as possible. After the groundwater level decreases and the wall has set sufficiently, the hastily backfilled sections can be re-excavated and properly backfilled.

5.8.3  Rock in Excavation

When a slurry trench must be excavated through material containing numerous or large boulders, hard rock layers, or into a hard aquiclude, construction delays are likely. The use of large equipment such as cranes may be required to remove very large boulders. Rotary or percussion drills may also be used to break up boulders prior to the use of smaller excavation equipment. All rock fragments should be removed from the trench bottom prior to backfilling.

The presence of boulders near the trench bottom, or the presence of an unrippable aquiclude may lead to variations in trench depth and inadequate aquiclude key-in. If trench excavation is not extended far enough into the aquiclude, the bottom of the slurry wall is inadequately sealed, and underseepage may result. When a permeable layer exists beneath the slurry wall, migration of water, wastes, or other materials is likely to occur (D'Appolonia 1980b). This reduces slurry wall efficiency and may lead to piping failure, as described later in this section.

5.8.4  Sudden Slurry Loss

Occasionally, slurry levels within a slurry trench will drop rapidly. This situation, termed sudden slurry loss, can be caused when the excavation encounters previous layers, such as gravel lenses or subsurface pipes.

5.8.4.1  Pervious Zones in Excavation

When sand or gravel layers are encountered, rapid slurry loss can occur. In this situation, lost circulation materials are used and large quantities of slurry are pumped into the trench to maintain high slurry levels. Factors that can reduce the flow of slurry into pervious soil such as rheological blocking and filter cake formation, are discussed in Section 2.

### 5.8.4.2  Pipes and Conduits

At some sites, subsurface pipes or other conduits have been encountered unexpectedly. This results in rapid loss of slurry from the trench. Two methods have been used to plug up the pipes and thereby slow or stop the rapid slurry loss. The first is applicable only to corrugated metal pipes, which can be pinched shut, using the excavation tool like a giant pair of pliers. The second method involves the rapid introduction of lost circulation materials, including "shredded cellophane flakes, shredded tree bark, plant fibers, glass, rayon, graded mica, ground walnut shells, rubber tires, perlite, time-setting cement and many others" (Xanthakos 1979). Coarse sand and crushed brick have also been used. These materials clog the pipe and allow the slurry to reseal the trench. In any case, additional fresh slurry must rapidly be pumped into the trench to avoid the loss of trench wall stability (Guertin and McTigue 1982b).

### 5.8.5  Slurry Flocculation

This situation may occur when cement is added to a bentonite slurry to form a CB slurry or when bentonite slurries come in contact with other high calcium materials. Several approaches can be taken when the slurry begins to form flattened clumps. Various thinners or dispersing agents can be added, as listed in Table 2-4. Additional fresh slurry may be added, or additional bentonite may be added, depending on the severity of the flocculation. A discussion of flocculation and its causes is presented in Section 2.

### 5.8.6  Trench Collapse

Trench collapse is caused by the loss of stability in the trench walls during excavation and before backfilling or CB slurry hardening. Causes of trench collapse include:

- Insufficient slurry head above groundwater

- Sudden or rapid loss of slurry due to contact with gravel, large pores, fissures, etc.

- Surface runoff into open cracks

- Insufficient agitation of slurry

- Overloading of the ground surface with stockpiles or heavy equipment in close proximity to the trench.

The underlying causes of trench collapse is the failure of the slurry to form and maintain a low permeability filter cake. Factors that interfere with filter cake formation or functioning were discussed previously.

Trench collapse can be either total or partial. Sometimes only partial collapse occurs, and the material from one wall slips partially into the trench without bridging the entire trench width, as shown in Figure 5-5. In this situation, the trench may still be salvageable.

If severe collapse of the trench side walls occurs, the trench can be backfilled as much as possible and left as is. Another trench parallel to the collapsed trench and at least 15 feet away is excavated using typical slurry trench construction techniques (Boyes 1975).

### 5.8.7  Inadequate Backfill Placement

Improper placement of the backfill can result in underseepage, excessive consolidation, or wall leakage. Specific backfill problems are described below.

#### 5.8.7.1  Sediments in Trench Bottom

The slurry can suspend small particles of sand as well as silt and clay particles due to the shear strength and gel structure of the slurry. Coarse sand and larger particles are not suspended. Instead they sink to the trench bottom and accumulate there. Excessive accumulations of heavy sediments mixed with slurry can interfere with backfilling if these sediments are close enough in density to the density of the backfill. Cuttings from broken boulders or gravel can also interfere with backfilling. The backfill cannot displace these sediments, so they remain after backfilling as a layer of sandy or gravelly slurry beneath the backfill. Studies of this type of material have shown that slurry-laced sand and gravel layers are much more susceptible to failure, leakage, and chemical degradation than are backfills containing a higher percentage of fines (D'Appolonia 1980b). At many sites, the removal of the sand from the trench bottom prior to backfilling is not necessary. This is because the slurry-encapsulated sand has a lower initial permeability and a higher density than the backfill. Thus the sand layer is not likely to interfere with backfilling operations.

The ability of a pure sand/bentonite layer to withstand permeation over time is, however, questionable. Even if a sand/bentonite backfill contained from 2 to 3 percent bentonite by weight, failure could occur due to permeation by calcium-rich solutions (D'Appolonia 1980b).

This situation is similar to the conditions at the trench bottom where bentonite concentrations may be minimal. Bentonite slurries usually contain from 4 to 7 percent by weight bentonite when introduced to the trench. As spoil particles become mixed with the slurry, the slurry density increases and

## Figure 5-5.
## Trench Collapse, Showing Plane of Weakness (a)
## and Block Slippage (b)

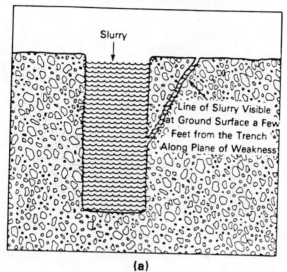

Slurry

Line of Slurry Visible
at Ground Surface a Few
Feet from the Trench
Along Plane of Weakness

(a)

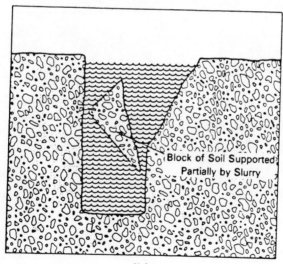

Block of Soil Supported
Partially by Slurry

(b)

the weight percent of bentonite is consequently reduced. The slurry is most dense at the trench bottom due to the presence of the settled sand and gravel layer. Thus the weight percentage of bentonite in the slurry at the trench bottom may conceivably drop to 3 percent or less, leaving the cut-off wall susceptible to failure should prolonged permeation with cation-rich solutions occur.

To prevent piping failures of soil-bentonite cut-off walls, D'Appolonia (1980) recommends that the backfill contain at least 20 percent fines. These fine particles effectively resist intergranular stresses and reduce the erosion of the bentonite particles from the backfill matrix. The backfill should be homogenous, both horizontally and vertically, to avoid piping failures and underseepage. Removal of the slurry-encapsulated sediments from the trench bottom prior to backfilling helps ensure vertical homogeneity and can contribute to the long term integrity of the cut-off wall.

### 5.8.7.2  Slurry Pockets in the Backfill

If the slump of the backfill is too high, the backfill does not flow to the trench bottom properly, but folds over itself during backfill placement and may entrap pockets of slurry. These slurry pockets remain in the wall and act like compressible layers with lower resistance to hydraulic gradients and chemical attack than the surrounding backfill. Because the slurry is less dense than the backfill, it gradually rises through the paste-like backfill until it reaches the trench surface. There, it is subject to desiccation and cracking if the clay cap has not yet been placed, or it may interfere with the connection between the clay cap and the cut-off. If the amount of entrapped slurry is excessive, the wall may need to be re-excavated and backfilled.

### 5.8.8  Cracking

It is well known that soils containing an appreciable concentration of clay can shrink, forming cracks, when allowed to dry. Even cement bentonite walls can crack "drastically" when allowed to dry (Jefferis 1981b). Some soils can, however, shrink and crack even when nearly fluid enough to flow. Nash (1976) and Tavenas et al (1975) noted the formation of cracks in silty clay soil mixtures only slightly dry of their liquid limits.

These cracks can be caused by several processes, including:

● Consolidation

● Hydraulic fracturing

● Syneresis.

### 5.8.8.1  Consolidation

Consolidation of soils occurs when water is squeezed from the soils pores (Hirschfeld 1979). This process is accompanied by a decrease in the volume of the soil mass due to a decrease in the volume of voids in the soil. (Baver, Baver and Gardner 1972) The amount of consolidation is maximal in fine-textured soils and minimal in coarse textured materials (Xanthakos 1979). The rate of consolidation depends on the soils permeability, the thickness of the layer being loaded and the magnitude of the soil mass's volume decrease. In fine textured soils, consolidation occurs at a much slower rate than in coarse textured ones. Most of the consolidation occurs rather quickly, however fine textured soils can continue slow minor consolidation for several months (Hirschfeld 1979). The soil-bentonite backfill in slurry walls has been found to continue consolidating for about 6 months, with minimal decreases in volume thereafter. (Xanthakos 1979)

The amount of consolidation in slurry walls is limited by the backfill's arching action along the trench walls and by grain to grain contact in the backfill (Xanthakos 1979, D'Appolonia 1980b). The amount of slurry wall consolidation depends on trench width, as well as on the amount of fines in the backfill. As the fines content increases, consolidation increases because fine particles are more compressible than coarse ones (Mitchell 1976). Wider trenches have been found to consolidate more than narrow ones. An 8-foot wide trench, for example, was reported by Xanthakos (1979) to have consolidated from 1 to 6 inches during the first few months after construction. In contrast to soil bentonite walls, CB walls consolidate very rapidly (Ryan 1976).

The process of consolidation in SB walls can produce many small cracks along shear zones in the soil mass (Mitchell 1976). Horizontal cracks that extend through the backfill can also be produced by the arching action mentioned earlier (Nash 1976). This cracking can occur even when the backfill is still quite fluid. Normally, the backfill contains from 25 to 30 percent water. This moisture content is slightly more than the liquid limit of the backfill (D'Appolonia 1980a). When soil is at its liquid limit, it contains so much water that it will flow under the influence of an applied stress (Baver, Baver and Gardner 1972). Even so, Nash (1976) observed the formation of horizontal cracks in a silty clay backfill that was only slightly dry of its liquid limit. The details of Nash's laboratory tests on this soil material were not given.

The arching that accompanies consolidation can also lead to the formation of another type of cracking due to a phenomenon called hydrofracturing. The relationship between hydrofracturing and consolidation is described below.

### 5.8.8.2  Hydrofracturing

When soils or rocks are subjected to excessive hydraulic pressures, cracks may form through which the excess water can flow. The pressure at which this cracking occurs can be less than the effective overburden pressure on the rock or soil in situ. This phenomenon has been used by petroleum geologists to fracture petroleum-containing strata and thereby increase the yield of oil wells (Bjerrum et al 1972).

The amount of pressure required to induce fracturing depends on the depth of the point receiving the pressure, and the ratio of vertical to horizontal pressures at that point. If is likely that other factors are also involved. Values used by petroleum geologists are 1 psi per foot of depth where the vertical pressures are less than the horizontal pressures, and 0.64 psi per foot of depth where the vertical pressures are greater than the horizontal pressures (Bjerrum et al 1972).

The cracks caused by this pressure extend vertically where the vertical pressures are greatest and horizontally where the horizontal pressures are greatest (Tavenas et al 1975). These cracks can continue to increase in lengh as long as the excess head is applied until they reach an area having greater permeability (Bjerrum et al 1972). When the pressure is decreased, the cracks will partially close, but will reopen when the pressure is again increased. (Tavenas et al 1975)

The effects of hydrofracturing on the functioning of a slurry wall can be severe. Where the vertical pressure exceeds the horizontal pressure (which is normally the case) the pressure exerted on the aquiclude can cause it to fracture. The vertical cracks will be immediately filled with slurry if this occurs during construction. Continued fracturing can, however, occur during backfilling. The backfill is less likely than the slurry to completely flow in and fill the cracks in the aquiclude, and the aquiclude's permeability may thus be increased. The overall effect of this type of fracturing may be minimal except at sites where the aquiclude is thin and/or overlies a very permeable strata.

A more detrimental effect of hydrofracturing may occur where the horizontal pressures on the wall are greater than the vertical pressures. If more than 1 psi of pressure per foot of depth is applied to the wall, horizontal cracks may form. These could allow significant amounts of water or leachate to flow through the wall. Hydrofracturing has been reported in both SB and CB walls (Bjerrum et al 1972 and Miller and Perez 1981).

The likelihood of slurry wall damage due to hydraulic fracturing is highest where:

● Significant amounts of consolidation occur

● Piezometers are installed in the wall to monitor the wall's permeability using constant head tests

● Large vertical loads are applied to the soils on either side of the trench

● Large hydraulic gradients are allowed to develop across the wall.

a.  Consolidation

When a great deal of consolidation and subsequent arching occur after
backfilling, the vertical loadings on the wall can be reduced to levels less
than the horizontal loadings.  This allows the wall to become susceptible to
horizontal cracking (Bjerrum et al 1972).  The amount of consolidation can be
minimized by reducing the content of fine particles, in the backfill (Mitchell
1976).  However, when additional coarse material is included in the backfill,
the wall's permeability is likely to be increased (D'Appolonia 1980b).  The
amount of permeability increase expected due to the inclusion of additional
coarse material in the backfill should be weighed against the risk of
hydrofracturing due to the anticipated pressure differential across the
trench.

b.  Piezometers

Where piezometers are placed in the wall to test the wall's permeability,
hydrofracturing may be induced when the excess head is applied.  Hydrofracturing due to the use of piezometers occurred when permeability tests were
being conducted on a series of dikes with soil-bentonite cores that were
installed in Israel.  The constant head permeability tests were designed so
that the maximum head applied did not exceed the effective weight of the soil
above the piezometer.  However, even at very low hydraulic pressures,
hydrofracturing occured.  This fracturing resulted in a thousand-fold increase
in the measured permeability (from $10^{-7}$ cm/sec initially to $10^{-4}$ cm/sec after
fracturing) (Bjerrum et al 1972).

Tests on an in situ, normally consolidated clay were conducted to see if
hydrofracturing were caused by arching along the walls of the soil bentonite
cores.  The normally consolidated clay that was not influenced by arching
along trench walls also fractured under the influence of an applied hydraulic
pressure that was less than the effective overburden pressure (Bjerrum et al
1972).  This indicates that the occurrence of hydrofracturing is not dependent
upon arching (and consolidation) along the walls of slurry trenches.

When large vertical loads are applied along the trench walls, the
horizontal stresses on the slurry wall can be greatly increased.  The vertical
loading can occur due to placement of stockpiles or heavy equipment along the
sides of the trench.  Depending on the other stresses acting on the wall at
the site, the horizontal stress may become greater than the vertical stress,
thus making the wall susceptible to horizontal hydrofracturing.

c.  High Hydraulic Gradients

A fourth potential cause of hydrofracturing is the presence of an
excessive hydraulic gradient across the wall.  If the pressure on the
upgradient wall exceeds 1 psi per foot of depth, and the horizontal pressures

acting on the wall are greater than the vertical pressures, it is quite possible that horizontal fracturing of the wall could occur.  Excessively high hydraulic gradients could be induced by:

- Failing to provide subsurface drains or extraction wells upgradient of the wall

- Installing extraction or injection wells too close to the wall

- Dewatering a site without deflecting groundwater around the site and away from the wall (via drains, ditches or extraction wells).

For this reason, the proper use and placement of auxiliary measures, such as wells, should receive careful attention during the wall's design stages.

### 5.8.8.3  Syneresis

Another process that can result in the formation of cracks in a slurry wall is syneresis.  According to Mitchell (1976) syneresis is a "mutual attraction between clay particles" that causes the particles "to form closely knit aggregates with fissures between."  It is the contraction that occurs in a gel that results in the extrusion of liquid (water).  Syneresis is often observed in gelatin after aging (Mitchell 1976).  Syneresis may take place in slurry walls, however, the extent to which this phenomenon affects the performance of slurry walls is not known.

### 5.8.9  Tunnelling and Piping

Two processes that can result in extensive breaching of a slurry wall are tunnelling and piping.  Both of these processes involve the formation of channels through the wall.  However, the causes and solutions for the two problems are different.

### 5.8.9.1  Tunnelling

Several dams have failed due to formation of very large pores that extend completely through the dam, from the upstream to the downstream face.  These failures occurred where the earthen dams were constructed of low to medium plasticity native clays that contained appreciable amounts of sodium montmorillonite (Mitchell 1976).  The process by which the failures occurred is termed tunnelling, and it can be described as a series of interrelated steps, as are listed below.

1. Differential consolidation of the wet and dry portions of several earthen dams led to the formation of stress cracks below the water line.

2. Water that contained calcium ions flowed into the cracks.

3. Calcium ions from the water replaced sodium ions on the exchange complexes of the clay particles in the dam. (See Section 2 for a more detailed description of cation exchange.)

4. The calcium ions caused the clay particles to decrease in size (shrink) and to form packets, or "flocs."

5. As the clay particles formed flocs, they became less dispersed, and the space formerly occupied by the dispersed clay particles became filled with water.

6. As the sizes of water-filled spaces (pores) increased, the rate of water movement in the pores increased.

7. The increased rate of water movement allowed the water to carry more particles in suspension.

8. As the particle-carrying capacity of the water increased, the number of clay particles eroded by the flowing water increased.

9. As the number of clay particles eroded from the dams increased, the sizes of the pores in the dams increased.

10. As the pore space size increased, the speed of the tunnelling process increased until extensive tunnelling had occurred (Mitchell 1976).

This tunnelling process has been found to take place in earthen dams and embankments that had initial permeabilities as low as $10^{-5}$ cm/sec. One method that has been used to reduce the likelihood of tunnelling is to mix the soil with lime prior to dam construction. This causes the clay particles to shrink and become less easily dispersed before any cracking or particle erosion can occur (Mitchell 1976).

The risk of tunnelling failures in slurry walls is greatest where ground-waters contain high concentrations of calcium. At these sites the calcium ions from the groundwater can disrupt the soil bentonite backfill and cause tunnelling failures that are similar to the ones experienced with the earthen dams described above. High calcium concentrations is groundwater are most commonly found in sedimentary aquifers, particularly limestone ones. Water from these aquifers can contain over 50 ppm dissolved calcium (Freeze and Cherry 1979).

The presence of stress cracks, high hydraulic gradients and permeable backfills are not prerequisites for the tunnelling process but these factors are likely to speed failure rate considerably. The causes of stress cracking were described previously. The hydraulic gradients across slurry walls at hazardous waste sites are not normally as high as the gradients across dams, so the rate of tunnelling in slurry walls should be much slower than in earthen dams. Another factor that operates in favor of slurry walls is their low permeability, which is normally 1 to 3 orders of magnitude less than the minimum permeability of the materials through which tunnelling had been reported (Mitchell 1976, D'Appolonia 1980b). This low permeability indicates that the initial rate of water movement through a slurry wall will be much less than through the earthen dams, consequently the particle carrying capacity will also be severely restricted, and the erosion rate will be minimal.

Despite the fact that tunnelling failures, if they occur in a SB wall are expected to require long time periods to develop, the potential for slurry wall disruption due to the presence of calcium ions should be kept in mind when evaluating the feasibility and design criteria for a slurry wall installation at a particular site.

### 5.8.9.2 Piping

Unlike tunnelling, which starts at the upstream side of the wall, piping begins at the downstream face and proceeds towards the upstream face (Mitchell 1976). It occurs due to the use of improper backfill materials or procedures. Variable wall thicknesses, poorly mixed backfill, or extensive quantities of coarse materials in the backfill can all contribute to piping failure.

Piping occurs where a high hydraulic gradient causes the rate of water movement through the wall to increase as the water nears the downgradient side of the wall. If the water movement is rapid enough, it could conceivably force the downstream filter cake into the pores in the soil along the trench wall. As the rate of water movement out of the wall increases, it can begin to erode the easily-dispersed backfill, creating even-larger pores and allowing the water movement rate to increase further (Anderson and Brown 1980). To avoid piping failures, the quality of the filter cake should be maximized, as described in Section 2, the backfill materials should be properly selected and mixed, the backfill should be carefully placed to avoid fold-overs and permeable areas, and the hydraulic gradient across the wall should be monitored and kept within designed levels.

### 5.8.10   Chemical Disruption

Chemical substances in soil and groundwater can affect the durability of the slurry wall once it is in place. Chemical destruction can affect the cement in CB slurry walls as well as the bentonite in CB and SB walls. The effects of alkali salts on bentonite slurries were described previously.

The action of the chemicals on cement or bentonite are similar to that of the tunnelling process. The cement may become slurry solubilized and the bentonite may become entrained in the solution as the chemicals eventually create a solution channel through the wall into surrounding soil. Thus, chemical destruction processes may create as well as accelerate the tunnelling process. Chemicals may also prevent the slurry from forming an adequate filter cake along the sides of the slurry trench by interfering in the slurry gelation process.  Additional information on chemical attack of slurry walls, and on testing compatibilities is contained in Section 4.

5.9  Summary

Design and construction activities for slurry trenches for the most part are relatively simple as long as thorough site investigation results are available and design and construction firms involved are experienced with slurry trench construction techniques.  Although many of the slurry quality control procedures are more applicable to drilling muds than slurry walls, experience has shown that they are adequate until improved procedures are developed.  ASTM is studying these procedures and is expected to make recommendations for changes.  However, trench excavation and backfilling processes, which many experienced design and construction people consider significantly more important than the slurry testing procedures, are governed chiefly by techniques that are practical and field proven.  Many depend on the physical dimensions and continuity of the trench and backfill properties which can be verified by good field inspection.

Therefore, when adequate foresight is used in the design stages, and good field inspection is practiced in the construction phase, existing slurry trench construction techniques should result in a quality installation that meets the criteria of providing a low permeability barrier to the migration of contaminants from waste sites.

# 6. Slurry Wall Monitoring and Maintenance

Upon completing the design, preparation and actual construction of a slurry cut-off wall, the next concern becomes the continuing effectiveness of the wall in the subsurface environment. The main question that arises subsequent to a wall installation is whether or not the wall material will remain resistant to the flow of the substances it is meant to contain. All three of the commonly used backfill materials are subject to attack by certain substances which can lead to an increase in permeability. In addition, failures may result from structural disconformities within the wall. The ability to detect and measure these types of performance failures is an important part of the slurry wall installation process. Performance monitoring is essentially the only means of determining the effectiveness of a cut-off wall over time, and some type of monitoring program should be instituted at all walls installed for pollution control.

The following section describes the different types of monitoring instrumentation used to evaluate wall effectiveness and discusses the various maintenance and restoration techniques which can be used to prevent and remedy the deterioration or destruction of the wall.

## 6.1 Effectiveness Monitoring

It is not possible to provide hard guidelines for the selection of a monitoring program at a particular cut-off wall site. Such a selection is dependent upon two aspects of a project: (1) the questions remaining in the designer's mind after completion of the design and (2) those problems that were encountered either during or after the construction phase. Every slurry wall design and subsequent installation has individual problems that are cause for unanswered questions. The monitoring program chosen for a project should reflect these questions, and the instrumentation selected should act as tools for providing data upon which additional judgements can be made.

Despite the emphasis that must be placed upon site specific characteristics in selecting a monitoring system, a few general guidelines are recommended and they are as follows:

- A solid knowledge should be attained of problems with the wall design and of those problems that were encountered during construction.

166

- A monitoring system should never be solely selected on the basis of what was arranged at a similar site.

- Selection should be preceded by as thorough an understanding as possible with current data, of the nature of contamination, both physically and chemically.

There are basically four types of potential geotechnical problems that require consideration after a slurry cut-off wall has been installed. These relate to the following parameters:

- Basal stability
- Ground movement behind the wall
- Groundwater level and chemistry
- Surface water chemistry.

Table 6-1 summarizes these parameters and possible measurement methods for each.

### 6.1.1  Basal Stability

A common method of determining the basal stability of an area is to measure the subsurface horizontal movement, either of the slurry wall itself or of the ground behind the wall. The instrument used for this purpose is an inclinometer (Dunnicliff 1980). An inclinometer system consists of a pipe installed in a vertical borehole, with internal longitudinal guide groves. A torpedo containing an electrical tilt sensor is lowered down the pipe on the end of a graduated electrical cable, the orientation being controlled by wheels riding in the guide grooves. The electrical cable is connected to a remote readout device indicating tilt of the torpedo with respect to the vertical. Tilt readings and depth measurements allow alignment of the grooved pipe to be determined. Charges measured in the alignment of the pipe provide horizontal movement data (Dunnicliff, 1980).

### 6.1.2  Ground Movement

There are several methods for measuring ground movement behind a cut-off wall and they are categorized according to the type of movement being measured. Horizontal ground movement can be measured using one of the following; an optical survey, a horizontally installed multi-point extensometer, a piezometer or an inclinometer system.

Vertical movement of the ground surface is yet another potential problem in the vicinity of a slurry wall construction site. There are two techniques available that can provide information on this type of movement; the optical survey and the subsurface settlement gauge.

TABLE 6-1.
POTENTIAL PROBLEMS RELATED TO SLURRY WALL
EFFECTIVENESS AND POSSIBLE ASSOCIATED MONITORING METHODS

| Potential Problem | Parameters | Possible Measurement/ Monitoring Method |
|---|---|---|
| Basal Instability | Horizontal Move- ment of Ground | • Inclinometer |
| Ground Movement Behind Wall | Horizontal Movement of Ground | • Optical Survey<br>• Inclinometer<br>• Horizontally Installed Multi-Point Extensometers<br>• Piezometer |
|  | Vertical Movement of Ground | • Optical Survey<br>• Subsurface Settlement Gauge |
| Groundwater | Groundwater Level | • Observation Well |
|  | Pore Pressure | • Piezometer |
|  | Chemistry | • Sampling Wells |
| Surface Water | Chemistry | • Direct Sampling |

Reference:  Dunnicliff 1980

In addition to the separate measurement of vertical and horizontal ground movement, it is also possible to combine instruments and gather both types of data simultaneously.

Detailed discussions of all these techniques can be found in Dunnicliff (1980).

The parameters discussed thus far are measured in order to determine the possibility of structural wall failure occurring due to changes in ground stability in the surrounding area. Basal instability and ground surface movement are both possible causes for premature wall deterioration. The monitoring of groundwater in the slurry wall area, on the other hand, serves a slightly different purpose and is probably the most important parameter to be discussed here. Data obtained through groundwater monitoring provides information on the present efficiency of the wall, instead of on possible reasons for its future ineffectiveness.

### 6.1.3  Groundwater Level and Chemistry

The slurry cut-off wall is by no means a totally impermeable structure. In practice, it is impossible to achieve complete water tightness (Telling et al 1978). There are, however, varying degrees of cut-off efficiency and the following section discusses the use of groundwater monitoring and pump-in testing methods to assess wall effectiveness.

#### 6.1.3.1  Groundwater Monitoring

The major steps necessary in establishing a groundwater monitoring network at a slurry wall site include the following:

- Measure groundwater contamination levels

- Design well and piezometer placement

- Design groundwater sampling and laboratory analysis program

- Data interpretation.

In assessing wall effectiveness, both the quality of groundwater prior to slurry wall installation and the background level of the groundwater quality immediately following wall construction are of primary importance. A solid groundwater background data base is necessary to ensure the validity of future comparative studies of sampling and chemical analysis results. Proper interpretation of chemical analyses conducted on samples taken on opposite sides of a wall is crucial in determining the ability of a wall to contain a contaminant plume. Differences in groundwater chemistry across a wall can be one indication of whether or not the wall is sufficiently containing the contaminant.

Another method of measuring wall efficiency involves the relative hydraulic head drop across the wall. The hydraulic head difference is generally measured using data obtained from piezometer readings, although observation well data can also be used. Equal numbers of piezometers or observation wells are normally placed on each side of the wall. Piezometer or well depth and distance from the wall will vary depending upon the surface and subsurface characteristics of the site. The optimal placement scheme would entail varying distances and depths to scan as large an area on either side of the wall as possible. With data collected over a large area, the formulation of a detailed groundwater flow diagram is possible. Using data obtained from piezometer readings, the increase in volume of water inside the cut-off during a particular time period and the effective permeability can be computed (U.S. Army Corps of Engineers 1978).

The design of a groundwater monitoring system to assess wall effectiveness at a slurry wall site can involve either groundwater monitoring wells or piezometers where monitoring wells are installed, the designated locations will depend upon the number and extent of the water-bearing zones to be monitored. A single well design is used only in the case where one aquifer system is to be monitored. If more than one aquifer or water-bearing zone is to be monitored, a well cluster system may be required at each well location.

The most easily used piezometer design for monitoring a cut-off wall in terms of groundwater levels across the wall is the open standpipe, the simplest of these being a cased or open observation well. The water level is measured directly with a small probe. However, the open standpipe does not function well in impervious soils because of time lag or in partially saturated soils because there is a problem with evaluating pore-air or pore-water effects. The simplicity, sturdiness, and over-all reliability of this type, however, dictates its use in many situations.

The electrical piezometer, consisting of a tip with a diaphragm that is deflected by the pore pressure against one face, is also used at slurry wall sites. This type of piezometer is most suitable for installation in quite impervious and very clayey, plastic materials. The remaining two piezometer types, the hydraulic and pneumatic piezometers are less frequently used for the purpose of monitoring groundwater levels across a slurry wall and will not be discussed here. However, a good source of information regarding piezometers and their applications is Wilson and Squier (1959). The choice of a groundwater sampling method will depend upon the frequency of sampling, the number of monitoring wells that have been installed and the specific conditions at the site.

The type of laboratory analyses to be performed for samples will be dictated by the type of wastes contained at the site.

### 6.1.4  In Situ Permeability Tests

Another means of monitoring wall effectiveness is by conducting in situ permeability tests. These involve sinking a vertical hole in the center of

the wall, and using this backhole for conducting pump-in or slug type
permeability tests. This procedure is not recommended for two reasons.
First, these tests are designed for use in permeable materials, and may give
erroneous values for low permeability SB backfill. Second, these tests have
been shown to cause hydraulic fracturing in fine-grained soil materials. Not
only would this give a falsely high permeability for the wall, it could create
planes of weakness, and lead to wall failure.

### 6.1.5  Surface Water Chemistry

The quality of surface water can be used as indication of cut-off
effectiveness if a contamination problem is located in close proximity to a
surface water body. An example of such a situation is where a cut-off wall
has been installed to prevent a contaminant plume from entering a stream. At
this type of site, monitoring the quality of stream water is an important and
necessary part of the monitoring program instituted. As with groundwater
monitoring, the background water quality must be established in order to
determine the effectiveness of the remedial action program undertaken. A
location far enough upstream to be unaffected by the site is necessary to
provide the most reliable background data. The number and location of
sampling points will depend primarily upon the suspected configuration of the
contaminant plume and also the level of criticality judged from knowledge of
the chemical characteristics of the contaminant. However, there should be a
minimum of three stream sampling sites:

- Background upstream
- Closest stream point to plume boundary
- Location downstream from site.

## 6.2  Maintenance

One claim that is very often seen in the literature, concerns the number
of advantages that the slurry wall construction method enjoys over competitive
systems. Among these advantages is that there is very little required
maintenance. The slurry wall system eliminates the mechanical problems that
are often involved with other remedial actions, such as pump breakdowns
electrical power failures risks due to worker strikes, etc. There do exist,
however, other possible causes for wall deterioration and there are measures
that can be taken to protect the wall from premature breakdown (see
Table 6-2).

A slurry cut-off wall's maintenance needs are very often determined
during the design and installation stages. Pervious zones in slurry walls are
possible, for example, due to improper mixing of the backfill, which then
results in pockets of permeable material within the wall. Failure to excavate
and subsequently key into the aquiclude properly, can also be the cause for

TABLE 6-2.
POTENTIAL CAUSES FOR PREMATURE WALL DETERIORATION
AND ASSOCIATED MAINTENANCE TECHNIQUES

| Potential Cause for Premature Wall Breakdown | Maintenance Method |
|---|---|
| Loading pressures | • Traffic capping<br>• Redistribution of load |
| Erosion | • Re-vegetation<br>• Capping |
| Hydraulic head | • Groundwater pumping |

wall inefficiencies, such as underseepage. Proper design and installation will greatly reduce the possibility that failures such as these will occur.

Chemical breakdown of the wall backfill material is another possible failure mechanism. However, if the proper steps are taken, during the design stages, including extensive compatibility testing, the chances of breakdown are greatly diminished.

Normal loading pressures and even catastrophic events such as earthquakes, are not generally seen as causing problems with slurry wall stability. The compressibility of slurry wall backfill is designed, in most situations, to allow for deformations without cracking (Ryan 1976). In addition, slurry walls tend to retain sufficient moisture to remain somewhat plastic. This is due to the fact that some portion of their structure is located below the water table. Stress and strain forces that change subsurface pressures would merely cause the wall material to flow, filling any cracks that might have otherwise developed (SCS 1981). In the rare case where lesions form due to excessive pressures, grout, of some type, can be used to seal the openings.

Despite the fact that loading pressures are not generally a major concern, the top of a wall should be covered with some type of vegetation or capping material to prevent application of concentrated loads (Ryan 1977). The cover or cap can also serve to reduce surface infiltration and control runoff and erosion around a wall particularly if the wall is located along a steep slope or where precipitation is normally high. The degree to which the wall cover should be maintained depends on the site location, i.e., whether the area is heavily trafficked, and on the physical and chemical nature of the contaminants.

The pressure exerted against the outer wall face by a large hydraulic head can be another cause for gradual wall deterioration. To counter this force, groundwater pumping can be used and is quite effective in diminishing potentially destructive pressures (Figure 6-1).

6.3   Wall Restoration

The need for wall restoration will arise due to reasons identical to those that necessitate wall maintenance. Wall failure can be due to:

• Chemical reaction processes between the wall and contaminant

• Stress/strain forces causing structural failure

• Improper design and/or construction methods.

It will be re-emphasized at the beginning of this discussion that in most cases, wall failure is due to poor design and construction specifications or lack of supervision during installation. Many problems can be avoided entirely with the proper knowledge and the ability to utilize it.

A breach in a wall caused by chemical attack usually originates in one small area of the wall. The cause for deterioration can be due to one of two factors: (1) there exists an area of weakness in the wall, such as the type produced by inadequate mixing of the backfill material during construction or (2) the contaminant concentration is greatest at one location, e.g., a floating solvent layer present in the groundwater column. In either case, the bentonite becomes dehydrated in one portion of the wall which causes an increase in porosity, as described in Section 2. These can result in a piping failure and an eventual breach in the wall (Figure 6-2). In the case where the cause for the breach is the nature of the contaminant and the wall material has the permeability specified in the design requirements, there is little that can be done to permanently restore the wall. A slurry wall is probably not the proper solution for that particular problem and a revision of the engineered solution should be required.

On the other hand, if a breach is due to a hole in the wall and the hole can be located with some accuracy, two restorative possibilities exist: (1) a synthetic liner can be placed along one side of the wall and (2) the breached area can be re-excavated and re-backfilled. There is one stipulation that must be made concerning the second option. In the case of a soil-bentonite wall, the soil-bentonite mixture tends to slide into any re-excavation, requiring that a long section of the trench be dug out and rebuilt (Ryan 1977). Cement-bentonite walls, however, are easily re-excavated by sections. Failure of a cement-bentonite wall would actually stabilize the surrounding soil, making it easy to excavate that section of the trench (Ryan 1977). In addition, new cement-bentonite slurry added to the breached section seals the wall to pre-existing segments (Ryan 1977).

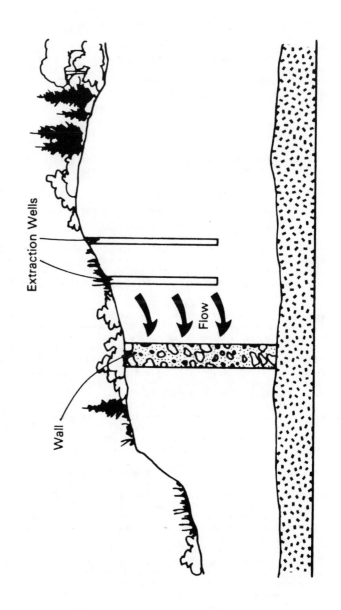

Figure 6-1.
Groundwater Pumping to Reduce Hydraulic
Head Pressure on a Slurry Wall

Wall failures related to physical stress/strain forces do not usually result in a breach. Instead, physical stresses can cause cracking, which then allows leachate seepage through the wall. As mentioned in the previous sub-section, this type of failure rarely occurs (Ryan 1977). If it does, however, there are three restorative actions that can be taken (1) grouting of the cracks, (2) the re-excavation and re-backfilling of the wall (if the wall material consists of cement-bentonite), or (3) placement of a synthetic liner.

The third type of failure is not a failure of a wall, but failure to properly construct a wall. This is due to either inadequate excavation and keying into the aquiclude, or poor backfill design and/or mixing. The most frequent result of not keying into the underlying aquiclude properly is the seepage of leachate under the wall. This can be remedied by re-excavation and re-backfilling, if the problem area can be located. The restrictions for this procedure are described above. Wall failure due to permeability higher than the design requirements is a problem that should never occur. Proper con-struction supervision and backfill design specifications will prevent this type of failure. Table 6-3 summarizes the available restorative methods for various wall failure problems.

TABLE 6-3.
POSSIBLE RESTORATIVE METHODS FOR
VARIOUS WALL FAILURE PROBLEMS

| Mechanism for Wall Failure | Resulting Problem | Possible Restorative Methods |
|---|---|---|
| Chemical reaction between contaminant and wall | Wall breach | • Re-excavation and re-backfill<br>• Second slurry wall installation |
| Stress and strain forces | Lesions or cracking | • Grouting<br>• Re-excavation and re-backfill |
| Improper design and installation practices | Low wall permeability --> contaminant penetration rate high | • Re-excavation and re-backfill |
| | Inadequate key-in --> underseepage | • Grout key-in |

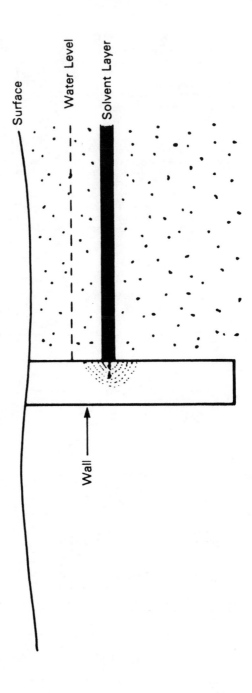

**Figure 6-2.**

**Wall Breach Due to Localized Chemical Attack**

6.4  Summary

The state-of-the-art of slurry wall use for pollution control, and of hazardous waste site remediation in general is such that few if any remedial measures can be assured of long term effectiveness without some degree of monitoring and maintenance. Such programs should be planned in advance of wall installation and continue through the design life of the wall. A monitoring program should be tailored to each specific site and should be able to detect significant changes in the wall's ability to serve its designed purpose. Although slurry walls require little maintenance, a program should be established to ensure the wall is not damaged by surface activity. If portions of a slurry wall are damaged or found to be incapable of serving their intended role, they may have to be restored by reexcavation and reinstallation.

# 7. Major Cost Elements

## 7.1 Introduction

The objective of this section is to present unit costs for activities and items associated with slurry cut-off wall construction. These costs may be used to prepare preliminary estimates for trench construction for comparison with alternative remedial measures at waste disposal sites. They can also be used to examine engineering cost estimates provided by contractors. Slurry trench construction is a specialized field of expertise, and the expense of installing a wall is highly dependent upon site conditions. Because of the dependence on factors which vary between sites, cost items presented herein should be used to develop costs for comparison purposes only. Qualified contractors experienced in this field should be contacted to provide more complete, detailed estimates for specific cut-off wall testing, design, and installation.

It should be noted that the costs presented here are examples only. Many site-specific factors, which could have significant impact on wall costs are not addressed here. Health and safety programs for protecting workers in a contaminated environment, for example, can more than double the time involved in on-site work. Additional information on the costs of working in a hazardous environment can be found in U.S. EPA (1983). These costs, and regional price differences must be considered in evaluating overall wall costs.

In developing unit costs, information presented in other sections of this report was used to develop specifications for material and equipment. These sections were also used to outline construction activities carried out during wall installation. This resulted in a list of items associated with cut-off wall construction. Industry representatives were asked to provide costs for specific items. This sometimes resulted in a range of costs for a specific item, along with a number of factors affecting costs. Industry representatives were contacted whenever an item had specific application to slurry trenches (e.g. bentonite manufacturers provided costs for several types of bentonite). Costs for equipment, materials or activities common to the construction industry and not significantly affected by factors peculiar to slurry trenches, were developed using standard sources. These include Means (1982), Dodge (1982), and NCE (1981).

178

The unit costs presented include standard overhead and profit. This does not include additional subcontractors overhead and profit. In several instances, EPA (1982) provides estimates for construction at hazardous waste sites.

### 7.1.1  Developing Preliminary Cost Estimates

There are several steps in developing cost estimates from unit costs. They are:

1.  Develop conceptual design including type and size of slurry wall.

2.  Develop plan listing all activities to be conducted as part of the job.

3.  Analyze activities, and determine type of equipment to be used and the size of the activity (e.g. number of cubic yards of earth excavated).

4.  Look up unit price for activity and size of equipment.

5.  Multiply size of activity (step 3) by unit cost (step 4).

6.  Add costs for each activity.

7.  Multiply total by contingency fee; usually between 5 and 20%, to account for unforeseen difficulties or problems.

For this report, unit costs are divided into 6 major categories to facilitate use:

1.  Feasibility Testing
2.  Construction Activities
3.  Slurry Wall Installation
4.  Maintenance and Monitoring
5.  Materials
6.  Equipment.

In developing a plan for installing a slurry wall, activities can be divided into four phases:

1.  Feasibility testing, which includes soil testing and hydrogeologic testing for the site, but does not include compatibility testing of the wall with local groundwater.

2.  Site preparation, which consists of all activities ancillary to wall installation. These include site clearing, grading and preparation of work areas, excavation of slurry holding ponds and backfill preparation areas, and temporary alterations in the site such as road construction.

3. Wall installation, including mobilization and demobilization of equipment, labor, shipping and mixing of bentonite, backfill preparation, trench excavation and site cleanup. Wall installation costs as provided by contractors are a function of the size and type of wall.

4. Site clean-up, including re-grading, re-seeding and security.

Once this plan is complete, unit costs presented in this section can be used to develop total estimated costs for the slurry wall installation.

Cost estimates for associated remedial actions as discussed in Section 2.4 are not provided in this report. Assistance in developing costs for these items can be found in the EPA (1982).

### 7.1.1.1 Cost Estimation Example

An example of the cost estimation process is provided below.

Based upon preliminary information, a slurry wall appears feasible as a remedial action at a given site. It is thought that the wall must be at least 50 feet deep to key into a clay layer, and that it must be between 700 and 800 feet long. Local materials will be used as a source of fines in the backfill. Access to the site will be difficult, as no road leads directly to the work area. The nearest access is 1200 feet from the site. There are few large trees in the work area; which is relatively flat and covered with tall weeds and grasses. After construction is complete, the area will be graded and revegetated.

Using this description, a preliminary estimate of costs can be made. First, a list of activities can be developed. This list includes:

- Feasibility testing
- Temporary road construction
- Site clearing and preparation
- Slurry wall excavation and completion
- Site re-grading and revegetation.

Costs for each activity are described below.

### a. Feasibility Testing

Testing is required to determine the continuity and depth of the clay layer to be keyed into, as well as to obtain data on the type of native material to be used as backfill.  It is estimated that soil borings of between 60 and 70 feet depth be set 50 feet apart in a line along that of the anticipated trench.  Specific tests to be conducted include:

- Sieve analysis, all locations, at 10 feet depth intervals
- Atterberg limits, all locations, at 10 feet depth intervals
- Permeability tests, all locations, depths of 20, 40, and 60 feet.

Costs are given in Table 7-1.

### b.  Temporary Road Construction

The road must extend at least 1200 feet from the nearest access. Vegetation and trees less then 6-inch diameter must be cleared and a gravel base laid.  It is estimated that the road must be 40 feet wide to accomodate heavy equipment.  Costs are presented in Table 7-2.

### c.  Site Clearing and Preparation

Brush and grass must be cleared to provide working space.  An estimated 10 acres must be cleared, and approximately 3 acres must be regraded to serve as a backfill preparation and slurry mixing and storage area.  Costs are given in Table 7-3.

### d.  Slurry Wall Excavation and Installation

Costs for slurry wall excavation and completion includes all activities associated with wall installation.  This includes such items as:

- Backhoes, dozers, and trucks, including mobilization/demobilization
- Bentonite and water
- Slurry mixing and preparation including mixers and hoses
- Backfill preparation and installation
- Site clean-up.

Costs are derived based upon discussion with industry representatives and published data.  Cost ranges for some slurry wall installation are shown in Table 7-4.

TABLE 7-1.

ESTIMATED COSTS FOR FEASIBILITY TESTING - EXAMPLE SITE

| Activity | Costs | |
|---|---|---|
| | Low Estimate | High Estimate |
| **1.  SOIL BORINGS** | | |
| 14 Sites (700 ft./50 ft. Intervals) x 60 ft. x $7.80/ft. - 8.89/ft | $ 6,552.00 | $ 7,468.00 |
| 16 Sites (800 ft./50 ft. Intervals) x 60 ft. x $7.80/ft. - 8.89/ft | $ 7,488.00 | $ 8,534.04 |
| **2.  SOIL TESTS** | | |
| Sieve Analysis - 6/site x 14 sites x $40.00 - $70.00 | $ 3,360.00 | $ 5,880.00 |
| Sieve Analysis - 6/site x 16 sites x $40.00 - $70.00 | $ 3,840.00 | $ 6,700.00 |
| Atterberg Limits - 6/site x 14 sites x $25.00 - $50.00 | $ 2,100.00 | $ 4,200.00 |
| Atterberg Limits - 6/site x 16 sites x $25.00 - $50.00 | $ 2,400.00 | $ 4,800.00 |
| Split Spoon - 6/site x 14 sites x $15.00      - | $ 1,250.00 | |
| Split Spoon - 6/site x 16 sites x $15.00      - | $ 1,440.00 | |
| Permeability Tests - 3/site x 14 sites x $50.00      - | $ 2,100.00 | |
| Permeability Tests - 3/site x 16 sites x $50.00      - | 2,200.00 | $ 2,200.00 |
| | $15,362.00 | $17,368.00 |

Reference:  Means 1982; Dodge 1982; and Smith 1982.

TABLE 7-2.

ESTIMATED COSTS FOR TEMPORARY ROAD CONSTRUCTION - EXAMPLE SITE

| Activity | Cost |
|---|---|
| 1.  CLEAR AND GRUB | |
| 1200 ft. x 40 ft. x sq.yd./9sq.ft. x $.26/sq.yd. | $ 1,386.00 |
| 2.  TEMPORARY ROADWAY - 4" GRAVEL FILL - NO SURFACING | |
| 1200 ft. x 40 ft. x sq.yd./9sq.ft. x $2.91/sq.yd. | $15,520.00 |
| | $16,906.00 |

Reference:  Means 1982, and Dodge 1982.

TABLE 7-3.

ESTIMATED COSTS FOR SITE CLEARING AND PREPARATION - EXAMPLE SITE

| Activity | Cost |
|---|---|
| 1.  CLEAR AND GRUB WITH DOZER | |
| 10 acres x 4840 sq. yds./acre x $.21/sq.yd. | $10,164.00 |
| 2.  REGRADE AVERAGE 2 FT. 75 H.P. WITH DOZER | |
| 3 acres x 43,560 sq.ft./acre x 2 ft. x | |
| cu.yds./270 ft. x $211/cu.yd. | $20,424.00 |
| | $30,588.00 |

Reference:  Means 1982, Dodge 1982.

TABLE 7-4.

ESTIMATED COSTS FOR SLURRY WALL INSTALLATION - EXAMPLE SITE

| Activity | Cost |
|---|---|
| 1. SLURRY WALL INSTALLATION<br>   SOFT TO MEDIUM SOIL<br>   DEPTH:  60 FT.<br>   SOIL BENTONITE BACKFILL | |
| 700 ft. x 60 ft. x $4.00 - $8.00/sq.ft. | $168,000.00 - $336,000.00 |
| 800 ft. x 60 ft. x $4.00 - $8.00/sq.ft. | $192,000.00 - $384,000.00 |

Reference:  Ressi de Cervia 1979.

e.  Site Re-grading and Revegation

After the wall is complete, the site must be re-graded and revegetated. Typical costs are given in Table 7-5.

f.  Total Costs

To arrive at total costs, all items are added.  A general contingency factor is added to account for unforeseen problems.  This usually is between 5 percent to 20 percent, depending upon the type of work conducted.  A contingency factor of 15 percent is usually more than sufficient.  Total costs are given in Table 7-6.

## 7.2  Unit Costs

Unit costs are presented under the following catagories:

- Feasibility testing
- Construction activities
- Slurry wall installation
- Maintenance and monitoring
- Materials
- Equipment.

Unit costs are based upon the discussions already presented.  The presentations here attempt to follow previous discussions as closely as possible.

The use of unit costs to develop estimates is relatively simple, but the result is still only an estimate.  In addition to the variations inherent in estimating costs for such a site specific construction technique as slurry cut-off walls, unit prices can vary depending upon a variety of factors. These include wage rates, labor efficiency, union regulations and material costs.  Other factors which may affect costs are weather, season of year, contractor management, and unforeseen difficulties.

Unit costs presented in the following pages give a range of equipment sizes and types which can accomplish the same activity.  Judgement must be used in deciding what type of equipment may be used.  Unit costs are given for a wide variety of activities which may be required as part of a slurry cut-off wall.  If a special activity is required and is not included in this section, one of the reference sources cited in this Section will probably contain the necessary information.

TABLE 7-5.

ESTIMATED COSTS FOR SITE REGRADING AND REVEGETATING - EXAMPLE SITE

| Activity | Cost |
|---|---|
| 1. REGRADE AT AVERAGE 2 FT. DEPTH WITH 75 H.P. DOZER | $ 7,414.00-<br>$20,424.00 |
| 2. REVEGETATE AND HYDROSEED, INCLUDING FERTILIZER<br>    10 acres x 4840 sq.yd. x $.46/sq.yd. | $22,264.00 |
|  | $42,688.00 |

Reference:  Means 1982, Dodge 1982.

TABLE 7-6.

ESTIMATED TOTAL COSTS - EXAMPLE SITE

| Activity | Cost |
|---|---|
| Feasibility Testing | $ 17,210.00 - $ 19,480.00 |
| Temporary Road Construction | $16,900.00 |
| Site Clearing and Preparation | $30,588.00 |
| Slurry Wall Excavation and Completion | $192,000.00 - $384,000.00 |
| Site Re-grading and Revegetation | $42,688.00 |
|  | $299,386.00 - $493,656.00 |
| 15% Contingency | $ 44,907.00 - $ 74,048.00 |
|  | $344,294.00 - $567,704.00 |

7.2.1   Feasibility Testing

To determine the feasibility of using a slurry cut off wall at a particular site, three types of tests are conducted.  They are:

- Geologic and soils tests
- Hydrologic tests
- Slurry wall tests.

The first two catagories provide a characterization of the site while the last determines the compatibility of the technique with specific site conditions, most notably the effect of the constituents present in the local groundwater upon the slurry cut off wall.  In general, feasibility testing for a slurry wall can run between 8 to 18 percent of costs (JRB 1979).

### 7.2.1.1   Geologic and Soils Testing

Geologic and soils testing is accomplished using a drill rig to extract samples from various depths.  Any type of drill rig may be used, but one of the more common type makes use of hollow stem augers to penetrate the subsurface and withdraw samples.  Costs presented here assume the use of hollow stem augers.

Factors which affect the cost of geologic and soils testing include:  the number and type of samples, the depth to which samples are taken, mobilization and demobilization of equipment, weather conditions, and the presence of contamination which may require careful handling techniques and special equipment.  Based on the presence of contamination, cuttings material brought to the surface by the advance of the auger may have to be disposed in secure landfills.  Drilling in contaminated areas can significantly affect the rate of sampling as well as the overall cost.

It is possible that a good deal of information is already available on many of the hazardous waste sites where slurry cut-off walls are being considered.  However, it will still be necessary to conduct special testing to determine the location and extent of the less permeable layer to be keyed into, and to fully characterize the content of the overburden which will be excavated.  Overburden characterization is especially important if native material is to be used as a source of fines for the backfill.  In this instance, test points relatively close together, both in the horizontal and vertical sense, may be necessary.  Where a cement-bentonite backfill is considered, soil testing can be kept to a minimum but cannot be discarded.  It is still important to know the characteristics of the key-in layer, and information on the overburden could prove useful at a later date if additional remedial measures are considered.

In general, test points of between 50 and 150 feet should provide more than sufficient information to characterize the subsurface material.  The test borings should extend at least several feet into the impermeable layer to confirm its suitability. Costs for geologic and soils tests are given in Table 7-7.

### 7.2.1.2 Hydrologic Testing

Hydrologic testing is designed to determine the characteristics of groundwater quality and flow at a site. Some hydrologic tests involve altering the condition of the aquifer and measuring the response to the change. Others merely monitor the existing conditions. In any event, it is necessary to install wells to conduct these tests.

Factors which affect hydrologic tests are almost identical to those which affect soils tests. Mobilization and demobilization, weather conditions, type and location of sample points and the presence of contamination all affect the cost of hydrologic testing.

Many hazardous waste sites have been studied to a degree that very good characterizations of the hydrology of the area already exist. Additional hydrologic testing may not be required at very many sites. Where more information is required, existing monitoring wells may be used to reduce costs. Costs for conducting hydrologic tests are given in Table 7-8.

### 7.2.1.3 Backfill Testing

Tests conducted to determine probable performance characteristics of a planned cut-off wall are important. Tests can be carried out by one of several contractors who specialize in slurry wall installation.

There are two types of tests carried out which are used to determine wall characteristics:

- Compatibility testing
- Permeability testing.

These tests determine the optimum mix of backfill materials to maximize wall strength and stability and minimize wall permeability. Usually, samples of soil and groundwater are taken from the site and used for the tests. These can be gathered as part of the soil and hydrologic testing programs. The tests are then run using these native materials. Ranges of costs as provided by a number of contractors are provided in Table 7-9.

TABLE 7-7.

EXAMPLE UNIT COSTS FOR GEOLOGIC AND SOILS TESTING

| Activity | Cost |
|---|---|
| **Soil Borings** | |
| Mobilization and Demobilization | $110.00 |
| over 100 miles, additional per mile | $  1.00/Mile |
| Auger Holes, 2.5" diameter | $  6.70/LF - 8.89/LF |
| 4" diameter | $  7.80/LF |
| Cased Borings, 2.5" diameter | $  9.45/L.F. - 11.41/LF |
| 4" diameter | $ 16.15/L.F. |
| Split Spoon Samples, 2 foot drive | $ 15.00 - $50.00 each |
| **Soil Testings** | |
| Atterberg Limits, Liquid and Plastic Limits | $ 25.00 - $90.00 each |
| Hydrometer Analysis and Specific Gravity | $ 50.00 |
| Sieve Analysis - Washed | $ 23.00 |
| - Unwashed | $ 40.00 - $70.00 each |
| Moisture Content | $  7.00 - $15.00 each |
| Permeability, Variable or Constant Head | $ 50.00 |
| Proctor Compaction, 4" Standard Mold | $ 80.00 - $95.00 |

Reference:   Means 1982, Dodge 1982, Smith 1982.

TABLE 7-8.

EXAMPLE UNIT COSTS FOR HYDROLOGIC TESTING

| Activity | Cost |
|---|---|
| **Well Installation** | |
| 1.  Boring and well installation, without casing[1] | |
|     2.5" auger | $ 7.23 – $ 9.00/foot |
|     4" auger | $11.50 – $14.40/foot |
|     6" auger | $17.34 – $21.60/foot |
| 2.  Casing | |
|     2" pvc.[1] | $ 3.00/foot |
|     4" pvc.[1] | $ 5.00/foot |
|     2" steel[2] | 4.50–5.50/foot |
|     4" steel[2] | 7.00–9.00/foot |
| 3.  Well Screens .010" Slot, 10' length | |
|     2" pvc. | $  6.47/foot |
|     4" pvc. | $ 18.98/foot |
|     2" steel, 5 foot length | $144.80 ea. + 26.00/ additional foot |
|     4" steel, 5 foot length | $238.70 ea. + 41.10/ additional foot |
| 4.  Submersible pump, 5 gallons/minute at 180 ft. lift[1] | $750.00 each |
| **Hydrologic Tests** | |
| 5.  Water Quality Tests – Includes sampling and analysis | highly variable depending upon site-specific conditions |
| 6.  Pump Tests | |
| 7.  Slug Tests | |

References:  (1) JRB 1979, (2) Smith 1982.

TABLE 7-9.

EXAMPLE COSTS FOR SLURRY WALL TESTING

| ACTIVITY | COST |
|---|---|
| 1. Compatibility tests | $800.00-$1,200.00 each test |
| 2. Permeability tests | $800.00-$1,200.00 each test |

Reference:  Various industry sources.


### 7.2.2  Construction Activities

Construction activities include all activities conducted which are not directly related to slurry wall installation.  Therefore, such items as slurry preparation, mixing and introduction into the trench; backfill preparation and placement; and slurry disposal are not covered in this section.  These items are covered in a following section.

Costs for the following activities are included in this section:

- Site clearing
- Excavation
- Backfill (excluding slurry trench backfill)
- Borrow
- Compaction
- Grading
- Hauling
- Mobilization and Demobilization
- Site Dewatering.

Costs for these activities are shown in Tables 7-10 through 7-18.


#### 7.2.2.1  Site Clearing

Slurry wall installation is made easier if a working area is cleared of trees, shrubs and bushes.  In urban areas, or where other factors may prevent

the removal of obstacles, the cost of slurry cut-off wall installation
increases dramatically.  Slurry wall installation or implementation of additional remedial actions is made easier if a working area can be prepared by
clearing the site of obstructive objects.  In rural areas the predominant
obstack is vegetation, ie, trees, shrubs, bushes, and site clearing can
usually be undertaken with minimal difficulty and at relatively low cost.  In
urban areas, however, where the obstacles are power lines, underground water
lines etc., site clearing is often difficult and as a result slurry cut-off
wall installation and any additional site work increases dramatically.  Costs
for site clearning are shown in Table 7-10.  Costs for clearing a site
containing wastes should not be significantly greater than normal costs,
however, if decontamination of personnel and equipment is required, costs may
rise significantly.

### 7.2.2.2  Excavation

Excavation may be required to prepare the work area.  Slurry may be
stored in excavated ponds to insure complete hydration of bentonite and to
provide a sufficient reserve of slurry.  In addition, "benches" may need to be
cut into hillsides to accomodate excavation equipment.  The type of equipment
chosen is dependent upon the size of the job, the type of excavation and site
conditions.

Costs for excavation are given in Table 7-11.  Costs will be affected by
the type of material being exhumed, and also by the presence of contaminants.
Contaminated material must be properly disposed, adding to overall costs.  In
addition, decontamination of equipment and health and safety precautions will
slow work, and increase costs.  Rental costs for equipment are presented under
the equipment discussion.  Unit costs provided in Table 7-11 include rental of
equipment.

### 7.2.2.3  Backfilling

Backfilling is required to "fill in" areas to insure level grade for
excavation equipment.  In slurry trench construction, below grade depressions
may need to be filled and compacted to create the level grade.  Backfill may
also be required to fill in slurry ponds after the job is complete.

Costs for backfilling are presented in Table 7-12.  The presence of
contaminants may influence costs, but not significantly if clean fill is used.
Health and safety precautions and decontamination of equipment may slow the
rate of backfilling operations.

TABLE 7-10.
EXAMPLE UNIT COSTS FOR SITE CLEARING

| ACTIVITY | UNIT COSTS ($) |
|---|---|
| Clear and Grub - Trees | |
| Light trees to 6" diam., cut and chip | 2,125/acre - 22.00 each |
|    grub stumps | 565.06 - 825/acre |
| Medium trees to 10" diam., cut and chip | 2,450/acre - 31.00 each |
|    grub stumps | 1,100/acre - 1130/acre |
| Heavy trees to 16" diam., cut and chip | 2,850/acre - 56.00 each |
|    grub stumps | 1,375/acre - 2260.00/acre |
| Trees over 16" diam., using chain saws and chipper | $100.00 ea. - 128.00 each |
|    For machine load, 2 miles haul to dump add | $18.00 - 38.00 each |
| Clearing-Brush | |
| With brush saw and rake | .27/square yard (S.Y.) |
|    by hand | .55/S.Y. |
| With dozer, ball and chain, light clearing | .27/S.Y. |
|    medium clearing | .31/S.Y. |

Reference:  Means 1982, Dodge 1982.

TABLE 7-11.
EXAMPLE UNIT COSTS FOR EXCAVATION

ASSUMPTIONS:

Medium earth piled or truck loaded
No trucks or haul added

| EQUIPMENT AND CAPACITY | UNIT COST (per Cubic Yard) |
|---|---|
| 1. Backhoe, hydraulic, crawler mounted | |
| 1.0 Cubic Yard | $2.17 – 2.71 |
| 1.5 Cubic Yard | $1.96 – 2.19 |
| 2.0 Cubic Yard | $1.93 – 1.98 |
| 3.5 Cubic Yard | $1.48 – 1.79 |
| 2. Backhoe, wheel mounted | |
| .5 Cubic Yard | $3.76 – 3.95 |
| .75 Cubic Yard | $2.62 – 2.92 |
| 3. Clamshell | |
| .5 Cubic Yard | $4.34 – 4.42 |
| 1.0 Cubic Yard | $2.93 – 3.39 |
| 4. 75 H.P. Dozer, 50' haul | $1.17 – 1.43 |
| 300 H.P. dozer, 50' haul | $ .57 – .98 |
| 75 H.P. dozer, 150' haul | $1.43 – 2.34 |
| 300 H.P. dozer, 150' haul | $1.08 – 1.48 |
| 5. 0.75 Cubic Yard Dragline | $2.47 |
| 1.5 Cubic Yard Dragline | $1.76 |
| 6. Front end loader, track mounted. | |
| 1.5 Cubic Yard | $ .98 – 1.05 |
| 2.5 Cubic Yard | $ .91 – 1.26 |
| 3.5 Cubic Yard | $ .72 – .82 |
| 4.5 Cubic Yard | $ .88 – .99 |
| Wheel mounted | |
| 0.75 Cubic Yard | $ .99 – 1.30 |
| 1.5 Cubic Yard | $ .84 – .89 |
| 5.0 Cubic Yard | $ .73 |
| 7. Shovel | |
| 0.5 Cubic Yard | $2.95 |
| 0.75 Cubic Yard | $1.66 – 1.88 |
| 1.5 Cubic Yard | $1.25 – 1.39 |

For soft soil or sand, deduct 15% for heavy soil or clay add 60%.

Reference:  Means 1982, Dodge 1982.

TABLE 7-12.
EXAMPLE UNIT COSTS FOR BACKFILL

| ACTIVITY | UNIT COST (Dollars Per Cubic Yard) |
|---|---|
| 1. Backfill by hand, no compaction, light soil | $8.83 - $11.10 |
| heavy soil | $12.95 |
| 2. Compaction in 6" layers, hand tamp | 7.55 - 11.02 |
| roller compaction | 3.90 - 4.67 |
| air tamp | 5.70 |
| vibrating plate tamp | 1.55 - 3.76 |
| 3. Compaction in 12" layers, hand tamp | 4.56 |
| roller compaction | 2.81 |
| air tamp | 4.10 |
| vibrating plate tamp | 2.63 |
| 4. Dozer backfill, bulk, up to 300' haul | 0.85 - 1.04 |
| Compaction air tamped | 4.81 Additional |
| - 6" - 12" lifts vibrating roller | 1.77 Additional |
| - Sheepsfoot roller | 1.92 Additional |
| 5. Dozer backfilling, trench, up to 300' haul | 1.09 |
| Compaction air tamped | 4.92 Additional |
| - 6" - 12" lifts vibrating roller | 2.11 Additional |
| - Sheepsfoot roller | 2.39 Additional |

REFERENCE:  Means 1982, Dodge 1982.

7.2.2.4  Borrow

Borrow is material taken from a nearby source to be used as a fill material on-site. Borrow can be used as a backfill, and as a source of material to construct berms, dikes, levees, or ramps. Borrow can also serve as a source of fines used in the preparation of cut-off trench backfill.

Cost for borrow are given in Table 7-13. These costs assume that a nearby source of material is available. If not, costs could rise substantially.

7.2.2.5  Compaction

Backfill or borrow used for haul roads, should be compacted to impart some strength to the material. This is especially important if heavy equipment is going to be moving over areas of loose or uncompacted material. Unless backfill or borrow is used at a site, compaction may not be necessary. Costs for compaction are given in Table 7-14.

7.2.2.6  Grading

Slurry trench construction requires a relatively flat working surface. In areas of sloping or uneven terrain, graders may be used to level the working area.

There are two types of graders, self-propelled and those towed by a dozer or some other suitable piece of machinery. Either can be used, but large, motorized graders are used primarily for larger jobs. Costs for various graders are presented in Table 7-15.

7.2.2.7  Hauling

Hauling material to the worksite may be a major cost factor if sources of material are not located nearby. Hauling may be required to bring borrow material to a site. Hauling costs presented in Table 7-16 do not give cost for rail or truck transportation of material for great distances (i.e., the shipping of large quantities of bentonite by rail). Manufacturers should be contacted to provide exact transport costs for these types of material.

The selection of equipment to haul material is dependent upon several factors. Of primary importance is the quantity of material to be hauled. For larger quantities, a larger capacity trailer should be used as they are usually more efficient. Limiting the type of equipment used are the physical constraints of the roads over which material will be hauled. Back roads or

TABLE 7-13.
EXAMPLE UNIT COSTS FOR BORROW

Assumptions:

Buy and load at pit, haul 2 miles to site, place and spread with 180 H.P. dozer with no compaction.

| MATERIAL | UNIT COST |
|---|---|
| 1. Bank run gravel | $6 - 6.25/Cubic Yard |
| 2. Common borrow | $4.63/C.Y. |
| 3. Crushed stone 1.5" | $6.65 - $10.70/C.Y. |
| Crushed stone 3/4" | $6.65 - $10.55/C.Y. |
| Crushed stone 1/2" | $11.88/C.Y. |
| Crushed stone 3/8" | $12.60/C.Y. |
| 4. Sand-washed- | $ 6.26 - $10.15/C.Y. |
| Dead or bank sand | $ 8.30/C.Y. |
| 5. Select structure fill | $ 6.87 - $8.35 |
| 6. Screened Loam | $ 8.80 - $12.35/C.Y. |
| 7. For 5 mile haul, Add | $1.40 - $2.30/C.Y. |

Reference: Means 1982, Dodge 1982.

TABLE 7-14.
EXAMPLE UNIT COSTS FOR COMPACTION

| ACTIVITY | UNIT COST |
|---|---|
| 1. Compaction, Rolling with road roller, 5 tons | $45.00/hr |
| 10 tons | $55.00/hr |
| 2. Sheepsfoot or wobbly wheel roller, 8" lifts | $ 1.56/C.Y. |
| for select fill | $ 1.31/C.Y. |
| 3. Terraprobe, deep sand | $.92 - 1.31/C.Y. |
| Mobilization-Demobilization | $4,650.00 - $6,100.00 |
| 4. Vibratory Plate, 8" Lifts, select fill | $1.55 - $2.56/C.Y. |

Reference: Means 1982, Dodge 1982.

TABLE 7-15.

EXAMPLE UNIT COSTS FOR GRADING

Assumptions:

Site excavation and fill, not including mobilization and demobilization or compaction

| Activity | Unit Cost (Dollars/Cubic Yard) |
|---|---|
| 1.  Dozer 300 foot haul-75  H.P. | 1.06 - 2.92 |
|                        ·    -300 H.P. | 1.08 - 2.11 |
| 2.  Scraper, towed, 7 C.Y.-300' haul | 3.53 |
|                                 -1000' haul | 7.75 |
|                        10 C.Y.-300'  haul | 1.88 - 2.33 |
|                                  1000'  haul | 1.96 - 3.96 |
| 3.  Self propelled scraper, 15 C.Y. 1000' haul | 1.95 |
|                                         2000' haul | 2.64 |
|                              25 C.Y. 1000' haul | 1.02 |
|                                         2000' haul | 1.27 |
| 4.  Dozer with ripper- 200 H.P. | 0.49 |
|                          - 300 H.P. | 0.99 |

Reference:  Means 1982, Dodge 1982.

TABLE 7-16.

EXAMPLE UNIT COSTS FOR HAULING

| Activity | | Unit Cost (Dollars/Cubic Yard) |
|---|---|---|
| 1.  6 C.Y. Dump truck, | 1 mile round trip | 2.03 - 2.28 |
| | 2 mile round trip | 2.64 - 2.91 |
| | 3 mile round trip | 3.42 - 3.64 |
| | 4 mile round trip | 4.28 |
| 2.  12 C.Y. Dump truck | 1 mile round trip | 1.71 - 2.00 |
| | 2 mile round trip | 1.96 - 2.11 |
| | 3 mile round trip | 2.21 - 2.47 |
| | 4 mile round trip | 2.65 - 2.96 |
| 3. 16.5 C.Y. Dump truck | 1 mile round trip | 1.50 |
| | 2 mile round trip | 1.85 |
| | 3 mile round trip | 2.17 |
| | 4 mile round trip | 2.42 |
| 4. 20 C.Y. Dump truck | 1 mile round trip | 1.31 |
| | 2 mile round trip | 1.64 |
| | 3 mile round trip | 2.94 |
| | 4 mile round trip | 2.19 |

5.  Hauling in medium traffic, add 20%
    Hauling in heavy traffic, add 30%

Reference:  Means 1982, Dodge 1982.

dirt roads may not stand up to larger trailers.  In addition, weight
restriction on roadways and bridges will limit the size of vehicle.

### 7.2.2.8  Mobilization and Demobilization

Mobilization and demobilization refers to the transportation of vehicles
and equipment to and from the job site.  These are primarily a factor of the
distance from the equipment storage site to the job location.  Mobilization
and demobilization costs for specialized, heavy equipment may be very high.
Average costs for representative pieces of equipment are shown in Table 7-17.
These figures assume a local source of equipment.

### 7.2.2.9  Site Dewatering

Dewatering may be required at sites where excavations intersect the water
table.  It is not anticipated that dewatering will be required during slurry
trench installation as little or no deep excavation is required other than
that of the trench.  Costs for dewatering systems are shown in Table 7-18.

### 7.2.3  Completed Wall Costs

Contractors have provided average costs for completed slurry cut-off wall
construction and installation.  These estimates may vary widely however, based
upon a number of site-specific factors.  Some of these factors are:

- Distance bentonite must be transported.

- Presence of contamination or high salt content in groundwater
  requiring special bentonite and excavation procedures.

- Type of overburden being excavated.

- Depth of excavation.

- Presence of physical constraints upon working area (i.e., buildings or
  other structures which must be worked around).

- Suitability of native materials for use as backfill constituents.

- Type of backfill (either cement or soil-bentonite).

Ressi di Cervia (1980) developed a chart (Table 7-19) which related
cut-off wall construction costs to type of backfill used, depth of excavation
and soil type present.  Costs are given in terms of square foot of wall since
the width of the excavation is a factor of the excavation equipment.  Although

TABLE 7-17.
EXAMPLE UNIT COSTS FOR MOBILIZATION AND DEMOBILIZATION

| | Equipment | | Cost |
|---|---|---|---|
| 1. | Dozer 105 H.P. | | $ 90.00 |
| | 300 H.P. | | $125.00 |
| 2. | Scraper-towed (include Tractor) 6 | C.Y. | $ 95.00 |
| | | 10 C.Y. | $130.00 |
| 3. | Self-propelled scraper | 15 C.Y. | $180.00 |
| | | 24 C.Y. | $290.00 |
| 4. | Shovel, Backhoe or dragline | 3/4 C.Y. | $130.00 |
| | | 1.5 C.Y. | $190.00 |
| 5. | Tractor shovel or front end loader | 1 C.Y. | $ 90.00 |
| | | 2.25 C.Y. | $125.00 |

Reference:  Means 1982, Dodge 1982.

TABLE 7-18.
EXAMPLE COSTS FOR SITE DEWATERING

| | Description | cost |
|---|---|---|
| 1. | Wells - large | |
| | dewatering excavation 10' - 20' deep, 2" steel casing | $5.00-22.00/Linear Foot |
| | submersible pump, 6", 1590 GPM | $1250.00/month |
| 2. | Wells - small | |
| | dewatering excavation 4" - 6" with casing | $12.95/Linear Foot |
| | submersibile 3"-300 GPM | $300/month |
| | 4"-560 GPM | $400/month |
| 3. | Wellpoints | |
| | Complete installation, operation, equipment rental, full and removal of system with 2" wellpoints | |
| | 100 foot header 6" diameter | $24,500-$32,000/month |
| | 200 foot header 6" diameter | $25,000-$27,000/month |
| | 100 foot header 6" diameter | $31,000-$69,000/month |

Reference:  Means 1982, Various Other Sources.

TABLE 7-19.
RELATION OF SLURRY CUT-OFF WALL COSTS
PER SQUARE FOOT AS A FUNCTION
OF MEDIUM AND DEPTH

| | Slurry Trench Prices in 1979 Dollars Soil Bentonite Backfill (Dollars/Square Foot) | | | Unreinforced Slurry Wall Prices in 1979 Dollars Cement Bentonite Backfill (Dollars/Square Foot) | | |
|---|---|---|---|---|---|---|
| | Depth $\leq$ 30 Feet | Depth 30-75 Feet | Depth 75-120 Feet | Depth $\leq$ 60 Feet | Depth 60-150 Feet | Depth > 150 Feet |
| Soft to Medium Soil N $\leq$ 40 | 2-4 | 4-8 | 8-10 | 15-20 | 20-30 | 30-75 |
| Hard Soil N 40 - 200 | 4-7 | 5-10 | 10-20 | 25-30 | 30-40 | 40-95 |
| Occasional Boulders | 4-8 | 5-8 | 8-25 | 20-30 | 30-40 | 40-85 |
| Soft to Medium Rock N $\geq$ 200 Sandstone, Shale | 6-12 | 10-20 | 20-50 | 50-60 | 60-85 | 85-175 |
| Boulder Strata | 15-25 | 15-25 | 50-80 | 30-40 | 40-95 | 95-210 |
| Hard Rock Granite, Gneiss, Schist* | --- | --- | --- | 95-140 | 140-175 | 175-235 |

Notes:

N is standard penetration value in number blows of the hammer per foot of penentration (ASTM D1586-67)

*Normal Penetration Only

For Standard Reinforcement add $8.00 per sq. ft.
For Construction in Urban Environment Add 25% to 50% of Price

Reference:  Ressi di Cervia 1980.

costs are given in 1979 dollars, contractors maintain that slurry trench costs have remained stable because of increased experience and new technology.

A breakdown of total cut-off wall costs according to several categories is shown in Table 7-20. As can be seen, costs for each element may vary widely.

Table 7-21 gives examples of costs for several walls as reported in the literature or otherwise available. A brief description of site characteristics which may have affected costs is included. This table also demonstrates the wide variation in unit costs depending upon site specific factors.

### 7.2.3.1  Monitoring

Once a slurry cut-off wall has been installed, monitoring should be conducted to assure that the wall is performing as designed. If the monitoring program indicates that the wall is not containing or isolating contaminants, maintenance to restore the integrity of the wall should be instituted.

There are two types of monitoring systems which are used to indicate the integrity of a cut-off walls; wall-stability monitoring and water quality monitoring. Effects on wall integrity due to ground movement is not considered a major problem as both SB and CB walls are normally flexible enough to withstand typical deformation. This type of monitoring is usually important if construction activities place a major load on the wall. Since it is not expected that slurry walls associated with hazardous wastes sites will be called upon to support major structures, costs are not provided for this type of monitoring.

Water quality monitoring will be the most important indicator of wall performance: the wall will either contain and isolate waste materials or migration of constituents will continue. Water quality monitoring systems usually consist of multiple wells installed at suitable locations up and downgradient of a wall. These walls can be sampled and analyzed to determine water quality. In addition to groundwater monitoring, surface water sources can also be sampled. Finally, water levels obtained from piezometers can be used as an indicator of wall integrity.

Table 7-22 presents estimated costs for monitoring well and piezometer installation. Costs for sampling and analysis are highly variable and depend upon the type of parameters analyzed, and therefore, have not been included.

### 7.2.3.2  Maintenance

Maintenance of a slurry wall begins immediately after installation. The wall should be capped with a clay or other capping material to reduce surface infiltration and control erosion. The cap should be properly graded.

TABLE 7-20.
BREAKDOWN OF COST CATAGORIES
FOR CUT-OFF TRENCH CONSTRUCTION*

| Activity | % of Total Costs |
|---|---|
| Testing - Hydrologic, Geotechnical, and Lab Tests | 8% - 18% |
| Equipment Mobilization | 8% - 18% |
| Slurry Trench Excavation and Backfill | 65% - 83% |

*Assumes soil-bentonite backfill with moderate soil conditions and depth not greater than 40 feet.

Referemce:  EPA 1982.

TABLE 7-21.
EXAMPLE RANGES OF UNIT COSTS FOR CUT-OFF WALL CONSTRUCTION

| | | Unit Cost | Conditions |
|---|---|---|---|
| Site I. | (1982) | $3/sq. ft. | 50 ft. x 11,000 ft. SB Backfill |
| Site II. | (1981) | 27.00/sq. ft. | 17 ft. x 700 ft. CB Backfill |
| Site III. | (1982) | $5/sq. ft. | 52 x 3900 ft. SB Backfill |
| Site IV. | (unk) | $6/sq. ft. | 30 ft x 300 ft. SB Backfill |

Reference:  Various Industry Sources.

TABLE 7-22.
EXAMPLE UNIT COSTS FOR MONITORING
WELL AND PIEZOMETER INSTALLATION

1.  Monitoring well installation

Boring  and well installation, without casing

| | |
|---|---|
| 2.5" auger | $ 7.23-9.00/foot |
| 4" auger | $11.50-14.40/foot |
| 6" auger | $17.34-21.60/foot |

Casing
| | |
|---|---|
| 2" PVC[1] | $ 3.00/ft |
| 4" PVC[1] | $ 5.00/ft |
| 2" Steel[2] | $ 4.50-5.50/ft |
| 4" Steel[2] | $ 7.00-9.00/ft |

Screen .010" slot, threaded flush joint
| | |
|---|---|
| 2" PVC | $ 6.47/ft |
| 4" PVC | $18.98/ft |
| 2" Steel[2], 5-foot length | $144.80 ea. + 26.10/ added ft |
| 4" Steel[2], 5-foot width | 238.70 ea. + 91.10/ added ft |

Submersible pump, 5 GPM at 180 ft. lift        $750.00/each

2.  Piezometer installation

Boring and installation (same as monitoring walls)
Piezometers, 24" screen, polyethylene        $65.54 each

Reference:  (1)  JRB 1979, (2) Smith 1982.

Other maintenance techniques include grouting, re-excavation of the trench or installation of a synthetic liner along one side of the wall. Costs for maintenance operations are shown in Table 7-23. Due to the technical difficulties in installing a synthetic liner near a slurry trench, unit costs could not be derived for this activity.

### 7.2.4  Materials

Materials essential for slurry cut-off wall construction includes

- Slurry consisting of a mixture of bentonite or suitable replacement and water

- Backfill consisting of a mixture of soil, bentonite and water and/or cement.

In many instances, borrow may be required on-site to serve as a source of fines or to be used in support of other construction activities. Costs are also incurred for disposal of spoils.

Supplies of bentonite can be obtained from a number of sources. Each vender has available a variety of bentonite types suitable for use in slurry cut-off walls. The costs for bentonite will be affected by the location of the site as transportation is a major expense item. Costs for bentonite as well as other materials such as concrete, sand, borrow, rip-rap etc. are also included in Table 7-24.

### 7.2.5  Equipment

Large construction projects like the installation of a slurry wall require varied types of equipment. Contractors usually provide much of this equipment themselves, especially specialty items like a modified backhoe. In some instances, equipment rented locally may prove more cost effective than shipping the same equipment for large distances. To provide a means of comparing equipment costs, the following tables present hourly operating costs and daily and monthly rental rates for earthwork equipment (Table 7-25), concrete and mixing equipment (Table 7-26), and general equipment (Table 7-27). No estimate of equipment requirements for a typical slurry wall are available as each project is site-dependent.

### 7.3  Summary

The development of costs for a slurry wall installation is an involved process and is highly site specific. This section has presented example costs that may be used to generate estimated total costs. Care must be taken in applying these example costs to a specific site. It is especially important

TABLE 7-23.
EXAMPLE UNIT COSTS FOR SLURRY WALL MAINTENANCE ACTIVITIES

| Activity | Unit Cost |
|---|---|
| 1. Grouting - soil stabilization with phenolic resin | $200.00-465.00/C.Y. |
| 2. Re-excavation of soil bentonite backfill with backhoe (Hydraulic crawler 1.5 C.Y. capacity) re-excavation of cement-bentonite backfill | $ 1.96/C.Y. highly variable |
| 3. Capping - buy, load, 2-mile haul, grade and spread Borrow - select fill Borrow - topsoil Compaction | $ 6.97 - 8.35/C.Y. $ 5.70 - 9.05/C.Y. $0.92-$1.31/C.Y. |
| 4. Revegetation - hydroseed | $0.46 S.Y. |

Reference:  Means 1982, Dodge 1982.

TABLE 7-24.
EXAMPLE UNITS COSTS FOR MATERIALS

| | |
|---|---|
| 1. Bentonite[1] Natural, "untreated" sodium bentonite Bulk rail (min 30 tons) Bulk truck (min 30 tons) Bag rail (min 21 tons) Bag truck (min 21 tons) | $42.00/ton $43.00/ton $50.00/ton $51.00/ton |
| 2. Cement, Portland, truckload, U.S. average[2] Cement Portland, less than truckload U.S. average[2] Portland Cement trucked in Bulk, U.S. average[2] | $ 4.62/Bag $ 5.55/Bag $ 3.57/100lbs. |
| 3. Borrow, bank run gravel[2] common borrow crushed stone, 3/4" sand - washed select, structural fill screened loam topsoil | $ 6.00-$6.25/C.Y. $ 4.63/C.Y. $ 6.65-$10.55/C.Y. $ 6.26-$10.15/C.Y. $ 6.87-$8.35/C.Y. $ 8.80-$12.35/C.Y. $ 9.05/C.Y. |

Note:  Does not include transportation costs.

Reference:  (1) Various industry sources:  does not include transportation,
            (2) Means 1982, Dodge 1982.

TABLE 7-25.
EXAMPLE OPERATING AND RENTAL COSTS FOR EARTHWORKING EQUIPMENT

| (Cost Without Operator) | Hourly Operating Cost | Rent Day | Rent Month |
|---|---|---|---|
| 1. Augers for truck/trailer mounting, vertical drilling 4" to 36" diam. 10' travel | $0.56 | $73 | $645 |
| 2. Backhoe diesel hydraulic, crawler mounted | | | |
|     5/8 C.Y. capacity | $6.55 | $450 | $3100 |
|     3/4 C.Y. capacity | $9.40 | $495 | $3500 |
|     1 C.Y. capacity | $12.15 | $735 | $3925 |
|     2 C.Y. capacity | $23.70 | $1075 | $7850 |
|     3 1/2 C.Y. capacity | $43.40 | $1650 | $13,800 |
| 3. Backhoe loader, wheel type | | | |
|     40 to 45 H.P. 5/8 C.Y. | $4.23 | $295 | $1100 |
|     80 H.P, 1 1/4 C.Y. | $7.65 | $400 | $2075 |
| 4. Bucket, clamshell, all purpose | | | |
|     3/8 C.Y. | $0.38 | $30 | $270 |
|     1/2 C.Y. | $0.50 | $35 | $335 |
|     1 C.Y. | $0.69 | $45 | $415 |
|     2 C.Y. | $1.13 | $75 | $680 |
| 5. Bucket, dragline, medium duty | | | |
|     1/2 C.Y. | $0.32 | $21 | $180 |
|     1 C.Y. | $0.44 | $33 | $290 |
|     2 C.Y. | $0.63 | $47 | $425 |
|     3 C.Y. | $0.88 | $73 | $605 |
| 6. Compactor roller, 2 drum | $2.12 | $70 | $735–1500 |
| 7. Vibratory plate, gas, 13" plate, 1000 lb blow | $0.48 | $39 | $330 |
| 8. Grader, self propelled, 25,000 lbs. | $10.60 | $325 | $3000–3450 |
|     40,000 lbs. | $19.15 | $540 | $4200–4850 |
|     55,000 lbs. | $25.00 | $845 | $5100–7550 |
| 9. Roller, towed type, vibratory, 2 ton | $2.05 | $80 | $700 |
|     Sheeps foot self propelled, 140 H.P. | $9.95 | $285 | $2750 |
|     Pneumatic tire, 12 ton | $7.40 | $120 | $1100–1500 |

(continued)

TABLE 7-25. (continued)

| (Cost Without Operator) | Hourly Operating Cost | Rent Day | Rent Month |
|---|---|---|---|
| 10.  Scrapers, towed 7 to 8 C.Y. | $2.45 | $115 | $1025 |
| Self propelled    14 C.Y. | $34.00 | $1050 | $8800 |
| Self loading    22 C.Y. | $46.00 | $1000 | $6675 |
| 11.  Tractor, dozer, crawler    75 H.P. | $6.20 | $375 | $1850 |
| 105 H.P. | 49.50 | $505 | $3525 |
| 200 H.P. | $17.20 | $765 | $6950 |
| 300 H.P. | $24.00 | $1025 | $9000 |
| 410 H.P. | $34.50 | $1250 | $11,750 |
| 700 H.P. | $60.30 | $1950 | $19,250 |
| 12.  Loader crawler 1.5 C.Y.    80 H.P. | $9.35 | $445 | $2550 |
| 1.75 C.Y.  95 H.P. | $11.10 | $475 | $2925 |
| 2.25 C.Y.  130 H.P. | $14.50 | $575 | $3950 |
| 5 C.Y.    275 H.P. | $31.00 | $1100 | $9850 |
| 13.  Truck, dump, tandem, 12 ton payload | $9.85 | $325 | $1625 |
| 3 axle, 16 ton payload | $14.35 | $410 | $2150 |
| Dump trailer only, 15.5C.Y. | $3.47 | $73 | $675 |
| Flatbed, single, 1.5 ton rating | $3.34 | $45 | $415 |
| 3 ton rating | $3.83 | $56 | $505 |
| Off highway, rear dump 25 ton | $21.85 | $4760 | $6600 |
| 35 ton | $30.25 | $1025 | $9300 |

Reference:  Means 1982, Dodge 1982.

TABLE 7-26.
EXAMPLE OPERATING AND RENTAL COSTS FOR CONCRETE AND MIXING EQUIPMENT

|  | Hourly Operating Cost | Rent Day | Rent Month |
|---|---|---|---|
| 1. Bucket, concrete, lightweight 0.5. C.Y. | $0.12 | $17 | $125 |
|     1 C.Y. | $0.12 | $20 | $165 |
| 2. Conveyor, concrete, 10" wide, 26' long | $1.10 | $64 | $505 |
| 3. Core driller, electric, 2.5 H.P. 1" - 8" bit | $0.56 | $39 | $290 |
| 4. Grinder | $.82 | $35 | $305 |
| 5. Mixer, powered, mortar and concrete | $1.92 | $26 | $255 |
| 6. Pump, concrete, truck mounted |  |  |  |
|     4" line, 80' boom | - | $640 |  |
|     5" line, 110' boom | - | $450 - $800 | — $4,750 |
| 7. Mud jack 47 cubic feet/hour | $0.99 | $20 | $180 |
|     225 cubic feet/hour | $2.84 | $125 | $1075 |
| 8. Portable Concrete Batch Plant | - | $1,500 | $15,500 |

Reference:  Means 1982, Dodge 1982.

TABLE 7-27.
EXAMPLE OPERATING AND RENTAL COSTS FOR GENERAL CONSTRUCTION EQUIPMENT

| | Hourly Operating Cost | Rent Day | Rent Month |
|---|---|---|---|
| 1. Air compressor, portable gas 60 cfm | $3.19 | $34 | $290 |
| 160 cfm | $3.87 | $48 | $430–840 |
| diesel engine, rotary screw | | | |
| 250 cfm | $6.20 | $78 | $700 |
| 360 cfm | $9.30 | $100 | $880 |
| 600 cfm | $15.45 | $150 | $1325 |
| 2. Barricade barrels with flashers | – | $.65 | $5.70 |
| 3. Generator, electrical    1.5 kw to 3 kw | $0.48 | $20 | $180 |
| 5 kw | $0.78 | $27 | $280 |
| 10 kw | $1.85 | $45 | $450 |
| diesel   20 kw | $3.11 | $54 | $525 |
| 100 kw | $7.73 | $180 | $1300 |
| 4. Hose, water suction with coupling 20' long | | | |
| 2" diameter | – | $7 | $45 |
| 4" diameter | – | $12 | $100 |
| 8" diameter | – | $34 | $255 |
| discharge hose with coupling, 50' long | | | |
| 2" diameter | – | $7 | $45 |
| 4" diameter | – | $12 | $90 |
| 8" diameter | – | $40 | $180 |
| 5. Light towers, portable with generator | | | |
| 1000 watt | $1.10 | $66 | $540 |
| 2000 watt | $1.63 | $94 | $845 |
| 6. Pumps, centrifugal gas pump, 1.5" diameter | $0.39 | $15 | $125 |
| 2" diameter | $0.95 | $20 | $175 |
| 3"diameter | $0.95 | $25 | $210 |
| 6"diameter | $1.52 | $75 | $655 |
| diaphragm, gas, single, 1.5" diameter | $0.41 | $13 | $115 |
| 3' diameter | $0.86 | $28 | $235 |
| double   4" diameter | $1.05 | $45 | $400 |
| Trash, self-priming  4" diameter | $1.16 | $55 | $520 |
| 7. Trailers, platform, flushdeck, 25 ton | $0.93 | $78 | $715 |
| 40 ton | $1.13 | $115 | $1025 |
| 3 axle, 50 ton | $2.14 | $145 | $1290 |

(continued)

TABLE 7-27. (continued)

| | Hourly Operating Cost | Rent Day | Rent Month |
|---|---|---|---|
| 8. Water tank, engine-driven discharge, 5000 gallon $8.40 | | $225 | $1975 |
| 10,000 gallon $9.95 | | $325 | $2875 |
| 9. Decontamination shower cost $2,400.00 each | | -- | -- |

10. Pipe, for excavation drainage
    (installation not included)

| | | Hourly Operating Cost | Rent Day | Rent Month |
|---|---|---|---|---|
| PVC 13"lengths | 4"diameter | $2.10 – $2.59/linear foot | -- | -- |
| | 8" diameter | $5.20 – 5.56/linear foot | -- | -- |
| | 12" diameter | $10.05 11.98/linear foot | -- | -- |
| | 15" diameter | $15.25/linear foot | -- | -- |
| Vitrified clay | 4" diameter | $3.25 – $4.10/linear foot | -- | -- |
| | 8" diameter | $4.85 – $7.20/linear foot | -- | -- |
| | 10" diameter | $6.99 – $9.45/linear foot | -- | -- |
| | 15" diameter | $19.75/linear foot | — | -- |
| | 24" diameter | 3-6.98/linear foot | -- | -- |

11. Security fence
    galvanized steel, 12 ga., 2" x 4" mesh with

| | Hourly Operating Cost | Rent Day | Rent Month |
|---|---|---|---|
| posts 5' o.c., 5' high | $3.25/linear foot | -- | -- |
| 12' high, prison grade | $32.00/linear foot | -- | -- |
| 12. Snow fence on steel posts 4' high | $3.36/linear foot | -- | -- |
| 13. Storage building, bulk, 180; diameter | $20/s.f. floor | -- | -- |
| 14. Survey, conventional topographic | $165.00-$1150/ acre (total) | -- | -- |
| aerial survey including ground control, 10 acres | $2200 /acre (total) | — | -- |
| topographic 2 ft. contours 10 acres | 200-600/ acre (total) | — | -- |
| 20 acres | 100-2300 acre (total) | — | -- |
| 50 acres | 6700 + 70.00 /acre (total) | — | -- |

15. Winter protection, reinforced plastic or wood $0.63/acres
    tarpaulin over scaffold without scaffold cost $0.29/s.f.

Reference:  Means 1982, Dodge 1982.

that site specific factors such as excavation obstructions or extremely hazardous working conditions be considered in costing. Factors such as these can double or triple the time spent on-site and can drastically affect total costs.

# 8. Evaluation Procedures

Numerous factors must be taken into consideration in evaluating proposed remedial actions, just as numerous factors must be considered in their design and installation. To evaluate slurry walls as remedial measures, an understanding of the currently accepted theories on the nature and function of the materials and techniques involved is essential. The early phases of the remedial planning process will center on characterization of the nature and extent of the environmental problems caused by the site in question. The later phases will focus on solutions to those problems. When a slurry wall is being considered as a remedial measure for a particular site, an evaluation must be made on the type and configuration of slurry wall to be used, as well as the other measures that must be taken to resolve the problems. In addition, the proposed construction techniques, quality control measures, and monitoring and maintenance programs must be evaluated carefully. Finally, the costs, both for the slurry wall and the related remedial measures must be analyzed, keeping in mind the degree of effectiveness or the safety factor gained for each additional cost incurred.

Each slurry wall installed for pollution control will be unique in many respects. It is essentially impossible to foresee every potential contingency of each site, however, the major site planning considerations can be listed. For this reason, this section presents a series of questions indicative of the type of thought process that should accompany the evaluation procedure. The evaluation procedures presented here parallel sections 3 through 7 of this handbook and are illustrated in Figure 8-1.

## 8.1 Site Characteristics

Both the surface and subsurface characteristics of a site influence the design and construction of slurry walls.

213

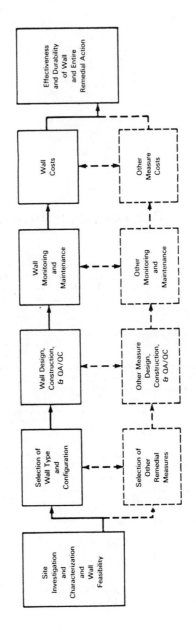

**Figure 8-1.**
**Flow Chart of the Evaluation Procedures**
**for a Pollution Control Slurry Wall**

8.1.1  Surface Characteristics

Important surface factors that can affect slurry wall installations
include:

- Topography
- Soils and vegetation
- Property lines, rights-of-way, and utilities
- Roads and structures.

Questions that pertain to a site's surfacial characteristics include the
following:

1.  Is the topography steep?  If so, CB walls can be used in steeper
    areas.  SB walls can be used where slopes are less than 1 percent, or
    site is graded to near level.

2.  Is sufficient area available for SB backfill mixing?  If not, back-
    fill can be mixed in mechanical batchers or pugmills, or it can be
    mixed in a central mixing area then trucked to the trench.  This will
    increase costs.

3.  Is the terrain too rugged to allow access of heavy construction
    equipment?  If so, access roads may need to be constructed prior to
    trench excavation.  This too will increase costs.

4.  Is there a preponderence of rock outcrops or boulders that will
    interfere with trench excavation?  If so, construction delays should
    be expected and drills and chisels should be available for rock
    fracturing.  In addition, the trench bottom should be cleaned of rock
    fragments prior to backfilling.

5.  Are the soils at the site stable enough to support heavy construction
    equipment?  If not, a work platform of compacted soil can be
    constructed along the proposed line of the trench.

6.  Are the areas to be excavated or used for hydration ponds and
    backfill mixing free of vegetation?  If not, these areas must be
    cleared and the organic matter removed so as not to contaminate the
    backfill.

7.  Have all property lines, rights-of-way and utility lines been
    located?  Have utilities been re-routed as necessary?  Have pipes
    such as sewers been closed off to avoid sudden slurry loss?  These
    procedures should be followed prior to excavation.

8.  If roads are to be crossed during trench excavation, have alternative
    routes been devised?  Has the structural strength of the cut-off in
    the area of the road been designed to withstand traffic loads?  CB

walls, concrete panel, or cast-in-place walls may be used where
structural support is required. Alternatively, a "traffic cap" may
be used. This cap is composed of compacted clay layers interspersed
with layers of geotextiles and topped with gravel.

9. If structures are nearby, what special design considerations were
   taken? Can groundwater levels be lowered? Must nearby foundations
   require reinforcement, such as by grouting or installing tiebacks?
   Are alternative remedial measures more cost effective?

8.1.2  Subsurface Characteristics

The subsurface characteristics of a site that affect slurry trench
cut-off design include:

- Properties of the subsurface strata
- Aquiclude type and location
- Groundwater regime.

Questions pertinent to a site's subsurface characteristics include the
following:

1. Does the material to be excavated from the trench have a favorable
   gradation? If not, suitable borrow areas must be located and
   provisions made for excavating the borrow and for hauling it.
   Ideally, the mixed backfill should contain from 20 to 60 percent
   fines.

2. Are the spoils contaminated? If so, will the contaminants interfere
   substantially with trench wall stability, or can the contaminated
   material be used? It has been suggested that if contaminated spoil
   is equal in quality to other available backfill material, that the
   contaminated soil be used in the backfill to minimize the detrimental effects of later permeation with pollutants.

3. Is all of the backfill contaminated, or are portions still
   uncontaminated? If only portions are contaminated with volatile
   organic chemicals to the point where they are not usable in the
   backfill, these portions can be disposed of and the uncontaminated
   material can be used. These materials can be distinguished by using
   an organic vapor detector to "sniff" each backhoe bucket or clamshell load. The contaminated material can then be dumped into
   trucks for haulage to disposal sites. The uncontaminated material
   can be used in the backfill.

4. Do the spoils contain other materials that may be detrimental to the
   integrity of the backfill? These materials include organic debris,
   construction debris such as pieces of concrete, and certain minerals
   such as caliche and anhydrite.

5. Will the trench be excavated through highly pervious zones such as gravel or coarse sand layers? If so, stipulations may be made in the design criteria to require the availability of lost circulation materials, as listed in Section 5. In addition, care must be taken in maintaining high slurry quality to avoid excessive slurry loss through the pervious layers. If certain fine grained sands become sufficiently lubricated, they may suddenly lose their stability and contribute to trench collapse.

6. How permeable is the aquiclude? Are there fissures, desiccation cracks, or other pervious zones within the aquiclude? If the aquiclude has permeable zones, the base of the backfilled trench can be grouted to decrease the walls permeability.

7. What is the hardness of the aquiclude? If it is extremely hard, removal of the rock for the key-in may be very difficult. Chisels or drills may cause the aquiclude to fracture, thus allowing under-seepage. In this situation, it may be better to scrape clean the surface of the aquiclude and install the backfill directly on it. The weight of the emplaced backfill should be sufficient to ensure wall integrity.

8. How deep is the aquiclude? This determines wall depth and the equipment required.

9. What is the key-in depth required in the design? Normally, it is between 2 and 3 feet in rippable aquicludes.

10. What is the nature of the groundwater contamination? Are the contaminants the same as those in the wastes or are they substantially different? At a minimum, the groundwater should be tested for pH and hardness. If any contaminants are suspected, tests should be run to determine their presence and concentrations. Similar tests should be conducted on all water sources to be used in the slurry.

11. What is the depth, volume, flow rate, and flow direction of the groundwater? These and other data on the groundwater regime should be obtained through site investigations as described in Section 4.

12. If groundwater levels get too high, such as during a flood, what contingency plans are included in the design to protect the trench prior to backfilling? One set of specifications recommended that excavations cease immediately and that the trench be immediately backfilled. After groundwater levels have returned to normal, the hastily backfilled portion of the trench should be re-excavated, then properly mixed and placed.

8.1.3  Waste Characteristics


Before slurry trench cut-offs are selected for use at a given hazardous waste site, the waste must be carefully characterized and the influences of the waste on the cut-off determined.  These interactions are described in Section 4.

Specific questions regarding waste characteristics are given below.

1.  What are the types and volumes of wastes known to be deposited at the site?  Are other wastes suspected at the site?  Certain types of wastes, such as pure xylene have been found to severely damage cut-offs.  If only small portions of these wastes are present, a slurry trench cut-off may still be feasible, however if major concentrations are present, other methods of isolating the site must be seriously considered.

2.  What, if any, are the known waste interactions?  Are dangers, such as explosions or sudden releases of toxic gases, likely?  Safety measures and trench wall siting must take these factors into account.

3.  How long have the wastes been at the site?  This information can contribute to the knowledge of plume characteristics and waste degradation, both of which are necessary for proper wall siting.

4.  How soluble are the wastes and how dense are they?  Immiscible wastes of low density can form lenses on the surface of the groundwater.  If these are present, skimmers can be used to remove them from the groundwater, thus lowering groundwater pumping and treatment requirements, as described in Section 3.  The presence of floating contaminants also affects wall design, in that aquiclude key-in may not be necessary at these sites.  If, however floating contaminants come in contact with the slurry trench cut-off, they are likely to be at high concentrations and thus are likely to adversely affect the wall.  Waste/wall interactions are described in Section 4.  Similar adverse effects may occur if extremely dense wastes are present.  Under these circumstances, aquiclude key-in may be of extreme importance.


8.2  Slurry Wall Applications


A critical evaluation of the type of slurry wall and how it is applied is very important.  Because slurry walls are rarely used alone, this evaluation must also focus on the other remedial measures to be used.

## 8.2.1  Wall Configuration and Type

All of the factors discussed above must be taken into account when selecting the location, configuration, and type of cut-off wall. Questions regarding wall configuration are listed below.

1.  Is the wall configuration consistent with what is known about the waste types and the groundwater regime at the site? As described in Section 3, walls can be placed downgradient if very limited groundwater flow is present; and upgradient if the groundwater can be effectively diverted from the site. Circumferential walls are used where maximum containment is required. In any case, the wall must be protected from contact with the wastes that cause increases in wall permeability.

2.  Are surface water diversions (i.e., dikes, ditches, berms, terraces, etc.) planned to protect the site from surface runoff? These features are particularly critical in humid areas and areas with sudden, extreme rainfall events.

3.  Where extremely low permeability is required, are SB walls with a high percentage of fines specified? Are the fines plastic or non-plastic? Research has shown that maximum cut-off effectiveness occurs in walls having 20 to 50 percent plastic fines and 1 to 2 percent bentonite, with 25 to 35 percent water.

4.  Where structural strength is required, is the wall designed to take the stresses applied? SB walls are more flexible and lower in strength than CB walls. Cast-in-place and panel walls have the highest strength, however they also have the highest permeability and cost.

5.  Are the site factors favorable for the use of SB walls? Site factors, described previously, include availability of suitable backfill and backfill mixing area, suitable terrain, and low strength requirements.

## 8.2.2  Associated Remedial Measures

Cut-offs are seldom used alone in controlling hazardous waste sites. The types of remedial measures used with cut-offs include:

* Surface Sealing
* Groundwater Pumping and Subsurface Collection
* Surface collection and runoff diversion
* Measures used to increase wall efficiency.

Questions useful in evaluating associated remedial measures are listed below.

1. Is surface sealing of the site planned? This reduces the influence of precipitation on the volume of groundwater at the site and thus can reduce the hydraulic pressure on the interior of the wall.

2. If well points or extraction wells are to be installed, are they close enough to the wall to influence wall stability? This is most important during trench excavation. If drawdown cones intersect the wall, the trench wall stability may suffer.

3. Is collection and diversion of surface water planned? If so, this water must not be allowed to erode, soften, or otherwise degrade the clay cap placed over the completed trench.

4. Is the use of other measures, such as grouting, sheet piling, or lining the trench with impervious membranes planned? If so, the location, construction considerations, and materials used must be compatible with the slurry, the backfill, and the wastes at the site.

8.3  Construction Techniques and QA/QC Requirements

The most carefully designed remedial action plan will not function properly if poor construction or QA/QC techniques are used. These factors must be carefully considered to ensure efficient wall installation. Questions regarding these criteria are given below.

1. Are the criteria used for selection of the contractor relevant and stringent enough?

2. Are the specifications overly stringent? Experience has shown that performance type specifications allow greater opportunity for innovation on the part of contractors. Because slurry trench construction is an evolving technique, there are many facets of the technique that are likely to be improved as greater field experience is obtained. For this reason, some leeway in the specifications is reasonable and may even be beneficial.

3. Do the specifications cover all the important design criteria, such as aquiclude selection and key-in, backfill composition and slurry viscosity? These specifications are described in Section 5. Theories explaining the importance of these factors are discussed in Section 2.

4. Are adequate QA/QC and documenation requirements included? Typical requirements are listed in Section 5.

5.  Are adequate safety precautions taken during cut-off construction? These are particularly important in a contaminated environment, especially during excavation.

## 8.4  Monitoring and Maintenance

Despite the care taken in design and construction, the overall performance of a slurry wall, as well as the other remedial measures, must be established through a monitoring program. The nature, extent, and frequency of the monitoring must be determined for each individual site. Although slurry walls require little maintenance, certain measures must be taken to ensure short and long-term effectiveness. Section 6 of this handbook presents these subjects in detail.

### 8.4.1  Monitoring

The monitoring program must provide answers to several geotechnical and geochemical performance questions. Some important geotechnical questions include the following.

1.  Does the monitoring data indicate that the wall is continuous and of the required permeability?

2.  Is the wall stable? If not what are the causes, impacts, and remedies?

3.  Has the groundwater regime been altered in the intended manner? If not, is this due to a poorly functioning cut-off, or an incomplete initial characterization of groundwater flow?

Given careful design and construction practices, there should be few geotechnical problems with a slurry wall installation. Nonetheless, these performance characteristics must be verified.

Because the chemistry and geochemistry of a site have a significant influence on successful slurry wall installation, questions similar to the following should be asked.

1.  Have the slurry wall and related measures halted or reduced to an acceptable level, the spread of contamination by groundwater and surface waters?

2.  Has leachate/wall contact been prevented? If not, is there evidence of chemical destruction of the wall?

The answering of such questions will help evaluate cut-off effectiveness and durability, and may alter the character of future site monitoring for that site.

### 8.4.2  Maintenance

Maintenance of a slurry wall primarily involves protecting the upper portion from damage.  Pertinent questions include:

1.  Is the wall protected from cracking by desiccation?

2.  Is the wall protected from breach by root penetration?

3.  Is the wall protected from traffic loading?

All of these are answered by investigating the integrity and maintenance of the capping method used and the condition of the vegetation or other material used to protect the cap.

### 8.5  Costs

Costs are a major concern with any project.  The cost of a completed slurry wall is dependent on a number of factors including the square footage of the wall, the characteristics of the site, and the materials used for backfill.  Section 7 presents costs for slurry walls and associated remedial measures.  Some relevant questions on costs should include the following.

1.  Is the total cost per square foot of the proposed slurry wall within the ranges for depth and excavation ease given in Table 7-19?

2.  If not, are there site characteristics which explain a higher or lower unit cost?

The quality of the finished product is often related to the cost, and it is important to understand the compromises involved between cost and quality. Although the cost for a proposed wall will likely be submitted as a fixed price lump sum, it is important to have any discrepancy between anticipated and bid cost adequately explained.  The possibility of an inferior product exists, particularly if a site has not been well-characterized.

The nature and extent of the other remedial measures needed to address a particular site's problems are difficult to generalize simply because they are so site specific.  Again, a compromise must be struck between the funds expended and the degree of pollution control achieved.  Some basic questions on the related measures used with slurry walls include the following.

1.  If costs are critical, where can costs be cut while reducing the effectiveness the least?

2.  If additional funds are available, where can they be best expended to increase the effectiveness or longevity of the remedial program?

In the majority of cases, the bids for a slurry wall installation will be quite close to one another. If a wide discrepancy is found, it should be explained. It should be kept in mind that greater costs for a wall do not necessarily indicate greater effectiveness of the final cut-off.

This section has provided a summary of the many aspects of slurry walls that must be examined during evaluation of slurry wall design and installation. These factors should be carefully considered to ensure that the proposed installation will perform its intended purpose over its design life in a cost-effective manner.

# Measuring Unit Conversion Table

| S.I. UNITS | LENGTH | METRIC |
|---|---|---|
| inch (in) | x 2.54 | = centimeter (cm) |
| foot (ft) | x 0.3048 | = meter (m) |
| mile (mi) | x 1.609 | = kilometer (km) |

| | VOLUME | |
|---|---|---|
| U.S. gallon (gal) | x 0.0038 | = cubic meter ($m^3$) |
| cubic feet ($ft^3$) | x 0.0283 | = cubic meter |
| acre-foot (ac.ft) | x 123.53 | = cubic meter |

| | AREA | |
|---|---|---|
| square inch ($in^2$) | x 6.452 | = square centimeter ($cm^2$) |
| square foot ($ft^2$) | x 0.09 | = square meter ($m^2$) |
| acre (ac) | x 0.4047 | = hectare (ha) |

| | MASS | |
|---|---|---|
| ounce (oz) | X 28 | = gram (g) |
| pound (lb) | x 0.45 | = kilogram (kg) |
| short ton | x 0.9 | = metric ton (t) |

| | DENSITY | |
|---|---|---|
| Pounds per cubic foot (pcf) | x 0.016 | = grams per cubic centimeter ($g/cm^3$) |

| | HYDRAULIC CONDUCTIVITY | |
|---|---|---|
| gallons per day per square foot ($gpd/ft^2$) | x $4.72 \times 10^{-5}$ | = centimeters per second (cm/sec) |
| Darcy | x $8.58 \times 10^{-4}$ | = centimeters per second |

# Glossary

Adsorption complex:  The adsorption complex is the group of substrates in soil
capable of attracting and exchanging other materials.  Colloidal
particles account for most adsorption in soils.

Apparent viscosity:  The apparent viscosity of a fluid is the viscosity it
exhibits under a given rate of shear and is equal to shear stress/rate of
shear.  This quantity can be measured using a Fann viscometer.

Aquiclude:  An aquiclude is a body of low permeability rock or other earth
material that does not transmit sufficient groundwater to supply a well
or a spring.

Aquifer:  An aquifer is a formation, group of formations, or part of a
formation that contains sufficient saturated permeable material to yield
significant quantities of water to wells and springs.

Attapulgite:  Attapulgite is a chain-lattice clay mineral having a distinctive
rod-like shape.  Syn: Palygorskite.

Backfill:  Backfill is earth or other materials used to replace material
removed during construction or mining operations.  For slurry walls, the
backfill is soil-bentonite, cement-bentonite, or concrete.

Bedrock:  Bedrock is the more or less solid, undisturbed rock in place either
at the surface or beneath superficial deposits of gravel, sand, or soil.

Bentonite:  Bentonite is a light-colored rock consisting largely of colloidal
silica and composed mostly of crystalline clay minerals.  It is produced
by the weathering of glassy igneous materials, usually a tuff or volcanic
ash.  When wet, it is soft and plastic.

Bleed water:  Bleed water is the water that separates from a cement or
concrete mixture before and during hardening.

Blowout gradient:  Blowout gradient refers to the hydraulic gradient at which
a slurry will be forced out of soil or other voids.

Borrow:  Borrow is soil material taken from a distant source to be used as
fill material on-site.

Cation exchange capacity:  Cation exchange capacity refers to the sum total or
exchangable cations that a soil can adsorb.

Confined groundwater:  Confined groundwater is under pressure significantly greater than atmospheric, and its upper limit is the bottom of a bed of distinctly lower hydraulic conductivity than the aquifer.

Confining bed:  A confining bed is a body of less permeable material overlying or underlying an aquifer.  "Aquitard" is a commonly used synonym.  The terms "aquiclude" and "aquifuge" are generally considered obsolete.  Confining beds have a high range of hydraulic conductivities and a confining bed of one area may have a hydraulic conductivity greater than an aquifer of another area.

Capillary fringe:  The capillary fringe is the zone immediately above the water table in which all or some of the interstices are filled with water that is under less than atmospheric pressure and that is continuous with the water below the water table.  The thickness of the capillary fringe is greater in fine-grained material than in coarse-grained material.  It ranges in thickness from a fraction of an inch to tens of feet.

Dewatering:  Dewatering is the removal of groundwater from an area by means of pumps or drains.

Discharge zone:  Discharge zone is a zone in which subsurface water, including water from both the saturated and unsaturated zones, is discharged to the land surface or to the atmosphere.

Dispersion:  Dispersion is the breaking up of compound particles into individual component particles.  It also refers to the distribution and suspension of fine particles in or throughout a dispersing medium, such as water.

Effective porosity:  Effective porosity refers to the amount of interconnected pore space available for transmitting water.

Fann viscometer:  A Fann viscometer is a device used to measure the viscosity of a slurry.  In this device the slurry is sheared between two rotating cylinders.  From the results of this test the plastic and apparent viscosities can be calculated.

Filter Cake:  Filter cake refers to the thin, very low permeability layer formed on porous media by slurry filtration. As the slurry is forced into the pores by the hydraulic head, the slurry particles plug the pores and build up a "cake".

Flocculation:  Flocculation is the aggregation of soils or colloids into small lumps called flocs, which settle from a suspension.

Flow net:  A flow net is a set of intersecting equipotential lines and flow lines representing two-dimensional steady-state flow through porous media.

Gel strength:  Gel strength is the stress required to break up a gel structure formed by thixotropic build up under static conditions.

Grout:  Grout is a fluid material that is pressure injected into soil, rock, or concrete to seal openings and to lower permeability and/or provide additional structural strength.  There are four major types of grouting materials:  chemical (silicates and polymers), cement, clay, and bituminous.

Hanging wall:  A hanging slurry wall is one that is completed several feet into the lowest water table level but is not tied into a low permeability zone.  These are used mostly to control floating contaminants.

Head (Hydraulic):  The height above a datum (sea level) to which a column of fluid can be supported by the static pressure at that point.

Hydraulic conductivity:  Hydraulic conductivity K, replaces the term "coefficient of permeability" and is a volume of water that will move in unit time under a unit hydraulic gradient through a unit area measured at right angles to the direction of flow.  Dimensions are $LT^{-1}$ with common units being centimeters per second.

Hydraulic gradient:  Hydraulic gradient is the change in head per unit of distance in the direction of maximum rate of decrease in head.

Keyed-in wall:  A keyed-in slurry wall is one which has been connected along its base to a low permeability zone such as a clay layer or hard bedrock.

Leachate:  Leachate is contaminated liquid discharge from a waste disposal site to either surface or subsurface receptors.  It is created by fluid percolation through and from waste materials.  The contaminated water then moves either into the ground below or as surface runoff or seepage.

Lithologic unit:  A lithologic unit is a stratigraphic unit having a substantial degree of lithologic homogeneity consisting of a body of strata that is unified with respect to adjacent strata by possessing certain objective physical features observable in the field or subsurface or consisting dominantly of a certain rock type or combination of rock types and considered completely independent of time.

Marsh funnel:  A Marsh funnel is a device used to measure the viscosity of a slurry.  The Marsh viscosity, in seconds, equals the time it takes 1 quart (946 cm$^3$) of slurry to pass through the funnel.

Montmorillonite:  Montmorillonite refers to a group of expanding-lattice clay minerals characterized by high cation exchange capacity and high swelling and shrinking.

Performance:  Used herein to describe a slurry wall's ability to function at or above design specifications.

Permeability:  Intrinsic permeability, k, is a property of the porous medium and has dimensions of LT.  It is a measure of the resistance to fluid flow through the medium and is often used to mean the same thing as hydraulic conductivity.

Permeameter:  A permeameter is an apparatus used in the laboratory to measure a material's permeability or hydraulic conductivity.

Piping:  Piping occurs as a result of seepage erosion in which flowing water has enough force to erode or carry away soil particles, creating localized channels and/or cavities in the soil.

Plasticity:  Plasticity is the quality of having the capacity to be molded or altered and the ability to retain a shape attained by pressure deformation.

Plastic viscosity:  Plastic viscosity is a measure of the resistance to flow caused by mechanical friction.  It is measured on a Fann viscometer and is dependent on solids concentration, size and shape of solids, and the amount of shearing within the liquid phase.

Porosity:  Porosity of a rock or soil is its property of containing interstices and is the ratio of the volume of interstices to the total volume.  It is expressed as a decimal, fraction, or percentage.  Total porosity is comprised of primary and secondary porosity.  Porosity is controlled by shape, sorting and packing arrangements of grains and is independent of grain size.

Potentiometric surface:  Potentiometric surface is an imaginary surface representing the static head of groundwater and defined by the level to which water will rise in a well.  The water table is a particular potentiometric surface.

Pozzolana:  Finely divided siliceous or siliceous and aluminous materials used to make strong, slow-hardening cements.  Pozzolanic cements are resistant to saline and acidic solutions.

Recharge zone:  A recharge zone is a zone in which water is absorbed and added to the zone of saturation, either directly into a formation, or indirectly by way of another formation.

Rheological blocking:  Rheological blocking refers to the inhibition of slurry flow into a soil or rock body due to the onset of gelation of the slurry in the large pores.

Saprolite:  Saprolite is a general term for earth materials formed by the disintegration and decomposition of rock in place.  "Saprolitic zone" refers to that zone where saprolite is present.

Saturation:  Water saturation is the percentage ratio of the volume of water to the volume of void space.

Saturated zone:  The saturated zone is that part of the water-bearing material in which all voids are filled with water under pressure greater than atmospheric.

Shear strength:  Shear strength is the maximum internal resistance of a
    substance to movement of its particles due to intergranular friction and
    cohesion.

Slump:  Slump refers to the vertical distance a cone-shaped mass of concrete
    or other plastic material will settle.  It is measured using a slump cone
    as specified in ASTM Book of Standards, Part 14.

Slurry:  Slurry refers both to colloidal suspensions of bentonite in water as
    well as mixtures of Portland cement and water.

Soil gradation:  Soil gradation refers to the frequency distribution of the
    various sized grains that constitute a particular soil.

Specific storage:  Specific storage, $S_s$, is defined as the volume of water
    that a unit volume of aquifer releases from storage because of expansion
    of the water and compression of the grains under a unit decline in
    average head within the unit volume.  For an unconfined aquifer, for
    all practical purposes, it has the same value as specific yield.
    Note the dimensions are $L^{-1}$.  It is a property of both the medium
    and the fluid.

Specific retention:  Specific retention of a rock is the ratio of the volume
    of water a saturated rock will retain against the pull of gravity to its
    own volume.

Specific yield:  Specific yield is the water yielded by gravity drainage as
    occurs when the water table declines.  It is the ratio of the volume of
    water yielded by gravity to the volume of rock.  Specific yield is equal
    to porosity minus specific retention.

Storage coefficient:  The storage coefficient, $S$, or storativity is defined as
    the volume of water an aquifer releases from or takes into storage per
    unit surface area of aquifer per unit change in the component of head
    normal to that surface.  Note it is dimensionless.

Structural discontinuity: Structural discontinuity refers to a sudden or rapid
    change in one or more of the physical properties of a rock mass.

Thixotropy:  Thixotropy is the property of various gels to become fluid when
    disturbed, and, later, to regain strength at constant water content.

Transmissivity:  Transmissivity, $T$, is defined as the rate of flow of water
    through a vertical strip of aquifer one unit wide extending the full
    saturated thickness of the aquifer under a unit hydraulic gradient.

Unconfined groundwater:  Unconfined groundwater is water in an aquifer that
    has a water table.

Underseepage:  Underseepage is the passage of water beneath a slurry wall as a
    result of an inadequate wall aquiclude key-in.

Unsaturated zone:  The unsaturated zone is the zone between the land surface and the water table.  It includes the capillary fringe.  Characteristically this zone contains liquid water under less than atmospheric pressure, with water vapor and other gases generally at atmospheric pressure.

Viscosity:  Viscosity refers to the ability of a fluid to resist shearing or flow due to counteracting, internal forces.

Weathering:  Weathering refers to the various chemical and mechanical processes acting at or near the earth's surface that bring about the disintegration, decomposition, and comminution of rocks.

Waste Plume:  Waste plume refers to a body of water, either surface or groundwater, that is contaminated by toxic or otherwise hazardous substances and moves as a coherent mass.

Water table:  The water table is an imaginary surface in an unconfined water body at which the water pressure is atmospheric.  It is essentially the top of the saturated zone.

# References

Alther, G. R.  The Role of Bentonite in Soil Sealing Applications.
International Minerals and Chemical Corporation, Des Plaines, Illinois.
[no date]

Alther, G. R.  IMC Corporation.  Personal Communication with C. E. Spooner of
JRB Associates.  April 1983.

ASCE.  American Society of Civil Engineers.  Subsurface Investigation for
Design and Construction of Foundations of Buildings.  ASCE No. 56.
Headquarters of the Society, NY, NY.  1976.

Anderson, D., and K. W. Brown.  Organic Leachate Effects on the Permeability
of Clay Liners, in Land Disposal of Hazardous Waste.  Publication No.
EPA-600/9-81-002.  U.S. Environmental Protection Agency, Municipal
Environmental Research Laboratory, Cincinnati, Ohio, 1981.

API.  American Petroleum Institute.  API Recommended Practice:  Standard
Procedure for Testing Drilling Fluids.  API RP13B.  American Petroleum
Institute, Dallas, Texas, 1982.

API.  American Petroleum Institute.  API Specification for Oil Well Drilling
Fluid Materials.  API Spec. 13A American Petroleum Institute, Dallas,
Texas, 1981.

Ash, J.L., B.E. Russel and R.R. Ronmmel.  Improved Subsurface Investigation
for Highway Tunnel Design and Construction, Vol. 1.  U.S. Department of
Transportation, Federal Highway Administration, Washington, D.C., 1974.

Ayres, J.  GZA Corp.  Personal Communication with G. E. Hunt of JRB
Associates.  September 3, 1982.

Baver, L.D., W.H. Gardner and W.R. Gardner.  Soil Physics.  John Wiley & Sons,
Inc., New York, 1972.

Bjerrum, L., J. K. T. L. Nash, R. M. Kennard, and R. E. Gibson.  Hydraulic
Fracturing in Field Permeability Testing, Geotechnique, Vol. 22, No. 2,
pp. 319-332, 1972.

Boyes, R. G. H.  Structural and Cut-off Diaphragm Walls.  Applied Science
Publishers Ltd., London, England.  1975.

Brady, N.C.  The Nature and Properties of Soils.  Macmillan Publishing Co.,
Inc., New York, 1974.

Brown, K. W., and D. Anderson. Effect of Organic Chemicals on Clay Liner Permeability. A Review of the Literature. In: Disposal of Hazardous Waste. Proceedings of the Sixth Annual Research Symposium. EPA 600/9-80-010. USEPA, Municipal Environmental Research Laboratory, Cincinnati, Ohio. 1980.

Case International Company. 1982. Case Slurry Wall Notebook, Manufacturers Data. Case Intn'l. Co., Houston, Texas.

Cavalli, N. J. ICOS Corporation of America. Personal Communication with P. A. Spooner of JRB Associates. December 1982.

Coneybear, R. Engineered Construction International, Inc. Personal Communication with C. E. Spooner of JRB Associates. September 1982.

D'Appolonia, E. Consulting Engineers Company. Results of Long Term Permeability Testing Rocky Mountain Arsenal. U.S. Army Waterways Experiment Station, Vicksburg, Mississippi. 1979. Contract No. DACW 39-78-M-3705.

D'Appolonia, D. J. Slurry Trench Cut-off Walls for Hazardous Waste Isolation. Technical Paper. Engineered Construction International, Inc., Pittsburgh, Pennsylvania. April 1980a.

D'Appolonia, D. J., J. and C. Ryan. Soil-Bentonite Slurry Trench Cut-off Walls. Engineered Construction International, Inc. Presented at the Geotechnical Exhibition and Technical Conference, Chicago, Illinois, March 26, 1979.

D'Appolonia, D. J. Soil-Bentonite Slurry Trench Cutoffs. J. Geot. Eng. Dir. ASCE, 106(4):399-417, 1980b.

D'Appolonia, D. J. Engineered Construction International, Inc. Personal Communication with P. A. Spooner of JRB Associates. June 23, 1982.

Dodge Manual. 1982. Building Construction Pricing and Scheduling. Edition No. 17, McGraw-Hill Cost Information Systems, Princeton, NJ, 302 pp.

Dunnicliff, J. Performance of Slurry Wall Construction. In: Proceedings of a Symposium on Design and Construction of Slurry Walls as Part of Permanent Structures. 1980.

Federal Bentonite. 1981. Suggested Standard Guideline. Technical Specifications; Soil/Bentonite Slurry Trench Cut-off Wall. Federal Bentonite, Montgomery, Illinois.

Freeze, R. A. and John A. Cherry. Groundwater. Prentice-Hall, Inc. Englewood Cliffs, N.J. 1979. 604 pp.

Geo-Con, Inc. Typical Specifications for CB Walls. January 1979.

Grim, R.E. Clay Mineralogy. McGraw-Hill Book Company, Inc., New York, 1968.

Grim, R. E., and N. Guven. Bentonites: Geology Mineralogy, Properties and Uses. Developments in Sedimentology 24. Elsevier Scientific Publishing Company, Amsterdam, 1978.

Guertin, J. D., and W. H. McTigue. Groundwater Control Systems for Urban Tunneling. Vol. 1. U.S. Department of Transportation, Federal Highway Administration, Washington, D.C., 1982a.

Guertin, J. D., and W. H. McTigue. Preventing Groundwater into Completed Transportation Tunnels, and Recommended Practice. Vol. 2. U.S. Department of Transportation, Federal Highway Administration, Washington, D.C., 1982b.

Guertin, J. D., and W. H. McTigue. Groundwater Control in Tunneling. Vol. 3. U.S. Department of Transportation, Federal Highway Administration, Washington, D.C., 1982c.

Hirschfeld, R.C. Soil Mechanics. In the Encyclopedia of Soil Science, Part I, Physics, Chemistry, Biology, Fertility, and Technology, pp 462-469, Edited by R. W. Fairbridge and C. W. Finkl Jr. 1979. Dowden, Hutchinson, and Ross Inc., Stroudsburg, PA., 646 pp.

Hughes, J. Use of Bentonite as a Soil Sealant for Leachage Control in Sanitary Landfills. American Colloid Company, Skokie, Illinois, 1975.

Hutchinson, M. T., G. P. Daw, P. G. Sholton, and A. N. James. 1975. The Properties of Bentonite Slurries Used in Diaphgragm Walling and Their Control. Paper in Diaphragm Walls and Anchorages. Institute of Civil Engineers, London. 1975. pp. 33-39. These are proceedings of the conference: (date of conference Sept. 18-20, 1974, London).

IMC, Imcore Division, International Minerals & Chemical Corporation. Bentonite product literature, specification and engineering reports: Mundelein, Illinois [no date].

Jefferis, S. A. Discussion of Soil-Bentonite Slurry Trench Cutoffs. J. Geotech. Eng. Div. 107:1581-1583, 1981a.

Jefferis, S. A. Bentonite - Cement Slurries for Hydraulic Cut Offs. In: Proceedings of the Tenth International Conference on Soil Mechanics and Foundation Engineering, Stockholm June 15-19, 1981b. A. A. Balkema, Rotterdam. pp. 435-440.

Jessup, W.E., Jr. and W.E. Jessup. Law and Specifications for Engineers and Scientists. Prentice-Hall, Inc., Englewood Cliffs, NJ, 1963.

Jones, J. C. Design and Safety of Small Earth Dams. In: Proceedings of the 26th Annual Soil Mechanics and Foundation Engineering Conference, Minneapolis, Minnesota. February 1978.

JRB Associates. Assessment of Alternatives for Upgrading Navy Solid Waste Disposal Sites. Final Report. JRB Contract No. 2-800-04-187-00. U.S. Navy Civil Engineering Laboratory, Port Hueneme, California, 1979. pp. 1-1--4-92.

Lager, D. C. Case International Co. Personal Communication with P. A. Spooner of JRB Associates. September 13, 1982.

La Russo, R. S. Wanapum Development-Slurry Trench and Grouted Cut-off. In: Grouts and Drilling Muds in Engineering Practice. William Clowes and Sons, Ltd., London, England, 1963. pp. 196-201.

Low, P. F. Viscosity of Interlayer Water in Montmorillonite. Soil. Sci. Soc. Amer. J. 40:500-504, 1976.

Matrecon, Inc. Lining of Waste Impoundment and Disposal Facilities. Publication No. SW-870. U.S. Environmental Protection Agency, Municipal Environmental Research Laboratory, Cincinnati, Ohio, 1980. 385 pp.

McCarthy, D. F. Essentials of Soil Mechanics and Foundations. Reston Publishing Company, Inc., Reston, Virginia. 1977. 505 pp.

McNeal, B. L. Prediction of the Effect of Mixed-salt Solutions on Soil Hydraulic Conductivity. Soil Sci. Soc. Amer. Proc. 32:190-193, 1968.

Means, R. S. Building Construction Cost Data. 1982. Robert Snow Means Company, Inc. Kingston, MA. 1981.

Meier, J. G., and W. A. Rattberg. Report on Cement-Bentonite Slurry Trench Cutoff Wall: Tilden Tailings Projects. In: Tailing Disposal Today. In: Proceedings of the Second International Tailing Symposium, Denver, Colorado, May 1978.

Miller, E. A., and G. S. Salzman. Value Engineering Saves Dam Project. Civ. Eng. 1980.

Miller, S. P. Geotechnical Containment Alternatives for Industrial Waste Basin F, Rocky Mountain Arsenal. Denver, Colorado; A Quantitative Evaluation. U.S. Army Engineer Waterways Experiment Station, Vicksburg, Miss. Technical Report GL-79-23. September 1979.

Millet, R. A., and J. Y. Perez. Current USA Practice: Slurry Wall Specifications. J. Geot. Eng. Div. 107(8):1041-1056, 1981.

Mitchell, J. K. Fundamentals of Soil Behavior. 1976. John Wiley & Sons, Inc. New York. 422 pp.

Moore, C. A. Design Criteria for Gas Migration Control Devices. In: Proceedings on Management of Gas and Leachate in Landfills, Cincinnati, OH. September 1977.

Mustafa, M. A. Dispersion Phenomena. In the Encyclopedia of Soil Science Part I, Physics, Chemistry, Biology, Fertility and Technology. pp. 124-127. Edited by R.W. Fairbridge and C.W. Finkl Jr. 1979. Dowden, Hutchinson, and Ross Inc. Stroudsburg, PA., 646 pp.

Namy, D. L.   Site Conditions Specific to Slurry Wall Construction.   Soletanche
    and Radio, Inc.   In:   Slurry Walls for Underground Transportation
    Facilities.   Proceedings of a Symposium at Cambridge, Massachusetts,
    August 1979.   Final Report.   U.S. Department of Transportation, Federal
    Highway Administration.   March 1980.

Nash, K. L. and G. K. Jones.   The Support of Trenches Using Fluid Mud.   In:
    Grouts and Drilling Muds in Engineering Practice.   William Clowes and
    Sons, London, England.   1963.   pp. 177-180.

Nash, K. L.   Stability of Trenches Filled with Fluids.   J. Const. Div.
    100(4):533-542, 1974.

Nash, J. K. T. L.   Slurry Trench Walls, Pile Walls, Trench Bracing.   In:
    Sixth European Conference on Soil Mechanics and Foundation Engineering,
    Vienna, Austria.   March 1976.   pp. 27-32.

NCE.   National Construction Estimator.   Edited by R. Saviel, ASPE.   Craftsman
    Book Company.   Solana Beach, CA   1981.   285 pp.

OCE.   Office of the Chief of Engineers.   Laboratory Soil Testing.   EM
    1110-2-1906.   U.S. Department of the Army, Office of the Chief of
    Engineers, Washington, D.C.   1970.

Oil Recovery Systems, Inc.   Product literature on equipment for recovering
    petroleum products and hydrocarbons from water.   Needham, MA.   1982.

Regan, T. J., Jr.   Critical Assessment of Slurry Wall Construction in the
    United States.   In:   Slurry Walls for Underground Transportation
    Facilities.   Proceedings of a Symposium at Cambridge, Massachusetts.
    August 1979.   Department of Transportation, Federal Highway
    Administration.   Final Report.   March 1980.

Ressi di Cervia, A. L.   Economic Considerations in Slurry Wall Applications.
    From:   Slurry Walls for Underground Transportation Facilities
    Proceedings.   U.S. Department of Transportation, FHA.   1979.

Rolfe, P. F., and L. A. G. Aylmore.   Water and Salt Flow Through Compacted
    Clays.   I. Permability of Compacted Illite and Montmorillonite.   Soil
    Sci. Soc. Am. J.   41:489-495, 1977.

Rovers, F. A., J. J. Tremblay and H. Mooij.   Procedures for Landfill Gas
    Monitoring and Control.   From:   Proceedings of an International Seminar,
    Canada, 1977.

Rowell, D. L., D. Payne, and N. Ahmad.   The Effect of the Concentration and
    Movement of Solutions on the Swelling, Dispersion, and Movement of Clay
    in Saline and Alkali Soils.   J. Soil Sci.   20(1):176-188, 1969.

Ryan, C. R.   Slurry Cut-Off Walls:   Design and Construction.   Geo-Con, Inc.,
    Pittsburgh, PA.   1976.

Ryan, C. R.  Slurry Cut-off Walls:  Design Parameters and Final Properties.
    Presented at:  Technical Course on Slurry Wall Construction, Design,
    Techniques, and Procedures, Miami, Florida.  February - March, 1977.

Ryan, C. R.  Slurry Trench Cut-offs to Halt Flow of Oil-polluted Groundwater.
    Presented at:  American Society of Mechanical Engineers, Energy and
    Technology Conference and Exhibition, New Orleans, Louisiana.  February
    1980a.

Ryan, C. R.  Slurry Cut-off Walls.  Methods and Applications.  Presented at:
    Geo-Tec. 1980, Chicago, Illinois.  March 18, 1980b.

SCS Engineers.  Memorandum on bentonite slurry walls as remedial actions at
    hazardous waste land disposal facilities.  Covington, Kentucky.  December
    1981.

Shainberg, I., and A. Caiserman.  Studies on Na/Ca Montmorillonite Systems.
    The Hydraulic Conductivity.  Soil Sci.  3(3):276-281, 1971.

Shallard, S. G.  Engineered Construction International, Inc.  Personal
    Communication with P. A. Spooner of JRB Associates.  January 1983.

Smith, D.  Soil Consultants, Inc.  Personal Communication with E. F. Tokarski
    of JRB Associates.  July 1982.

Soletanche Corp. Product Literature.  Use of Slurry Trench Cut-off Walls in
    Construction and Repair of Earth Dams.  Soletanche, 6 Rue de Watford B.P.
    511, 92005 Nanterre Cedex, France.  1977.

Sommerer, S., and J. F, Kitchens.  Engineering and Development Support of
    General Decon Technology for the DARCOM Installation Restoration Program.
    Task 1.  Literature  Review on Groundwater Containment and Diversion
    Barriers.  Draft.  U.S. Amry Hazardous Materials Agency, Aberdeen Proving
    Ground, Maryland.  1980.

Tamaro, G.  Slurry Wall Construction, Construction Procedures and Problems.
    In:  Slurry Walls for Underground Transportation Facilities.  Proceedings
    of a Symposium at Cambridge, Massacuhsetts.  Final Report.  U.S.
    Department of Transportation, Federal Highway Administration.  March
    1980.

Tavenas, F. A., G. Blanchette, S. Leroueil, M. Roy, and P. LaRochelle.
    Difficulties in the In Situ Determination of $K_o$ in Soft Sensitive Clays.
    Proceedings of a Specialty Conference on In Situ Measurement of Soil
    Properties, Vol I., North Carolina State University, Raleigh, NC., June
    1-4, 1975, pp 450-476.

Telling, R. M., B. K, Menzies, and H. E. Simmons.  Cut-off Efficiency
    Performance and Design.  Ground Eng.  1978. pp. 30-43.

US EPA.  NEIC Manual for Groundwater/Subsurface Investigations at Hazardous
    Waste Sites.  EPA-330/9-81-002.

US EPA. Environmental Protection Agency. Office of Research and Development. Handbook for Remedial Action at Waste Disposal Sites. EPA-625/6-82-006. U.S. Environmental Protection Agency, Cincinnati, OH. 1982. 497 pp.

US EPA. Costs of Remedial Actions at Uncontrolled Hazardous Waste Sites, EPA Contract No. 68-03-3028, MERL, SHWRD, Cincinnati, OH. 1983.

U.S. Army Corps of Engineers. Excerpt from Aliceville and Columbus Locks (Alabama). Bid Package, Mobile District. 9. Quality Control. February 1975.

U.S. Army Corps of Engineers. Excerpt from Lake Chicot P.S. (Mississippi). Bid Package, Vicksburg District, Section 2 Slurry Trench. June 1976.

U.S. Army Corps of Engineers. Foundation Report. Design, Construction, and Performance of the Impervious Cutoff at W. G. Huxtable Pumping Plant, Marianna, Arkansas. Volume I. April 1978.

Veder, C. Excavation of Trenches in the Presence of Bentonite Suspensions for the Construction of Impermeable and Load-bearing Diaphragms. In: Grouts and Drilling Muds in Engineering Practice. Butterworth's, London, England. 1963. pp. 181–88.

Villaume, J. Philadelphia Power and Light Co. Personal Communication with C. A. Furman of JRB Associates. August 4, 1982.

Weber, W. J. Physiochemical Processes for Water Quality Control. Wiley-Interscience, New York. 1972. 640 pp.

Wetzel, R. Memorandum. Trip to Slurry Trench Installlation (Soil-Bentonite). JRB Associates, McLean, Virginia. August 4, 1982.

Wilson, S. D., and R. Squier. Earth and Rockfill Dams. In: State of the Art Volume. Seventh International Conference on Soil Mechanics and Foundation Engineering, Mexico. 1969. pp. 137–223.

Winter, C. D. Slurry Trench Construction. Mil. Eng. (446):437–440, 1976.

Xanthakos, P. P. Slurry Walls. McGraw-Hill Book Company, New York. 1979. 621 pp.

Zoratto, E. M. Engineered Construction International, Inc. Personal Communication with C. E. Spooner of JRB Associates. September 1982.

*Other Noyes Publications*

# GROUNDWATER CONTAMINATION AND EMERGENCY RESPONSE GUIDE

by

**J.H. Guswa**
**W.J. Lyman**
Arthur J. Little, Inc.

**A.S. Donigian, Jr., T.Y.R. Lo,**
**E.W. Shanahan**
Anderson-Nichols & Co., Inc.

*Pollution Technology Review No. 111*

An overview of groundwater hydrology; a technology review of equipment, methods, and field techniques; and a methodology for estimating groundwater contamination under emergency response conditions are provided in this book. It describes the state of the art of the various techniques used to identify, quantify, and respond to groundwater pollution incidents.

Interest in the causes and effects of groundwater contamination has increased significantly in the past decade as numerous incidents have brought the potential problems to public attention. Protection of our groundwater resources is of critical importance, thus making the book both timely and relevant.

Part I assesses methodology for investigating and evaluating known or suspected instances of contamination. Part II surveys groundwater fundamentals, state-of-the-art equipment, monitoring methods, and treatment and containment technologies. It will serve as a desk reference and guidance manual. Part III details possible emergency response actions at toxic spill and hazardous waste disposal sites.

A condensed table of contents listing **part and selected chapter titles** is given below.

**ISBN 0-8155-0999-5 (1984)**

**490 pages**

*Other Noyes Publications*

# VADOSE ZONE MONITORING FOR HAZARDOUS WASTE SITES

by

**L.G. Everett**          **L.G. Wilson**          **E.W. Hoylman**

Kaman Tempo

*Pollution Technology Review No. 112*

This document is an extensive state of-the-art review and evaluation of vadose/unsaturated zone monitoring. The particular applicability of selected vadose/unsaturated zone monitoring methods to hazardous waste disposal sites is also described.

The vadose, or unsaturated, zone is that ground layer, beneath the topsoil and overlying the water table in which water in pore spaces co-exists with air, or in which the geological matter is unsaturated.

A major concern at all hazardous waste disposal sites—abandoned, active, or planned—is potential pollution of the underlying groundwater system. Current federal regulations require both groundwater monitoring and vadose zone sampling at land treatment installations.

This book will serve as a compendium of monitoring techniques from which the user may select a method to develop a vadose zone monitoring program. Each of the methods presented is quantitatively described according to physical, chemical, geologic, topographic, hydrologic, and climate constraints. The monitoring techniques are also evaluated as to preactive, active and postclosure assessment applications.

The condensed table of contents listed below includes **chapter titles and selected subtitles.**

ISBN 0-8155-1000-4 (1984)                                    358 pages